BRITAIN
3000 BC

BRITAIN
3000 BC

RODNEY CASTLEDEN

SUTTON PUBLISHING

First published in the United Kingdom in 2003 by
Sutton Publishing Limited · Phoenix Mill
Thrupp · Stroud · Gloucestershire · GL5 2BU

British Library Cataloguing in Publication Data
A catalogue record for this book is available from the British Library.

ISBN 0-7509-2693-7

Typeset in 11/15 pt New Baskerville.
Typesetting and origination by
Sutton Publishing Limited.
Printed and bound in England by
J.H. Haynes & Co. Ltd, Sparkford.

CONTENTS

TO
DON KLIPSTEIN

FOREWORD

The world of the neolithic is with us still. Its creations are features of the landscape that challenge us whenever we see them: Stonehenge, the Orkney stone circles, the houses at Skara Brae, round barrows and long barrows and the mysterious etchings of aerial photography. These sites are here and now, a part of the intricate tapestry of time and industry that is the landscape of today, but they are also then – they are a coded message from another age. Anyone who responds to them wants to decode the message; we are, after all, ourselves the descendants of the megalith builders, these inscrutable, short-lived, manipulative people.

My own early apprehension of a distant past came when I was far from this country. I grew up in Egypt. I have a compelling memory of being taken to visit a place in the desert where archaeologists were excavating what I now know to have been a pre-dynastic burial site. I was shown a shallow depression in the sand in which lay the faint impression of a curled skeleton – fragile bones, the fan of ribs, an eggshell skull. This had once been a person; this person had lived thousands of years ago. I glimpsed time, and continuity, and was awed; I think I was about seven. All my life, I have been intensely interested in the complexities of past landscapes, and hence in archaeology; perhaps that was a seminal moment. The neolithic has always seemed especially emotive, ever since I first saw the Orkney sites and felt their extraordinary resonance – emphatic statements against the green slabs of the islands and the grey sea.

Our response to the enigmatic survivals of ancient societies is a need to deconstruct. We ask questions of the monuments; all this tantalizing visible evidence that someone has been here before us is provocative. Landscape is not just scenery; it is a narrative. And one in which the people of the Stone Age wrote an early chapter. Rodney Castleden analyses the way in which neolithic people interacted with their physical world, and then expressed this complex and imaginative relationship in their own constructions. We can never have more than a glimmer of how the neolithic mind worked, but attention to this intense connection that they felt with their backdrop does give some insight into a distant ancestry. We notice our surroundings; they lived in some kind of significant communion with theirs. The Britain evoked by this book is recognizable in its basic structure. The rivers and the coast are there, much as we know them, and the contours. And, of course, the resources (birds, beasts, vegetation, timber – though far more of all of these than today) and soil and many kinds of stone. The rest is conjured up from the known evidence, a fascinating exploration of a land covered in the wildwood, amidst which the scatter of monuments that we know today would have stood out in pristine splendour, an assertion of human presence. For this is a place that is peopled, with all that that implies – the long process of landscape manipulation has begun.

They were young, they were tough and strong, they were craftsmen. We cannot know how they thought, but we can have some idea of how they may have looked, where they went, what they did. As they moved about the place, they 'rustled, clinked and clattered', slung about with the necessary equipment for daily life – for making arrows, sharpening flints, repairing clothing. An Orcadian Stone Age family would have had a dresser in the home, on which to display choice household goods. But against these homely practicalities can be set that other, inaccessible aspect of their psyche which impelled them to build the megaliths, to drive great cursus monuments miles long across the landscape, to bury their dead in conspicuous earthworks. Rodney Castleden calls the monuments mnemonic devices, and likens them to the cathedrals of our own age, in which each feature has a meaning and a reference for those who can read the place. They tethered the people of the Stone Age not only to the landscapes in which they existed but also to their own pasts. Like us, they needed to relate to those who came before; in the prehistoric world, constructions took the place of the written word.

They must have been given to ritual, perhaps to the point of obsession. The cursus and the stone circle echo the two basic forms of primitive dance, the processional and the round dance. In a time when life expectation was brief, death was a commonplace; many of the monuments are references to death – burial places. But they are also about continuity, about the turning of the world – even if that was a concept unknown to their builders. And, knowing this, it is impossible not to think of the great neolithic landscapes – the Wiltshire sites, Orkney – as places that reverberate still with lost sounds and sights, with song and dance, with chanting and enacting.

That said, I have no time for mystical responses to landscape. The value of *Britain 3000 BC* is that it enables the reader to arrive at a more informed understanding of those many places in this country from which the Stone Age sends out a signal. Any landscape is meaningless until you can read its codes; it is simply an assemblage of hill and valley, field and road, assorted lumps and bumps in the ground. Only when you know that this is an Iron Age hill-fort, those are the ridges of medieval ploughing, that distortion of a hilltop is a neolithic long barrow, can you start to imagine your way into these half-vanished worlds.

PENELOPE LIVELY

ACKNOWLEÐGEMENTS

Many people helped me to write this book, some consciously, when I approached them for advice, others quite unconsciously, when they made some observation about the past or present that set off a train of thought. Some of the most influential are now dead, which makes it all the more important to acknowledge the debt.

The late Sir Harry Godwin back in 1980 gave me a useful firsthand perspective on the revolution in prehistory brought about by radiocarbon dating and pollen analysis, and encouraged me to develop a new synthesis. The first great exponent of the British neolithic, Stuart Piggott, made encouraging comments about my earlier writings. His 'successor', Colin Renfrew, was kind enough to discuss the Orkney tombs with me when we met, by chance, in the rain as he emerged, like the White Rabbit, from one of them. The composer Sir Michael Tippett was a great encourager; he felt I had given him an ancestry in the people of the barrows.

I am grateful to the staff at the Sackler Library, formerly the Ashmolean Library, Oxford, for their help; Alison Fraser for her thoughts on prehistoric ailments and advice on relevant literature; John and Celia Clarke for their hospitality during my reading weeks in Oxford; Rupert Harding for his invaluable detailed advice at the planning stage of the project; Christopher Feeney, my editor at Sutton Publishing; and Mick Sharp for being willing to let me use some of his wonderful images of neolithic sites.

I am glad to have this opportunity to thank some of the writers whose ideas have influenced me over the last twenty years; names such as Colin Renfrew, Ros Cleal, Richard Bradley, Alex Gibson, Aubrey Burl, Tim Darvill, Chris Scarre and Francis Pryor spring immediately to mind. There are also the correspondents who have written to me with their responses to my writings on various subjects, encouraging me, correcting me and supplying me with all manner of stimulating ideas and useful updates about sites. It may be invidious to name names, but I would like to mention some: Nigel Rose, John Miller, John Darrah, Don Klipstein, Laurence Nowry and, more than any other, Aubrey Burl.

PREFACE:
PALACES OF THE LOST CITY

This synthesis of landscape and culture in the British neolithic is written in the eddying wake of a tremendous surge of progress made by archaeologists during the last twenty years. We often forget that the neolithic lasted a very long time – as long as the Christian era – and it seemed from an early stage in the project that a sharper image would emerge if I made the book focus on what was happening at a particular moment. I chose 3000 BC – a pivotal moment in the middle of the neolithic when major changes were under way.

What would it be like to travel back in time to 3000 BC? What landscapes, what buildings would we see, what activity? What kinds of people would we meet there? Would we be able to understand what they were doing? Would we be surprised at the way they lived their lives?

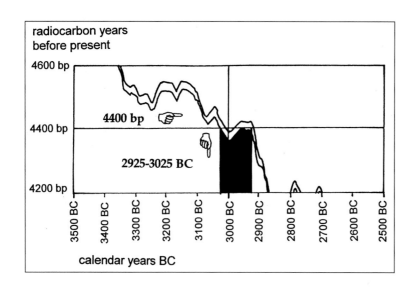

The radiocarbon conversion graph (after Stuiver and Pearson 1993).

Can we reach the year 3000 BC?

For fifty years we have been able to date bone, wood and other once-living materials using radiocarbon dating, and this has given a much clearer picture than before of the way things changed during the neolithic; for one thing, radiocarbon dating showed that the neolithic was two thousand rather than five hundred years long. But even with refinements to radiocarbon dating, which is still our main source for a neolithic chronology, it is difficult to give accurate calendar dates.

Raw radiocarbon dates come from the laboratory with a 'health warning'; each is expressed as a range of dates, and we can be only 95 per cent certain that the true date lies within that range. The raw date then needs to be converted in the light of tree-ring dating, which counts backwards year by year from the present and enables us to check on the accuracy of radiocarbon dates. The conversion graph we use[1] throws up further problems; because there are waves or ripples in the graph, a single raw date may convert to three different calibrated dates. The real, calendar, date is lost in the ripple among the three dates.

Unluckily for us, there is a ripple in the conversion graph around 3000 BC. Any event falling between the calendar dates of 3100 and 2900 BC is likely to yield the raw (uncorrected) radiocarbon date of 4400 bp. Two hundred real calendar years of prehistory have been replaced by just one radiocarbon date. This may be why so many chamber tombs appear to have been built all at once. This is why the middle neolithic gives an impression of a period of stagnation ending in a sudden spasm of activity and change; the reality is more likely to have been a dynamic evolution – faster than before, but not a convulsion.

In the circumstances it is probably more realistic, for most purposes in this book, to look at the period 3200–2800 BC rather than try to pinpoint a particular date. Radiocarbon dating cannot find 3000 BC for us.

But before we write off the two centuries straddling 3000 BC as a 'lost world', a time zone we are forbidden to enter, we must remember that there are other dating methods. Tree-rings record variations in British weather year by year, every year through that period and ice layers entombed in the Greenland and Antarctic ice sheets similarly show a continuous stored record of global atmospheric changes. Dendrochronology and ice cores show that those two centuries existed like any others, and in tree-rings from the Lancashire bogs we *can* find Britain 3000 BC exactly.

I stumbled on this 'foreign country' while I was researching landscape processes in the Midlands, trying to unravel the biography of an obscure river valley and detect order in the wildness of its winter floods. I discovered in the Radcliffe Science and Ashmolean Libraries in Oxford not only a wealth of information and ideas about the past, but a knack for getting what I wanted out of a wall-full of books, a skill not easily acquired. I also found, at Ecton in Northamptonshire, a moongate that transported me from geography into archaeology. At the bottom of a gravel pit beside the river I found the sand bars the River Nene had laid down in its channel long before Stonehenge was dreamed of, the boulders it had rolled along its bed in the summer snowmelts of twenty thousand years ago. Halfway up, between the layers of modern silt and the ice age sand bed, was an old land surface where trees had been felled or burnt down – they had certainly been charred by fire – and nearby a handful of neolithic knives. People had visited this river bank five thousand years before, perhaps to collect river cobbles for tool making, perhaps to clear a bit of woodland for a settlement site. This meeting with ancestors was a formative moment. Until then I had been using archaeology to follow through the story of the river, but from then on I was pursuing the elusive people of the new stone age for their own sake. The more I found out, the more excited I became, and the more I wanted to share what I had discovered. Out of that came *The Stonehenge People*, and now this book.

In South Africa the Sun International hotel group built a fake archaeological site based on a fake myth concocted to order by a Californian design team. *The people of a nomadic tribe journeyed from North Africa to Bophuthatswana, built a rich civilization with a great city there, only to have it destroyed in an earthquake, its ruins lying undiscovered and unrestored until now . . .*[2] The recognizably Californian agenda of destruction by earthquake is an importation, a piece of geographical chauvinism, a salutary warning to writers like me. I have to be sure that the neolithic Britain that I am assembling for you is not another Palace of the Lost City, a construct that covertly contains the Trojan horse of my own past, a 'preoccupied' version of the prehistoric past that might persuade you, and yet be unreal. I have to try to put myself neutrally into the past, to see it, as far as possible, as it was seen at the time. Inevitably, the story of the past can never be how things were seen at the time, only how they came to be seen when the story was written. I am nevertheless striving to reach a closer approximation to what *we* would see and understand if we could travel back in time and watch our ancestors with the greatest measure of empathy we are capable of mustering.

CHAPTER ONE

INTRODUCTION: THE CREATIVE SURGE

J ust five thousand years ago was the heyday of the new stone age, the 'high' neolithic. It was one of those rare and highly significant moments in the development of the human race, when many changes and great creative surges were under way – not just in Britain but elsewhere. It was that crucial landmark moment when civilization began, with the invention of writing in Mesopotamia. Towns had been growing steadily in the Middle East for five hundred years, becoming fully fledged cities where architecture, sculpture, pottery and metal-working were achieved amid landscapes transformed by irrigation systems and agriculture. Great and imposing buildings had been created, such as the White Temple of Uruk. An historic change happened in Egypt. In 3100 BC a ruler of Upper Egypt became the first to unite into a single kingdom the whole of the Nile valley from the First Cataract to the Mediterranean; in effect Egypt itself was created.

On the other side of Europe, in the British Isles, a cultural revolution manifested itself in a flurry of monument building: great stone tombs at Newgrange and Maes Howe were built, earth circles at Avebury and Stonehenge, and the huge chalk mound of Silbury Hill shortly afterwards.[1] Ten thousand years ago the last cold stage ended, the point in time where dramatic and rapid environmental changes finally shook the human race out of its palaeolithic habit and into a phase of cultural development without parallel in its rapidity and variety. There were earlier interglacials, maybe twenty of them, but none of them saw the human race develop as fast as it has done during the current warm stage. 3000 BC was the halfway point between the end of the last cold stage and today. How far had we in Britain travelled by that halfway point?

Archaeologists are used to digging from the earth pieces of bone, stone, pottery and wood and seeing, with their mind's eye, the living reality of the long-gone past. Non-specialist onlookers are often disappointed with the visible finds, which are incomplete, in a poor, weathered and damaged state and look divorced from any living human endeavour. Only occasionally do we uncover something that grips us all with its immediacy. The discovery of Tutankhamun's tomb was such a moment. When

I started researching the neolithic, I lived in the continual hope that peat extraction in the Somerset Levels would uncover the preserved body of a neolithic hunter who had lost his footing on one of the narrow slippery wooden trackways that crossed the reed-beds. Then we should have been able to see what neolithic clothes were like, how neolithic people actually looked. So far no neolithic bog people have been discovered, though the Somerset peat layers have yielded a significant number of neolithic artefacts. It was a few years later that my wish came nearly true: a well-preserved neolithic man was found, not in Somerset but in the Alps, preserved not by peat but by freezing. So now it is possible to meet the gaze of a neolithic person who died in 3200 BC, to establish a sense of intimacy and kinship that bridges the five thousand years separating Them from Us. 'Oetzi' has made a huge impact on us. My hope is that we can develop that sense of rapport with the past. We need answers to some big questions. *Was* it a foreign country, and *did* they do things differently there?

A problem is that in becoming 'familiar' with an individual, past or present, we may lose sight of larger-scale social, political and economic processes: we may lose sight of the culture. Initially, archaeologists studying Oetzi's remains assumed he had been caught out by the sudden onset of bad weather while on a seasonal visit to high alpine pastures or on a routine hunting expedition. Now it seems more likely that he was an exile, an outcast, possibly a man chased out of his village for committing some crime, fatally wounded and driven up into the mountains to die; in other words what happened to him was not normal at all. It is often difficult to assess how far an individual event in the past (which is what turns up in any archaeologist's excavation trench) is representative.

I once worked with Les Sandham, who, as a young bandsman in the Second World War, suffered badly at the hands of the Japanese on the Burma Railway. I also had a neighbour, Bob Bartholomew, who served in the Royal Navy at the same time in the same war and, by chance, saw no hostile action; he had a wonderful time, on what was for him a free five-year world cruise. Two personal histories of the same period, the same conflict, both true. Which of the two men had the experience that more meaningfully represents the 1940s? Historians wisely draw back from this sort of question, from the individual anecdote, in order to see more clearly the larger processes at work – and prehistorians do the same. Yet in doing so they lose something important, the sense of sharing an experience with the people of the past, and that special sense of ownership of the past that most of us need.

I hope to unfurl before you a panorama of the past, but also to provide some glimpses of moments in other people's lives, long lost. How else can we tell whether life was different for them? Or whether *they* were in some significant way a different sort of people?

CHAPTER TWO

A NEW HEAVEN AND A NEW EARTH

BRITAIN – A NEW ISLAND

Five thousand years ago the ice age was over. Five thousand years before that the glaciers had melted in the highlands; the temperature had risen steeply and small bands of hunter-gatherers had become established in the lowlands and round the coasts.[1] Not that the coasts of 8000 BC would be recognizable today. Huge volumes of ocean water were still locked up in land-ice in Canada, the level of the sea was 30–40 metres lower than it is today[2] and a great deal of what is now shallow sea off the south and east coasts of England was exposed as a dry treeless plain.

People and animals were able to walk to and fro between Britain and the European mainland, crossing the exposed and dried-out floor of the English Channel and southern North Sea, until as late as 5000 BC. Only then did Britain become an island. To the east, like stepping stones between the Netherlands and Norfolk, an archipelago of five small islands remained, together with one large island in the middle of the North Sea, later submerged to form the Dogger Bank. The fast-rising sea had swamped those stepping stones by 3000 BC, making a North Sea coastline recognizably like today's. The sea crept in like a slow relentlessly rising tide, drowning many of the hunter-gatherers' settlements – which is one reason why we know relatively little of the background to the neolithic transformation.[3]

When the neolithic began, in around 4500 BC, the first farmers must have ferried their livestock and plants to Britain across the Channel or the southern North Sea.[4]

In 3000 BC the climate reached its optimum. In the English Midlands summers reached their warmest ever (17.4°C on average) and winters their mildest ever (5.0°C);[5] both summer and winter temperatures were to drop by at least one degree by 2000 BC. It was the warmest it would get – a degree or two warmer than today. There were, even so, big contrasts in weather from year to year, just as there are now.[6]

The sea had certainly risen to within 4 metres, and possibly 2 metres, of its present level.[7] In south-east England the rising sea created a ragged submergent coastline with many headlands and islands, such as Sheppey, Thanet, Wight and Selsey, separated from one another by winding estuaries, inlets, backwaters and broad shallow bays. Subsequent wave action has eroded away many of the headlands, trimmed back the islands and silted up the estuaries, inlets, bays and creeks to make a straighter, smoother coastline. Flooded river mouths that were long fingers of the sea in the neolithic have become broad floodplains (such as the Arun, Adur, Sussex Ouse and the Stour in Kent), while shallow bays have become extensive alluvial plains: Pevensey Levels and the Romney and Walland Marshes.[8] Along the coast of the Fens, Firth of Forth and Somerset Levels there were large areas of marshland with reed-beds; the reeds were both a refuge for wildfowl and a valuable resource in themselves – for roof thatch.

The unresistant cliffs of glacial sediment that stretch along the North Sea coast from Holderness southwards to Suffolk were significantly further to the east in 3000 BC. In many places the coastline is retreating by around 2 metres per year, and in some places, like Covehithe, by nearly 6 metres. The mid-neolithic coastline of eastern England was probably 5 kilometres or more to the east.

Christchurch harbour. The rising sea drowned the Avon valley to make a perfect natural harbour.

The west coast of Britain is made of tougher rocks and rates of both erosion and silting have been much slower. The main changes there have been caused by the land rising as a result of glacial unloading. Although the ice caps covering Wales and Scotland melted away long ago, the recovery still continues. In Scotland the coastal flooding caused by rising sea level reached a maximum in 3000 BC, creating a drowned coastline. Since then the rising land has outstripped the rising sea, so the Highland coastline has emerged from the sea and the neolithic coastline is stranded inland, but there are many local variations. Loch Lomond was a sea-loch in 3500 BC, but by 3000 BC the rising land level had cut it off from the sea, turning it into a huge freshwater lake. Loch Sheil remained a sea-loch for a time, and did not become a lake until 2200 BC.[9]

Time line: environment and culture.

1. Long-term average temperatures for central England, derived from various sources.

2. Mainly from the work of Mike Baillie.

3. The names for cultural phases are by no means definitive. Others could be proposed, but they underline the growing dissatisfaction with the names on the first column.

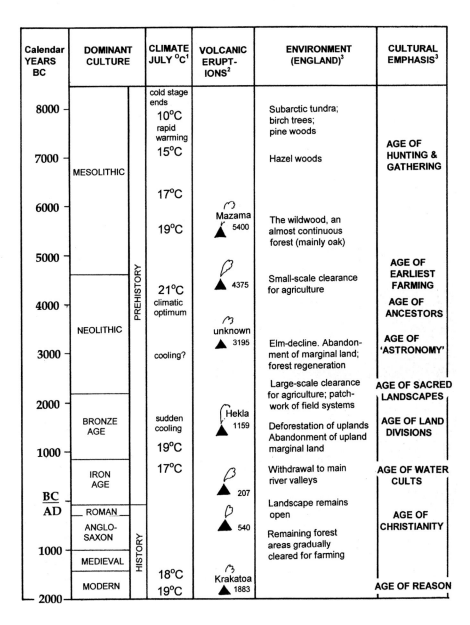

Calendar YEARS BC	DOMINANT CULTURE		CLIMATE JULY °C[1]	VOLCANIC ERUPT-IONS[2]	ENVIRONMENT (ENGLAND)[3]	CULTURAL EMPHASIS[3]
8000	MESOLITHIC	PREHISTORY	cold stage ends 10°C rapid warming		Subarctic tundra; birch trees; pine woods	
7000			15°C		Hazel woods	AGE OF HUNTING & GATHERING
6000			17°C	Mazama 5400		
			19°C		The wildwood, an almost continuous forest (mainly oak)	
5000	NEOLITHIC		21°C climatic optimum	4375	Small-scale clearance for agriculture	AGE OF EARLIEST FARMING
4000				unknown 3195		AGE OF ANCESTORS
3000			cooling?		Elm-decline. Abandonment of marginal land; forest regeneration	AGE OF 'ASTRONOMY'
2000	BRONZE AGE		sudden cooling	Hekla 1159	Large-scale clearance for agriculture; patchwork of field systems	AGE OF SACRED LANDSCAPES
1000			19°C		Deforestation of uplands Abandonment of upland marginal land	AGE OF LAND DIVISIONS
	IRON AGE		17°C	207	Withdrawal to main river valleys	AGE OF WATER CULTS
BC AD	ROMAN	HISTORY		540	Landscape remains open	AGE OF CHRISTIANITY
	ANGLO-SAXON				Remaining forest areas gradually cleared for farming	
1000	MEDIEVAL		18°C	Krakatoa 1883		
MODERN			19°C			AGE OF REASON
2000						

Watersmeet.

Then, as now, the people of Britain were living in an environment that was changing and new. The forces of nature were gradually wearing away hills and mountains and building up valley floors, but in most places these changes were imperceptibly slow. Over most of Britain, especially inland, the land surface was very close to its present shape; in most places the neolithic land surface was within a metre of its present position. The broad features of the landscape, the shapes of the hills and valleys, the views and the lines of intervisibility would have been just as they are today.

In 3000 BC large-scale climatic and ecological shifts were under way. Britain shared in a continent-wide change in vegetation. Was this a result of human impact, or some external cause? There were several big volcanic eruptions, at least nine in the twenty-eight years beginning in 3201 BC, and those are likely to have brought on serious environmental changes.[10] Water levels in African lakes dropped abruptly, which led on to other disastrous ecological changes in Africa.[11] By 3000 BC there was a huge drop in methane levels in the atmosphere (about 8 per cent), which resulted from a reduction in the tropical wetlands. It is not clear if this was a result of the eruption sequence or, as has been suggested, the collapse of the system of ocean currents in the Atlantic, which also led to a large-scale expansion of the Sahara.[12] Environmental systems around the world were in upheaval. In Britain it looks as though the spate of major volcanic eruptions was directly responsible for ecological problems in the shape of three phases of impeded tree growth, in 3200–3191 BC, 3183–3176 BC and 3172–3161 BC. Around 3193 BC tree growth came to a virtual standstill.[13]

THE WILDWOOD

The wildwood that covered Britain in 3000 BC was nevertheless still the richest ecological resource imaginable. The hunter-gatherers had colonized a meagre subarctic tundra. A few birch trees crept in and then, as the climate warmed, a few pine trees, then an open pine wood. By 4000 BC woodlands covered nearly all of Britain with a leafy canopy at about 15 metres, except for a few small patches of grassland in infertile areas like the Norfolk Breckland. By 3000 BC the woodlands had reached their most complete development, and even then the clearance had begun.[14]

Only mountains rising above 500 metres peeped out above the sea of trees; the summits of Snowdonia, the Pennines, Cumbria, the Cheviots and the Scottish Highlands were bald, bleak and bare. Some landscapes now windswept and treeless were then wooded, like Shetland. Coastal wetlands like the Fens were covered with pine, oak and yew woods.[15] Orkney seems never to have been wooded, though specimens of yew, oak and hawthorn did grow there, providing a skimpy supply of firewood; probably dried seaweed was the main fuel.[16] When the great tomb of Maes Howe was raised in 2900 BC, it was built on heathland; only later was the surrounding land turned over to agriculture.[17]

The wildwood was richly varied. In the highlands generally, the sessile oak dominated. Along the Great Glen and on the mountains on either side lay the already ancient Caledonian Forest, a relic of the pine forest that had briefly covered Britain in

Remnant of the ancient Caledonian Black Forest at Glenlyon (Jean Williamson/Mick Sharp).

older, colder times. The birchwoods in Caithness were similarly left over from a colder past. Blanket bog had begun to develop on the Welsh mountains, but only in small areas; it did not dominate as it later would.

The wildwood is often described as an oakwood, but over large areas of poorly drained lowland, such as the Lowlands of Scotland and the waterlogged clay areas of the English Midlands, the wet-loving alder was dominant. Alders grew in East Anglia and south-east England too, but there warmth-loving lime was dominant. In the West Country mixed oak forest covered everything except the high moors where only cotton-grass and sphagnum moss grew on blanket-peat.[18] In the Fens great bog-oaks were drawn up, like rhubarb, in the pine woods with their 30-metre canopy, to make abnormally tall, straight oak trunks – forest giants such as are seen nowhere today.

When an old tree died or blew down in a gale, sunlight reached the otherwise dark forest floor to make a small woodland glade where low-growing plants could flourish: scabious, cuckoo-flower, bugle. This was important in maintaining bio-diversity because, apart from these clearings, the forest continuously covered large swathes of landscape. In the English Midlands even the river floodplains were forested. The Nene floodplain at Wellingborough had a covering of alder, oak and hazel woodland in 3000 BC; clearings were opened up later, either by deliberate tree-felling or by wind-throw, and here more grasses and herbs grew, with bracken dominant.[19] Peat dating from 3000 BC at Narborough Bog on the River Soar shows a floodplain partially cleared of its woodland cover, and herbs and bracken on the increase.[20]

But Britain was not completely covered by forest from coast to coast. Natural processes, such as attack by disease, insects or storms, would have generated clearings all over the place. And then there was fire. The idea of a primeval forest was borrowed from North America, where early white settlers thought they were encountering a virgin wilderness, but they were mistaken; the native peoples had been altering the forest for thousands of years by setting fire to it. Fire was a way of keeping ground open for travel, of improving hunting by stimulating grass growth and flushing out game, of clearing sites for camps and famously of communicating with people a long way off. Probably fire was used in some or all of these ways in Britain too.[21] Some of the Nene floodplain woodland was burnt down; the tree trunks were left where they fell, so perhaps this was an accidental firing.

The forest was a rich food source for hunter-gatherers. They could collect acorns, barberries and blackberries, sloes, crab-apples and hazelnuts, and there were many plants they might collect for food too, such as knotgrass and chickweed. There was plenty of meat on the hoof: red deer, roe deer and the fearsome aurochs, a wild bull, roaming through the forest and grazing in the glades.[22] The site of the Stonehenge car park, where totem poles were raised as early as 8000 BC, may have been an artificial clearing purposely designed to lure deer – a place made special, marking the beginning of the long story of Stonehenge.[23] The impact of the hunter-gatherers on the environment appears to have been small, but in some areas they may have set fire to the forest,[24] perhaps to flush out prey, perhaps to create clearings for grazing or settlement.

The wildwood. Main tree species. 1 – montane grassland; 2 – birch wood; 3 – pine wood; 4 – hazel wood; 5 – alder wood; 6 – oak wood; 7 – elm wood; 8 – lime wood.

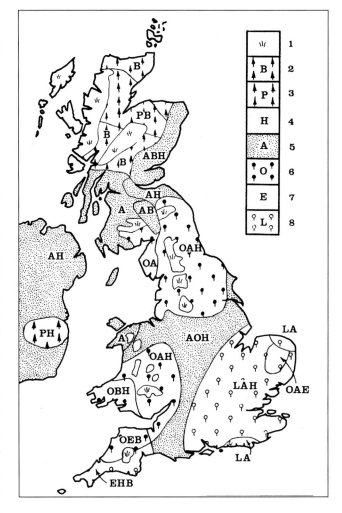

They may have turned parts of the Black Mountains in Wales from woodland to moorland as early as 5000 BC.

The hunter-gatherers harvested the air, catching cranes, storks, lapwings, guillemots and flightless great auks, and the sea, where they caught seals, whales, dolphins and many kinds of fish. The only animal the hunter-gatherers domesticated was the dog, invaluable as a hunting animal in the forest where prey could more easily be scented than seen. It is often forgotten that the hunting and gathering continued unabated through the neolithic. Red deer were especially valued for their antlers which could be used for picks and mallets, sleeves for axe-heads and handles for tools. A cache of antler fragments found at Fletton near Peterborough included several short lengths that were carefully smoothed off and used as handles. I have held them, and was surprised how comfortable and fit-to-purpose they are to grip.

There were wild horses, wild boar, wild cats, badgers, foxes, polecats, pine martens, red squirrels, brown hares, beavers, field voles, bank voles, water voles, wood mice, yellow-necked mice, common shrews, moles, bats, common toads, frogs and grass snakes. Relatively few remains of birds have survived, but enough to give an idea of the range of the wildlife that teemed in and over the wildwood and in the marshes beyond: bitterns, curlews, eagles, buzzards, falcons, carrion crows, blackbirds, jackdaws, thrushes and starlings. Along the coasts there were cormorants, shags, skuas, great auks, guillemots, gannets, whooper swans, ducks and sea eagles.[25]

Large areas of the wildwood remained undisturbed.[26] Even though there were gaps, it was at that time still more continuous than it would ever be again. The great stone monuments that for most of us *define* the neolithic were often built in small woodland clearings. Several of the Welsh tombs were built either in small grassy clearings or actually in woodland.[27] To neolithic people the forest must have seemed endless in

Bryn Gwyn stone circle, Anglesey.

space and time, smothering the world like a great green ocean. It was still the primary source of fulfilment, providing shelter, food, medicine, protection, raw materials, folklore and mythology. Wood fuelled the cooking fires, expanding the variety of food. Wood lit up the evening darkness, lengthening the day. Wood warmed the chill night air and made surviving winter possible.[28]

Some woodlands were carefully managed. In Somerset a great shallow bay had filled with silt, peat and water to form the Somerset Levels, a flat expanse of fen woodlands with stands of birch, alder and willow and lots of marshy pools and reed-beds where wildfowl might be caught. Large areas of alder, birch and willow were coppiced to generate a supply of straight, flexible osiers to make baskets, hurdles and houses – and to build elaborate trackways across the marsh. The oldest built roadway in Europe, the 2km long Sweet Track connecting two of the marsh islands, was already immemorially old, disintegrated and sunk in the swamp.[29]

Mount Caburn in Sussex was covered with lime forest in 4000 BC, managed perhaps by pollarding in 3800 BC, with cereals grown in clearings on the lower slopes from

3750 to 3450 BC. After that there was forest regeneration, but this time of yew, and the Caburn yew wood was maintained on into the bronze age.[30]

Evidence for forest clearance came to light in Norfolk half a century ago, and gradually other areas have added more detail to the picture.[31] From the Lake District comes evidence of forest clearance in the form of soil erosion, which was under way by 3000 BC in several of the Lakeland valleys.[32] An area of forest intended for cultivation was cleared by felling or burning, the exposed soil hoed and sown with seeds. After a few years under cultivation the clearing was turned over to pasture for a while before the forest was allowed to reclaim it.[33] In the Wye valley there were at least two episodes of cereal cultivation followed by soil exhaustion. This happened within a twenty-year period and was part of a longer sequence by which open conditions were gradually established; the whole process probably went on for hundreds of years.[34]

Several sites in the Thames valley tell the same story of woodland clearance. The lime wood on Hampstead Heath was cleared in successive phases in the neolithic, eventually to be replaced by a holly wood.[35] The lime and elm forest extended down on to the lower valley sides near the Thames at Egham, giving way to alder woodland on the wetter parts of the floodplain near Runnymede, where small sun-warmed clearings may have been man-made or the result of wind-throw.[36] Forest fallow farming opened small temporary clearings like wounds, creating a mosaic of secondary woodland in various stages of healing. Agriculture was subtly, discreetly folded into the older, woodland-dependent way of life, supplementing it with new foods, and only gradually changing it with new tasks and new imperatives. Woodland ecosystems were modified but not destroyed. By 3000 BC many of the clearings had been left to grow back; the widespread woodland regeneration at this time[37] might suggest an economic implosion of some kind – a dark age.[38]

Some areas of forest were cleared specifically to make way for monuments. The swathe of open country required for the Dorset Cursus, a processional way marked by chalk banks and ditches, was created by clearing a huge corridor of pasture passing through the virgin forest.

The marked decline in elm pollen around 3200 BC is often quoted as evidence for human modification of the woodland, but the elm decline affected the whole of northern Europe at the same time, including northern Norway, which was then uninhabited, and this makes human interference an impossibility.[39] The arrival of Dutch elm disease in the UK in the 1970s alerted archaeologists to an alternative mechanism. Maureen Girling's 1980s discovery of wing cases of the elm bark beetle (*Scolytus scolytus*) immediately below the elm decline in a soil sample from Hampstead Heath seemed to clinch elm disease as the likeliest explanation.[40] Meanwhile, it is certainly not sensible to see the elm decline as a marker for the beginning of agriculture.[41]

In the past the neolithic 'revolution' has often been represented as a conquest of the forest. The truth is that agriculture, at a very small scale, was bolted on to a well-established hunter-gatherer culture. The forest continued to be very important to people, both economically and spiritually. The flint mines in the South Downs were in woodland.[42] In some areas, like Avebury, forest clearance was large in scale, but still the forest was never far away and always in view, always a physical and psychological presence in the human landscape.[43]

Evidence of extensive clearance comes from snail shells under the long barrows in southern England. In other areas, such as the Cheviot Hills, the clearance was smaller in scale, with cereal cultivation on valley floors, pastures higher up, while all around lay the encircling forest teeming with wild resources. The bald, treeless mountain tops rose out of the forest, bare, stark and conspicuous.[44]

It was the forest that gave the landscape its visible seasonal variation. The architectural framework of boughs, branches and interlacing twigs was wholly visible in winter, the skeletal trees letting a lot of light through to ground level, possibly making travel easier by improving visibility. More of the sky became visible too, with the moon shining and stars twinkling among the bare black branches. In summer the forest was clothed in a dense mass of foliage that cut off distant views and much of the sky, and focused attention on the local; in effect by reducing visibility foliage reduced the scale of the landscape. It also created an infinite variety of diffuse and intensely localized lighting effects; clearings would have become significant meeting places, special places to which people as well as wild animals would naturally gravitate.

The forest had a mythic presence in the neolithic imagination. Maybe isolated great trees regularly formed foci for ceremonial landscapes; the line of totem poles erected at Stonehenge in the mesolithic is thought by some to have been rooted in the veneration of a living tree standing in the westernmost of the line of pits,[45] but it is usually an impossible task to reconstruct alignments with trees, or even distant clearings, that have long-since vanished.

The forest was one of the great prehistoric landscape archetypes – the forest labyrinth – taking its place in the human heart alongside the glacial wasteland and the primordial sea.[46] It embodied the cyclicity of the seasons and was full of ready-made metaphors of the life cycle and the wheel of human fortune. From earliest times the forest was a universal presence in European folklore and myth, sometimes as a great mother, a place of tranquillity and refuge, safety and protection, sometimes as a threatening demonized wilderness full of dangerous predators and hobgoblins, but always as a place of adventure and quest, full of danger and delight. Above all, the forest was an enduring and ever-present symbol of the immutable realm of the grandfathers and grandmothers, of the immeasurable ancestral past and the unforeseeable future.[47]

CHAPTER THREE

HOUSE AND HOME: THE HUMAN HABITAT

DISAPPEARING BUILDINGS

Few people would expect houses built by neolithic people to have survived as part of the visible landscape. Most of us are deeply impressed when we see an intact Roman building, like the Pantheon in Rome, or a Saxon building, like Brixworth Church in Northamptonshire, still standing after one-and-a-half or two thousand years; we would not expect any building to last five thousand years. All of us have seen in the landscape the evidence of the process of disappearance, sometimes rapid, sometimes imperceptibly slow: the urban development schemes where almost overnight a clutch of 200-year-old shops is cleared to make way for a superstore; the slowly sagging roof of a medieval barn; the restoration appeal board outside a crumbling church; the ruins of an abbey; the footings of a Roman fort. In time, weather, decay, neglect, malice and the natural disintegration of materials will cause a building to fall apart, however well made it is; some houses are accidentally destroyed, by landslide, subsidence, coastal erosion or fire; some are deliberately destroyed out of malice or to make way for a new land use or a new building. Sometimes houses are rebuilt on the same spot, sometimes a settlement is abandoned in favour of a new site altogether. This process has been going on continuously through the last five thousand years. We walk across fields or moors, through villages or down city streets for the most part unaware that we are walking through the invisible walls and doors of other people's houses, treading on their invisible hearths, beds and prized possessions.

With that process of disappearance in mind, it is amazing that in a country as densely peopled as Britain over a dozen neolithic houses have somehow survived, as a result of the chance convergence of favourable circumstances. Understandably, they have attracted a lot of interest from archaeologists because they allow us to see something we could not have expected to see – where and how neolithic people actually lived, where they sat warming their hands before the fire and told stories,

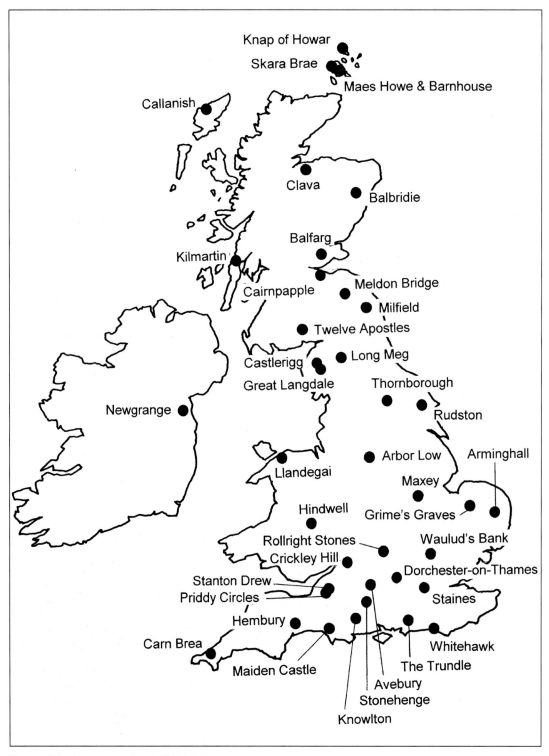

Some of the important sites in 3000 BC.

where they slept, made love and reared their young, and something of what it must have been like to live at that remote time.

HEBRIDEAN AND ORCADIAN HOUSES

Perhaps we should begin somewhere geographically remote; to travel a long way is to travel far through time – another neolithic idea. Loch Olabhat is on the western edge of North Uist in the Outer Hebrides. Here, at Eilean Domhnuill, we can see the footings of an early settlement on a tiny man-made island called a crannog. For several centuries, beginning in 3500 BC, a small community lived on that island, rebuilding their houses and sheds several times, within a timber and wattle palisade probably built to keep the wind out. They reached the island from the lake shore by walking over a wooden footbridge 40 metres long. In the first phase two houses about 6 by 4 metres stood side by side. Archaeologists were able to make out their bases from stone footings which supported light timber-frame structures. They were often modified, possibly because of damage by the weather. The people who lived on Eilean Domhnuill had stone querns to grind grain and used a lot of pottery. They may have avoided taking livestock onto the island because of the lack of space, or because it would not have been easy to get animals safely over the bridge.

This was probably but one of a string of occupation sites they used; there would have been others along the shell-sand coastal strip, the inhabitants staying in each of them for a time as their foraging activities took them across the landscape. This semi-nomadic behaviour is suggested by the way their chamber tombs are scattered around the landscape.[1]

In the Orkney islands extraordinary developments were taking place in monument-building, even though relatively few people lived there. Two well-made drystone semi-

Loch Olabhat. A reconstruction of one of the phases of the neolithic crannog (developed from Parker Pearson 1993).

'Jelly-baby' houses in the Shetlands

The Shetland houses are simple oval drystone structures 10–15m long. Each one encloses a single large oval chamber 7–8m long with a smaller chamber 3–4m in diameter opening out of it like an apse at the inner end. The more elaborate structure sometimes called the Stanydale Temple is probably just a larger farmhouse. The ruined farmhouses are dispersed, not grouped into villages, and stand among the still-visible remains of their walled gardens.

The neolithic Shetland houses were very similar in plan to the figure-of-eight or jelly-baby houses still being built three thousand years later in the Western Isles. One of these pre-Norse houses was rebuilt as an experiment at Bosta on Great Bernera in 1998. The roof timbering began as two cones, with the taller cone covering the main chamber. When it became clear that water would be trapped in the gully between the cones, their apices were joined by a ridge pole. This made a ridge roof that was strong, waterproof and windproof, as it tapered down into the north wind (Neighbour and Crawford 2001). Interestingly, the neolithic houses in the Shetlands are oriented in the same way, with the smaller chamber to the north; perhaps we now have the explanation.

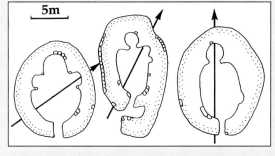

The Gairdie   *Stanydale*   *Gruting School*

Plans of jelly-baby houses in the Shetlands.

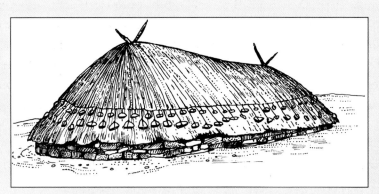

A newly built reconstruction of a jelly-baby house at Bosta, showing how a thatched roof was probably held on at windy coastal sites.

The thatch selected for the reconstructed Bosta house was double-skinned heather and turf thatch, held down by a web of strings weighted down by stones. It is this giant hairnet that gives the Bosta house its distinctive texture. Maybe the neolithic houses of Orkney, Shetland and the Western Isles were thatched in the same way.

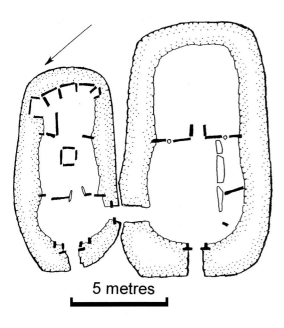

Knap of Howar. Plan of the house (after Ritchie 1983).

Knap of Howar. The front doorway, still intact after five thousand years.

detached houses still stand at Knap of Howar on the shore of the island of Papa Westray. They were so well made and well preserved that for a long time they were thought to be iron age, but Anna Ritchie's excavation and the radiocarbon dates she obtained showed that they were not only neolithic but the earliest buildings in the Orkneys, dating to 3500–2700 BC. They were rebuilt repeatedly on the same spot through that long period, so the remains we see today are those of the last phase, built around 2800 BC, and we do not know what the earlier houses looked like. They were built in a midden which was deep enough to provide heat insulation – possibly even heat itself. The larger southern building is divided in two by a partition of four upright slabs of flagstone, and posts between each outer pair of stones may have held up a wooden roof. The outer room was partly paved and had a broad bench which could have been a bed against one wall. The inner room had no paving, just domestic rubbish scattered on the ground; there was a central fireplace and a big quernstone. The smaller northern building had three rooms, the inner one evidently a storage area, well equipped with slab-built recess-cupboards, and there was a square hearth in the centre of the middle room.

The Knap of Howar people fished for their food, venturing some distance out to sea, probably in skin-boats, to catch their fish – cod, ling, turbot, flounder, conger eel and halibut. Rather surprisingly, deep-sea fishing was not uncommon at this time: people living in the Rhine Delta took to the sea to catch dolphins and whales. Along the coast from the Knap of Howar the more modest Orcadians collected oysters, winkles, cockles and razor-shells, but sometimes took seals. The people who lived here

---

Skara Brae

Until 1850 a high grassy sand dune stood unnoticed in the southern corner of the Bay of Skaill. It was called Skara Brae. In a storm in that year the grass and upper layers of sand were ripped off to reveal the ruined houses beneath. William Watt, the laird of Skaill, excavated and cleared four of the houses by 1868, acquiring a wealth of neolithic artefacts. Ten houses have now been excavated, and traces of stonework showing in the eroded seaward face of the dune imply that there may be several more still buried. Both the rooms, with their smoothly flowing lines, and the unique stone furniture are well made and aesthetically pleasing, showing an accomplished handling of material. The excavated houses, complete except for their roofs, convey better than any other place I can think of what it was like to live in the neolithic. The architecture is nothing short of wonderful; the domestic finds are comprehensive; the whole site is a veritable neolithic time capsule.

---

were not just fishermen, they were farmers. They cultivated cereals and raised sheep very like those that can still be seen grazing today on North Ronaldsay. They also caught birds in large numbers, especially the great auk, because it was easy to catch while it was nesting in the cliffs.

It was only from 3000 BC onwards that larger settlements appeared on Orkney, and they were associated with the making of the mysterious Grooved Ware pottery. They include some settlements that were massively built of stone and so have lasted much better than the wooden houses that were built in other parts of neolithic Britain. In the stone houses of the neolithic village at Skara Brae it is possible to see clearly how people lived.

Each house is rectangular, 6m across, with rounded corners. The walls are thick, well built and very strong, still standing in some places to well over 2 metres high. The doors are narrow and low-lintelled, and were originally fitted with doors; jambs, sills and bar-holes survive. The walls corbel in slightly, especially at the corners, but it is unlikely that the houses ever had beehive vaults. It is thought the roofs were spanned by the ribs of stranded whales or conifer trunks carried across by ocean currents from North America, and the basic framework was then covered with brushwood, skins and turves. When complete, the houses were warm and cosy, the soft rounded corners of the masonry lit by the glow of firelight, and the space filled with the pleasant smell of food, cooking and peat smoke. The built-in furniture is remarkable. It includes – for each house – a seat, a large square hearth, box beds, a dresser, wall cupboards and tanks for water or shellfish. The way the people used stone is particularly illuminating. Skara Brae shows us the sort of furnishings which were almost certainly made out of wood at other settlements elsewhere in Britain, but which have perished without trace.

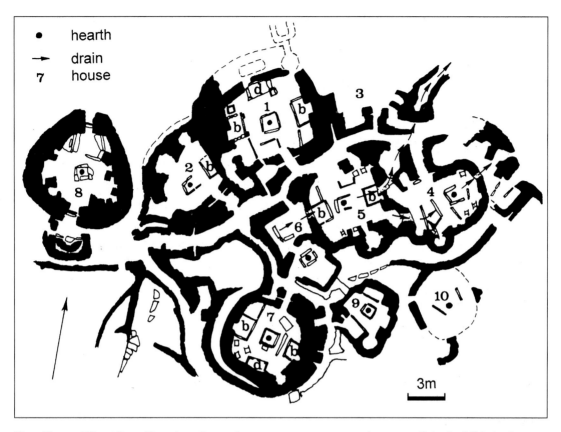

The village of Skara Brae. Remains of more houses, as yet unexcavated, are tantalizingly visible in the sand cliff to the west. Stone beds (b) and dressers (d) are shown (after Childe 1931).

Not all the houses were used in the same way. One was closed from the outside and had the bodies of two women buried under the floor. Possibly this house was reserved for menstruating women; in many societies right down to the present day menstruating women have been segregated and confined in a special house.[2]

Unexpectedly, there is pride at Skara Brae, pride in ownership of possessions. In each house opposite the door is an imposing stone dresser. House 7 shows this particularly well. If I travel back through time and visit House 7 in 3000 BC, I find myself stooping in the dark, low-roofed passage outside the house; I knock at the wooden door and wait to be admitted while the securing draw-bar inside is removed; meanwhile, I sniff the acrid smell of decaying domestic refuse seeping down from the entrance passage roof. Too tall, I have to bend double to get through the low door without braining myself on the stone lintel. Rising from this enforced bow, I see in the smoky gloom across the big square grate, his face underlit by a blazing fire, the greeting smile of the young head of the family sitting on a stone seat, *his* seat, in front of the huge dresser, *his* dresser, where his family's prized possessions are on display for me to admire. I hear the giggling of his children, playing hide-and-seek among the heather and animal skins in the box beds on either side.

People lived at Skara Brae at least from 3200 BC. They rebuilt their houses more than once and stayed there for generations; the settlement continued in use for about 450 years. Gradually the rubbish accumulating round the houses completely engulfed them and stone-roofed passages had to be created to provide an accessible pathway between the dwellings. Still the rubbish piled up, covering the passage roofs until the village disappeared, still living, beneath its own midden. Whatever else, neolithic people were not clean and tidy. But there was a point to their filthy ways. The accumulating layers of refuse sealed any gaps in the stonework, kept out the wind and the rain and insulated the houses, turning Skara Brae into an almost subterranean village; from a distance it would have been invisible in the landscape, given away only by the smoke drifting up from its fires, like a huge smouldering bonfire.

In a more sheltered location 8 miles to the east was the settlement of Barnhouse. Newly discovered surprisingly close to the great tomb of Maes Howe, this was a less congested village, straggling along the treeless shore of the Loch of Harray, close to the Stones of Stenness. The remains of about ten drystone houses of various sizes were uncovered in 1985–6. Open spaces separated the houses, which were very regular and orderly. House 2, a well-made two-roomed structure, has received a lot of attention, but to the south of it was a larger and slightly later square building, Structure 8, which measured 7m by 7m internally and was fitted with a massive enclosure wall. Some archaeologists suggest that this was a temple, because of its great size, because its doorway appears to have been deliberately aligned on the midsummer sunset, because the central hearth and porch features are also to be seen in the stone circle a stone's throw away, because the floor was clean and because a Grooved Ware vessel was embedded into the floor. On the whole, though, it seems to me there is no reason to see it as anything other than a big house; other houses, here and at Skara Brae, had square central hearths and Structure 8 had a dresser built against the wall opposite the door just like House 7 at Skara Brae. The matter of alignment is a perennial problem and one to return to later.

The varying sizes of the Barnhouse dwellings may reflect the varying requirements or aspirations of different families living at the same time, or changing material expectations through time.

The fact that the houses were freestanding – detached, as it were – suggests that they are contemporary with the first houses to be built at Skara Brae, around 3200 BC. The earliest houses at Skara Brae were similar to the Barnhouse dwellings, showing that the people living in the two villages were drawing on the same house-building tradition and had the same ideas about architecture, as we would expect. The difference between the villages is that at Skara Brae a long process of evolution caused the dwellings to merge and combine. Barnhouse was not occupied for as long and the houses remained separate. Why the people living at Barnhouse abandoned it and what happened to them is a mystery; its key position close to the centre of a ceremonial complex that included the Ring of Brodgar, the Stones of Stenness and the magnificent, cathedral-like tomb of Maes Howe might have been expected to

The Barnhouse settlement was discovered on a cold December morning in 1984. Colin Richards and his assistant Miranda Schofield were field-walking in the field next to the Stones of Stenness when she chanced upon a scatter of flints and some burnt bone a short distance east of the stone circle. Colin's dog Rufus, also a keen digger, found the first walling down a rabbit burrow. The excavation that followed revealed the footings of several well-made stone houses. They were radiocarbon dated to around 3200 BC, broadly contemporary with Skara Brae. Even more excitingly, they contained Grooved Ware identical to that found in the ditch of the stone circle, which identified the inhabitants of Barnhouse as the selfsame people who created and used the stone circle just 150m away. Only very rarely can we tie a specific settlement and a specific monument together in this way.

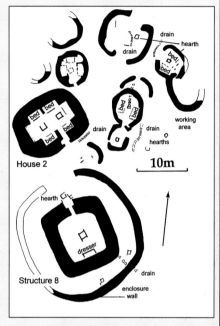

The excavated part of the Barnhouse settlement (after Parker Pearson 1993).

The carefully made square hearths, the use of big flagstone slabs for partitions and the stone beds all recall the architecture of Skara Brae. What Barnhouse lacks is the stone cupboards, and tanks; the design is cleaner, and it is tempting to see it as rather sharp, minimalist architecture, but of course there is no way of knowing how much wooden, textile and other perishable clutter the occupants may have had.

The overall design of House 2 is symmetrical, two interconnecting square rooms, each with its central hearth and each with three substantial rectangular bed recesses. Two of these recesses were connected by an L-shaped passage that was screened from the communal area to create a private area – the master bedroom, perhaps? Since its discovery House 2 has been singled out for theoretical interpretations of Orcadian buildings generally. Architecture is not just a way of organizing space but of organizing people's movement through it, so a close study of a well-preserved house plan may tell us much about people's patterns of domestic activity – and their ideas about that activity.

The bed immediately to the right of the entrance passage may have been the man's bed, specifically positioned there to guard and answer the door. Analysis of phosphate levels in the Barnhouse beds shows that the bed on the left regularly had higher levels than the one on the right. Urine is a source of phosphates, and the higher levels of phosphates may be the result of nursing mothers sharing their beds with incontinent infants.

guarantee its success. The answer may lie in some untraceable accident of prehistory, such as an epidemic.

Orkney provides such a promising beginning to this review of neolithic houses and homes that moving on to the mainland of Britain must inevitably seem an anticlimax. Traces of houses here are comparatively rare. Some prehistorians have understandably assumed that this indicates uneven patterns of survival in the archaeological record, that originally there were similar stone remains in mainland Britain, but that subsequent events, like erosion and stone-robbing, have obliterated them. Other prehistorians have assumed that it was the use of perishable timber, wattle and thatch which proved fatal to the record of habitation. Either way, it does seem odd that there is so little evidence of neolithic houses over such large tracts of Britain. Even large-scale surveys supported by trial excavations and sustained investigation round key sites like Stonehenge and Avebury have not produced settlement evidence anywhere near as abundant as we see on Orkney.[3]

A GREAT TIMBER HALL

Even so, from time to time we get a startling insight into the diversity of houses that people were building in the middle neolithic. At Balbridie near Banchory in Grampian a large, strong and symmetrical timber hall was built on well-drained rising ground near the River Dee. This was a very substantial rectangular building 25m by 13m with a door in each of its bowed ends. There were long curving timber walls immediately inside; these may have been screens designed to ensure that people did not walk straight into the central space but approached by way of one of the two side aisles; it was a feature of many of the more modest houses that entrance was by way of one of the corners and this may be a variant of the practice. Alternatively, the curving wall may represent the main wall, rising the full height of the building, while the outer wall was low, with its own separate pentise roof, and represented a porch. It would be possible to reconstruct several distinctly different-looking buildings from the arrangement of post-holes.[4] It seems very likely in any case that it had a ridge roof rising to a height of 9m – quite an imposing building. It was also used to store grain. The timber house stood in pasture, with on the side towards the River Dee an area of marsh and alder/hazel woodland, and on the other side, beyond a belt of hazel/birch woodland, fields of cereals, more pasturage and beyond that untouched oak woodland. The house itself probably served as a farmhouse, byre and barn, and was very solidly built.

Balbridie was so like a dark age hall that the excavators initially thought that that was what it must be, but four radiocarbon dates confirmed the amazing truth – that it was built as early as 3650 BC. Although it is just possible that a dark age hall might be made of ancient timber such as bog-oak that would give an early date, it is not really credible to regard the presence of Unstan Ware pottery on the site as just a coincidence; common sense says this confirms that the building was created and

The Balbridie timber hall.

occupied in the middle neolithic. The Balbridie hall is a rare but very significant example of a type of dwelling that was common on the European mainland five hundred years earlier, the timber longhouse. Remains of three more longhouses of the same size have been found in Scotland, two at Balfarg and a third at Auchenlaich near Callander.[5] Similar houses were built further south, too.

ENGLISH AND WELSH HOUSES

A typical example of the scant evidence for houses in England and Wales comes from Honington in Suffolk. Here there was a hamlet of eight huts 3m across, inferred from discoloured patches in the soil containing concentrations of tools and pottery. Each hut seems to have had a cooking hole – a small pit in the ground containing animal bones and showing signs of burning. There is very little here on which a reconstruction might be based, but since there are no post-holes and no masonry it may be assumed that the walls were raised on a foundation course of turves, with a light frame of branches or wattles planted into that. This type of farming hamlet consisting of up to ten simple dwellings was probably very common all over neolithic Britain, but as we have seen there were also much larger and stouter houses, with conveniences such as properly built indoor hearths. It looks as if there were big variations from place to place in people's standard of living.

The remains of another humble settlement were found at Hurst Fen near Mildenhall. Again the evidence for houses was indirect, shown this time by a scatter of two hundred small food storage pits, although it has not been possible to decipher the shapes of the buildings.

At several English and Welsh sites it is possible to reconstruct the plan and likely elevation of the houses from the pattern of post-holes. The timber houses themselves

The European longhouse

On the Northern European mainland in the fifth millennium BC it was quite common for timber houses to be 20m or 30m long. A few were twice that length and truly monumental in scale; they must have housed extended families and all their livestock. They often consisted of flanking drainage ditches and five rows of posts, of which the outer rows were often set in continuous bedding trenches. Some were trapeze-shaped, with a wide frontage to draw attention to, and show off, the entrance.

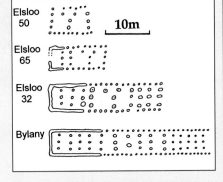

European longhouses. Houses 50, 65 and 32 at Elsloo in the Netherlands and one of the early houses at Bylany in the Czech Republic: short, medium, long and very long longhouses (after Modderman 1970 and Champion *et al.* 1984).

These very long longhouses were not built after about 4000 BC. By the time we reach 3000 BC shorter longhouses were the norm. In Denmark there were houses 10–15m long, consisting of just three rows of posts. A longhouse built at Zeewijk in west Frisia may have been reserved for non-domestic use, as a meeting-house; perhaps it was deliberately built in an old-fashioned style to make a link with the past, like the mock-Gothic churches and town halls the Victorians liked to build – such as the Guildhall in Northampton. One question often arises in people's minds: were full-length longhouses really never built in Britain? That would be odd, as long barrows are British 'houses for the dead' that seem to be modelled on the European house type, complete with trapezoid plan and flanking trenches, rather than on the shorter British type.

The longhouses were often monumental in scale. The weighty timber frames were topped by elaborate thatched roofs. The walls were fitted with wattle-and-daub panels to keep out the wind and rain. The clay daub was modelled into relief patterns. An entire panel from a gable end was found among the remains of a neolithic house in Hungary; the pargetting includes horizontal bars, apparently imitating wooden beams, and a geometric maze pattern. The aesthetic effect of a finished house would have been very rich.[6]

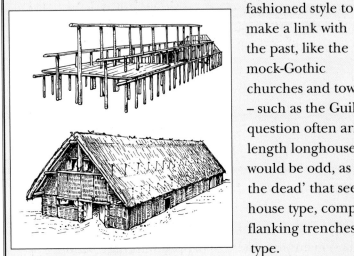

Reconstruction of a European longhouse. Above: the timber skeleton of posts, ridge poles and purlins (after Luning 1982). Below: the nearly completed building. The hurdle wall-panels were probably coated with a layer of clay to make them wind- and waterproof. The doors were made of big wooden panels hinged on leather thongs tied round the door jambs; these are based on the neolithic door found at Robenhausen in Switzerland (Cunliffe 1994, 178).

Hard primitivism

John Aubrey's view of Britain's prehistoric past was unromanticized and hard. He described the neolithic people of Wiltshire as 'almost as savage as the beasts whose skins were their only rayment . . . They were 2 or 3 degrees less salvage [*sic*] than the Americans.' That view of neolithic people recurs in the writings of one generation of archaeologists after another.

In 1861 the worshippers at a stone circle were described as 'one array of trembling votaries, swayed by terror, or blind hope, or ruthless savagery, at the will of the stern interpreters of a dark and merciless superstition'.

E. Cecil Curwen was one of the major figures in Sussex archaeology in the 1930s; among many other sites he excavated the great causewayed enclosure at

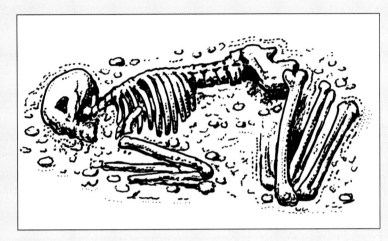

A woman buried in a ditch at Whitehawk.

Whitehawk in Brighton. He found evidence of occupation debris and human remains in the shallow ditches that marked out the enclosure, and this led him to a pessimistic (and mistaken) conclusion: that neolithic people lived in ditches on windswept hilltops. 'Life at Whitehawk Camp must have been at a very low level . . . not in the least civilized,' he concluded, painting the bleakest possible picture of people squatting among uncleared domestic debris, huddled round meagre fires. There were human remains too, so these people must have been cannibals, eating their own children. Curwen's picture is representative of a particular view of the distant past, one which we call 'hard primitivism'. For Curwen, the neolithic was indeed 'those savage times'. When he turned his attention away from his grotesque caricature of cannibal squatters in Brighton and thought more generally – and gently – about the neolithic, he described it in slightly more positive terms as 'the first lapping on our distant shores of the ever-widening ripples that brought us the benefits of [Near Eastern] civilization'.[7]

disintegrated and rotted away long ago, but the supporting posts were set in sockets that have survived. The post-hole patterns show that the houses were commonly rectangular, 5–9m long and 4–5m wide. Often a row of posts down the central axis shows that there was a ridge pole to support, and that in turn tells us the shape of the roof. Sometimes there were two rows of posts, presumably to support the centres of the rafters and prevent sagging, creating a high, roomy central space that was clear of posts. Presumably beds and other furniture were pushed back to the sides against the walls, where the roof was lower. Often the posts were set in a foundation layer of gravel set in clay, making a dry footing for the wattle-and-daub wall that was fixed to the vertical posts. These quite spacious, stoutly made and serviceable houses were made right through the neolithic. The fact that examples have been found in several regions suggests that they were widespread.

A classic example is the house at Llandegai in North Wales. The design of this three-part rectangular house was almost identical to that of the house at Ballyglass in Ireland, where the floor, complete with hearths and other occupational evidence, was preserved. The Llandegai house was 13m long and 6m across, and divided into three compartments: a big central living room (probably with a hearth) and a smaller room at each end. One of the end rooms had many posts within it, suggesting a store room with a first floor or sleeping platform above.[8] Closer still to the European longhouse tradition, both in length and in geographical location, is the house found under 4m

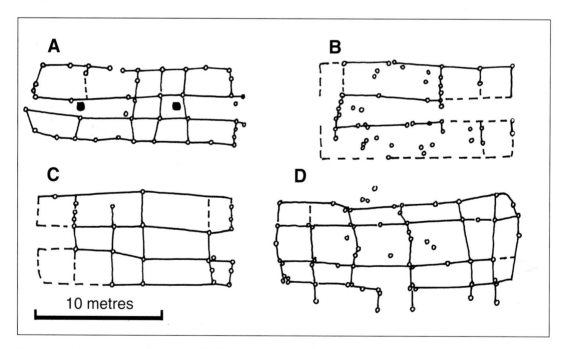

Four British longhouses. A: Lismore Fields, Derbyshire; B: Chigborough Farm, Essex; C: Llandegai, Gwynedd; D: White Horse Stone, Kent. The circles are post-holes. The lines show likely timbering (exterior walls and the rafters and purlins of the roof space).

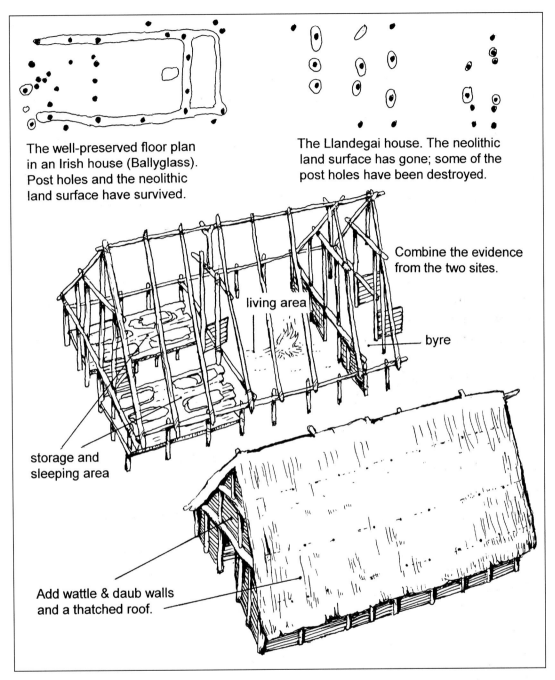

The well-preserved floor plan in an Irish house (Ballyglass). Post holes and the neolithic land surface have survived.

The Llandegai house. The neolithic land surface has gone; some of the post holes have been destroyed.

Combine the evidence from the two sites.

living area

byre

storage and sleeping area

Add wattle & daub walls and a thatched roof.

Stages in the reconstruction of a neolithic house at Llandegai. Information from other similar sites can help us to make sense of the post-holes.

of slopewash at White Horse Stone in Kent. This rectangular post-built house was 18m long and 8m wide, with an entrance porch halfway along one side.[9]

The evidence is startlingly uneven and far from complete, but the emerging picture is one of considerable diversity. The evidence for settlements in lowland England is scanty; at many locations there is little more than a scatter of flint flakes. Perhaps people did not stay at these locations for very long; perhaps they were still as mobile as their hunting predecessors, and depended for their communal foci on the houses of the ancestors and the ceremonial enclosures where they sky-buried their dead. Sky-burial was the exposure of corpses in special enclosures, often on wooden platforms supported by three stout posts. Bodies disintegrated rapidly, picked clean by scavengers, and what remained decomposed quickly in the open air. Maybe in these areas it was the local long barrow or causewayed enclosure that constituted the main focus for bonding with other people and with the land.[10] Or maybe the remains of substantial houses have been lost or overlooked, eroded away or buried under layers of later deposits. The discovery of the White Horse Stone longhouse seems to point in this direction.

In many parts of Britain ordinary people were living in well-made houses that were at least as comfortable as the dwellings of ordinary people in the middle ages, four thousand years later – without the problems of urban overcrowding – and some people were living rather better than that. Some of the settlements were inhabited for a long time, many spanning what used to be thought of as a great divide – the boundary with the middle stone age.[11] Whether it was the same families or kinship groups living in these settlements for hundreds, even thousands, of years we cannot tell, but the relationship between people and place was a deep and enduring one.

CHAPTER FOUR

NEW FOOD SOURCES

AN ECONOMY BASED ON AGRICULTURE?

Why did the ancient Britons start growing cereals? It was assumed for a long time that agriculture was adopted because in terms of food supply it was an obvious improvement on what was going on within the forager societies. Environmental problems or population growth put pressure on resources to the point where new strategies had to be tried; agriculture gave more reliable and predictable harvests and improved the calorific scores of people's diets.[1] But there is little evidence of environmental disaster, and the mesolithic communities seem to have been successful. The most advanced pre-neolithic communities in western Europe were three clusters of settlements in Portugal, Brittany and southern Scandinavia, where hunter-gatherers were living not only in settlements but with formal cemeteries nearby. These three locations were in effect cradles of neolithic megalithic culture, and they were stimulated by contact with societies to the east and south-east that had adopted agriculture. They got hooked into the farmers' exchange networks; the Scanian foragers received axes from their neolithic neighbours on the North European Plain and saw that agriculture was the way to make impressive surpluses. That desire to impress, by display (megaliths), by extravagant gift-giving (pottery and stone axes) and by hosting great feasts, triggered the neolithic revolution.[2] Perhaps it was partly because cereals were plants that they had a special magic; because, grown with human help, they occupied the mysterious boundary between culture and nature. The production of cereals was seen as being associated with the production of food surpluses, and that was the key to accumulating status.[3] Cereals were to be flaunted in tournaments of produce, a source of social, political and ideological power.[4] Meat from domesticated livestock would be offered in feasts. Later in the neolithic there would be huge pork feasts at Durrington Walls, near Stonehenge.

Windmill Hill causewayed camp, Wiltshire, looking out from the bank of the outermost circuit towards the Marlborough Downs. (Mick Sharp).

Once forest clearance was involved, a new sense of place emerged. Communities needed to claim the plots they cleared, ploughed, manured, sowed, weeded and hoped to harvest. Increasing population pressure might later lead them to consolidate their claim in terms of an inheritance from their ancestors, building conspicuous tombs in key positions to emphasize that claim.[5]

The neolithic people were the first farmers, but both settlement and land use patterns of the neolithic were to an extent continuous with what had gone before, and the real agricultural revolution – in terms of huge clearances of forest for farming – did not come until the middle bronze age.[6] There was, for instance, a hunter-gatherer settlement at Avebury Trusloe, the precursor of neolithic Avebury; the whole elaborate neolithic complex at Windmill Hill and Avebury may be seen as a glorification of an old, pre-neolithic woodland hunting camp.[7] The ceremonial focus at Stonehenge can in a similar way be traced back to an origin in a hunting shrine in a woodland clearing. Hunting went on through the neolithic; pitfalls were made in the forest to catch deer and more elaborate wooden snares were made to catch smaller forest animals.[8]

The ancestors had also fished from lake, river and sea, and fishing too continued. Dog whelks and oysters were taken many miles up the Avon valley to be consumed at Windmill Hill, so seafood was not just consumed on the coast.[9]

Given the almost continuous forest cover, the adoption of agriculture took a long time. Forest clearings took a while to create with stone axes alone – experiments using stone axes show that it takes five people two weeks to clear a hectare of forest[10] – and the earliest of them were abandoned and allowed to revert to forest after a few years or decades. The initial clearings were small, no more than gardens, and created mainly by ring-barking and burning.[11] Burning was certainly an easier way of clearing forest, and it brought the additional benefit that all the plants that might compete with the crops were destroyed, reducing the need for weeding.[12] The ash was easy to hoe into the soil as a preliminary to sowing. At the same time the forest would mostly have been too damp to burn, implying that the trees were either ringed first or laboriously felled; the dead, dry trunks would burn well in the second year.[13] Later the clearings became bigger, around 40–80 sq km.

After the trees were removed, the ground was prepared by hoeing or ploughing. The primitive plough, or ard, was armed with a simple stone point which broke the soil into a furrow. The ard was built to a design similar to the later plough, a heavy wooden implement that was almost certainly dragged by a pair of oxen, with a man steering it from behind. When the South Street long barrow near Avebury was excavated there were clear traces on the neolithic land surface beneath of the criss-cross pattern of deep-ploughing with a rip-ard.[14] Arding was quite quick – as fast as 4km of furrow per hour – but the parallel furrows could not be ploughed too close

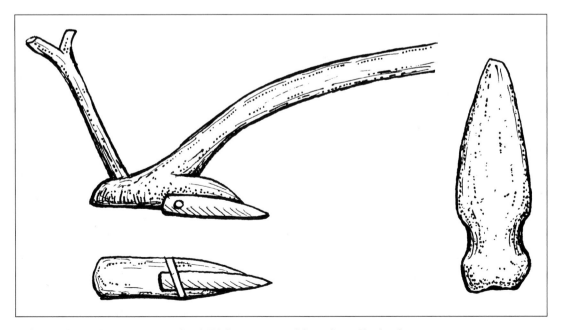

Left: two views of a reconstructed ard. Right: a stone ardshare from Shetland.

together without the point slipping sideways. The normal spacing of 30cm meant that a second set at right angles was needed and this cross-ploughing was the standard method for breaking up the ground ready for sowing seed of wheat and barley.[15] Ard-marks have been found at locations as widely separated as Orkney, the Tyne valley, Rudgeway near Bristol, Gwithian near Penzance and four Wessex sites;[16] given the spread of the evidence, the ard was probably used over the whole of Britain. Probably most agriculture was transient, informal, no more than horticulture, and producing cereals was part of a broader programme of food production.

In southern Britain emmer wheat, hulled six-row barley and naked six-row barley were grown; these were common in Europe generally. There was a single yearly sowing, with no winter wheat. Spelt wheat, rare in Europe as a whole, has been found at one British site (Hembury), and elsewhere there have been isolated finds of einkorn wheat and club wheat.[17] Beans were grown too.[18] Even in go-ahead Wessex, though, plenty of wild foods were gathered from the woods: hazelnuts, crab apples, raspberries, blackberries, sloes, hawthorn berries. The primitive crops were hardy, requiring little care, so there was plenty of time to go hunting and gathering.[19] In the South Midlands there was a very similar mix of cereals and wild foods: emmer wheat and hulled six-row barley alongside hazelnuts, apples, sloes and blackberries.[20] In Essex too people were as dependent on produce from wild plants as they were on harvests from domestic cereals.[21]

There were lots of regional and local variations, some related to soil types. People preferred light chalky soils for barley cultivation, and heavier soils for pasture.[22] Even within Orkney there were differences of economy that led on to significant cultural differences. The glacial till was heavy, hard to plough and hard to drain. The settlements at Rinyo and Barnhouse are on these heavy clay soils and both have elaborate drainage systems consisting of clay-lined drains made out of flagstone slabs. But occupation and exploitation of the machairs necessitated different strategies. Soils on the shell-sand are deficient and tend to blow away once the surface is broken. This was addressed by adding a thick midden layer, as at Links of Noltland and Skara Brae.[23] In the Western Isles the west-facing coastal strips may in the early neolithic have been sand-free and treeless, and so have favoured agriculture and settlement, though now these areas are unproductive machair. Expansion into the inhospitable interiors would not have been an option once the sandy coastal soils started to deteriorate. As a result, throughout the Western Isles, and on North Uist especially, there was increasing pressure on resources, and people appealed to the spirit world to help them by building ever-larger chamber tombs. Hence the high concentration of chamber tombs on North Uist.[24]

As we might have expected from the impressive size of the Balbridie hall, it sat in a rich landscape offering a wide range of food options. There was the River Dee, where salmon might be caught. Close at hand there was marshland where fowling might produce some more wild food. The oakwood offered game. Land cleared for pasture yielded milk, hides, wool and two kinds of meat, while arable land yielded barley for bread, biscuits and beer.[25]

Analysis of people's bones, five thousand years on, can show us the kind of food they ate, and even identify the source of protein. Although people far inland at Windmill Hill ate shellfish,[26] the inhabitants at Hambledon Hill, only 30km from the sea, consumed no fish. People in general ate large quantities of meat, and there were no dietary differences between men and women. The Parc le Breos Cwm chamber tomb stands only a kilometre from the sea, which makes all the more surprising the total absence of marine protein from the diet of the people buried there; they lived next to the sea yet did not eat anything from it. At Avebury, even though considerable preferential treatment was given to their bones after death, there was no significant difference in the food people ate while they were alive.[27] Protein analysis shows that neolithic agricultural systems were not uniform, and by no means dependent on cereals. Seafood was eaten at some places, not others, and its presence was not always connected with distance from the sea. Mussels were eaten at the Whitehawk enclosure in Brighton, then only a kilometre from the sea, and limpets were eaten at Maiden Castle near Dorchester.[28] Different communities followed different feeding regimes, which seem to have been based on preferences rather than on mere availability.[29]

Nowhere did agriculture wholly replace the old hunting and gathering way of life. The same was true on the European mainland. The rock carvings in Val Camonica in Italy show that hunting was as important as agriculture right into the iron age.[30] All the way through the neolithic the older techniques of collecting food continued. The forests, lakes, rivers and seas were still there to be exploited as food sources. It was a mixed economy, with farming communities consuming large quantities of hazelnuts and other gathered wild food,[31] as well as hunted deer meat; they also harvested rushes and osiers from the wetlands to make baskets and textiles, including the coasters that were used, before the days of the potter's wheel, to turn the pot.[32] The patterns on some of the pottery, Grooved Ware especially, imitate basketry. Rushes were harvested in early July, before the cereal harvest, dried and turned for fifteen days, then stored for up to two years. They needed only an overnight soaking to make them ready for weaving. Willows were harvested as osiers (i.e. coppiced willows) mainly in winter; these too were stored for basket-making. The wooden forks found at the Etton causewayed enclosure were perhaps used for picking soaking bundles of rushes, osiers or bark out of streams to check whether they were pliable enough for working. The fact that these objects were found at a ceremonial enclosure implies that elaborate artefacts and costumes were made on site specially for ceremonial purposes.[33]

Cattle, sheep and pigs were raised for a variety of products including meat, milk and skins. Many communities were rearing cattle, a small breed with big horns, though there is no way of knowing how big their herds were.[34] Whether they used cattle as draft animals has not been proved; there is no archaeological evidence that they used bullocks,[35] though it seems to me likely that they did. Cattle were normally slaughtered after three or four years, which means that stock was normally given gathered fodder for three or four winters, so clearly people did not regard the task of

Maiden Castle, with a bronze age barrow in the foreground (Mick Sharp).

Maiden Castle viewed from the south. The neolithic causewayed camp was at the east (right) end. (Jean Williamson/Mick Sharp).

collecting winter feed as burdensome.[36] Maybe there was enough land to provide foggage, which is grass that is allowed to grow long during the summer and left uncut for stock to graze in winter.[37]

This extensive approach to farming, putting in the lowest possible investment of time and effort, is what would be expected if the population density was low. It would also fit in with the idea that people had plenty of leisure for devising and carrying through large-scale monumental projects. 'Spare time' was an essential part of the culture.

People in different areas had preferences for different types of livestock. This may be to do with a liking for particular meat flavours, or it may be to do with the totemic significance attributed by some communities to certain animals, and not always animals that would be a likely food source. In a tomb at Hanging Grimston the jaws of twenty pigs were deposited.[38] Along the southern coast of Rousay in the Orkney group there is a succession of closely spaced chamber tombs, each belonging to a family living and farming nearby. Each family took joints of meat to eat at the funeral feasts that were held at the ancestral tomb. At one it was beef, at two it was venison and at two others it was mutton.[39]

Sheep were an introduced species, not native to Europe at all.[40] Numbers of them must have been brought in boats across the Channel or the North Sea; there is no question of their being domesticated *de novo* from feral stock in Britain.[41] They were small and long-legged, like the long-tailed Drenthe heath-sheep bred today in the Netherlands, which may be where they came from.[42] Like cattle, sheep were kept for their meat. Mutton was well suited to wind-drying, which made it the meat of choice as a reserve for lean seasons.[43] Another advantage of sheep was that they could look after themselves outdoors under harsh weather conditions. They could go on grazing during the winter and therefore generated relatively little work for gathering winter feed. They were not shorn but combed for their wool,[44] a distinctive short hair covering a fine woolly undercoat, like the Corsican mouflon.

People exploited wild animals side by side with tame: aurochs, red deer, roe deer, brown bear, cat, fowl and fish. Relatively few bones of wild animals have been found at settlement sites, and this may be because many neolithic people still led a semi-nomadic existence in which freshly killed wild animals were consumed mainly at hunting camps out in the forest.

A single burnt grape pip, the only one known in Britain at this time, was found at Hambledon Hill and has led to a lot of discussion. Was it an exotic import from overseas, possibly as dried fruit, or were vines grown in Wessex?[45] Or does it represent contamination from some later period? Or was it a hoax by a mischievous archaeology student? A piece of charcoal in the enclosure ditch turned out to be a burnt vine, so we now know that vines *were* grown in Dorset, after all.[46]

The large areas of grassland the neolithic people created simply gave scope to plant species that were already here. Possibly a few low-growing plants were brought in from mainland Europe, such as white clover, but most were growing in the woodland, survivors from the more open conditions that prevailed at the end of the last cold

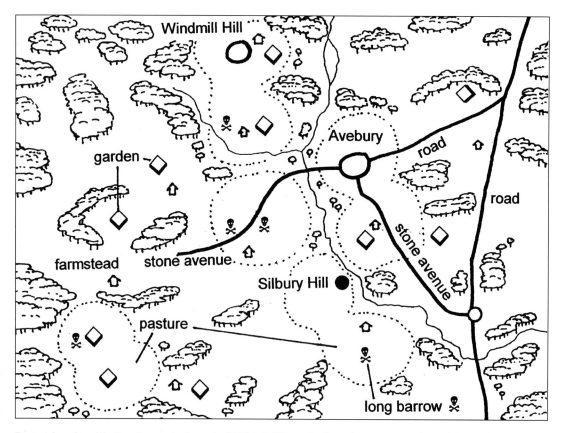

Pastoral and arable farming at Avebury in 3000 BC. When the long barrows were in active use for burial in
the early neolithic, people built their houses well away from them. As the barrows went out of active use
they lost this taboo (after Smith 1984).

stage. Plants that were to flourish in the neolithic pastures, like meadowsweet, self-heal
and ragged robin, had for a long time been growing unobtrusively under the canopy
of the wildwood.[47]

Organized field systems were more characteristic of the later neolithic, but not all
were late; some ordered systems of fields were laid out by 3000 BC, such as those
surrounded by drystone walls and preserved under peat at Behy and Glenulra in
Ireland. Next to Carn Brea in Cornwall, a defended enclosure dating to the same
period, there are small fields, thought to be contemporary, which have been cleared
of stones and these would appear to be the oldest identifiable fields in Britain.[48] It has
been suggested that it was no coincidence that the laying out of large-scale field
systems happened just after the period of monument-building ended.[49] Perhaps it was
an inevitable sequel to the process of punctuating the landscape with monuments to
mark out the spaces between them.

There is a problem, a resistance to overcome. The idea of the neolithic as a settled
mixed farming lifestyle appeals to our nostalgia for an idyllic, once-upon-a-time

English countryside and the simple bucolic way of life that went with it. But the reality of the landscape was different. It was not a cleared landscape but still a mainly forested one. Nor was it even a predominantly agricultural way of life, but a more complex one deeply rooted in the ways of the hunter-gatherer ancestors – literally our hunting fathers – and in the understanding of the wildscape inherited from that long and educative past, the knowledge of all the resources available in the seas, rivers, marshes, moors and above all the everlasting forest.

We come full circle now, back to the cereals and why they were adopted. It has often been assumed that the grain was ground to make flour, which in turn was made into porridge, bread, cakes and biscuits. Certainly barley was used to make barley cakes: the remains of some were found at Yarnton in Oxfordshire.[50] Barley cakes are sweet, coarse, granular, rather like crunchy muesli biscuits – or the Trackers I never tire of eating. And there are other possibilities: beer, for instance.

Balfarg henge monument, Glenrothes, Fife (Mick Sharp).

Stone circles on Machrie Moor, Arran (Mick Sharp).

Residues of fermented alcoholic drinks have been identified on neolithic pottery at a significant number of sites, in Orkney, at Balfarg, on the isle of Rhum and at Machrie Moor on Arran. The initial discovery was made on Rhum in 1985, when a black crust inside a neolithic pot was found to be the remains of a heather ale containing an unusual combination of cereals and herbs collected in late summer or early autumn. The heather suggests that honey was an ingredient. William Grant & Sons produced some experimental brews from these ingredients, producing a pleasant, pale golden drink, rather like an after-dinner wine. It was 9 per cent proof.[51]

The drink at Balfarg contained meadowsweet, henbane and deadly nightshade – hallucinogenic as well as intoxicating. Henbane induces intoxication, hallucination, blurred vision, rapid heartbeat, euphoria, dizziness and an illusion of flying. Here we have the first solid evidence that the ceremonies at stone circles and henges involved quaffing spiked alcoholic drinks that produced weird and other-worldly experiences. Spiked or unspiked, alcohol was also probably a major feature of the bigmen's display feasts.[52] The several tons of Grooved Ware pottery found at Durrington Walls may have been used in these display feast drinking bouts. The bigman is the oldest type of leader, the headman who unobtrusively and without any authority other than personal charisma holds a tribe together. He has no hereditary rights and his role is to act as a chairman, foreman and spokesman for the community – and to host feasts.

Brewing need not have involved any elaborate technology, though special items and spaces would have been set aside for it. Ale was fermented in a large closed vessel, a large jar with a close-fitting lid. Other equipment and facilities included a shovel, a quern, hot stones, a hearth or oven, baskets, a water supply, washing facilities and a hut in which to carry out the simple process. Maybe caretaker communities living at the ceremonial enclosures saw to the production of the ale.

Cereals can be made into sweet malts and malt extracts, and it may be that these were the products people were initially most interested in making; they are both nutritious (rich in B-vitamins) and delicious to eat on their own. They can also be mixed with milk to make a tasty drink exactly like Horlicks.

But this was no Eden. By 3000 BC some areas cleared for agriculture were suffering from soil depletion. People were letting them go, allowing them to revert to woodland. People working marginal lands were giving them up and there was a withdrawal, at least as far as farming was concerned, to the more productive areas – Orkney, eastern Scotland, Anglesey, Yorkshire, the upper Thames valley, Wessex, Essex and the valleys draining to the Fens. In these core areas cultivation intensified, but across large areas even in the chalklands of southern Britain arable farming was shutting down and the land being converted to pasture. This economic shift sent ripples through the social structure and affected a whole range of practices that now seem far removed from food production.

CHAPTER FIVE

A LAND WITHOUT LEADERS

HOW MANY PEOPLE?

What people say about neolithic society depends to a great extent on their assumptions about the size of the population, especially the number of people available to carry out work on major communal projects, such as building stone circles or chamber tombs. Prehistorians with ideas about large-scale changes in prehistoric societies frequently call upon 'population pressure' as a key mechanism, by which they mean the increase of population density to a point where a critical pressure is put on resources, forcing the socio-economic system to change. It seems likely that technological changes and many social, economic and political events did in fact spring from such shifts in population pressure, but unfortunately we do not know what the population density was at any time, nor can we easily estimate how many people lived in any particular community. Various approaches to an estimate have been tried, using the number of settlements and their size, the number of tombs and the number of dead they contain, and the number of people needed to build the monuments. Yet the information we have to go on is, in every case, incomplete.[1]

Concentrations of tombs can highlight areas of high population density, but their absence from certain areas should not be taken to mean certain areas were deserted. In some areas the dead may have been buried close to home, in a family tomb overlooking the family plot, but in other areas the dead may have been carried or even ferried to a special 'central' place many miles from the dwelling places. The scatter of stone axes may well be a better general indicator of the presence of people in an area. In Wales, for instance, a thin scatter of axes covering all parts of the country shows that people went everywhere, though they were especially interested in the lowlands and the valleys: the mountains and moors were less visited.[2] It is what we would expect.

The death rate was certainly high, probably around 40 per 1,000 per year, compared with 14 today.[3] Living close to livestock, people would have been more vulnerable to tuberculosis, brucellosis and anthrax. They were eating and drinking from unglazed pottery, and food contamination would have led to gastro-enteritis.[4] People died young. A survival chart for several communities in neolithic Switzerland shows only 30 per cent of people surviving to the age of 18, only 5 per cent to the age of 45.[5] It was no different in Britain. Infant mortality was high and there was a low life expectancy for women because of the perils of childbirth. Archaeologists frequently come across the pathetic remains of young women with new-born infants or foetuses.[6]

Colin Burgess arrived at a population of 16,000 for Wessex 'at the time of Stonehenge', basing the estimate on the existence of four thousand barrows, but also arrived at a figure twice as high, based on the carrying capacity of the fertile chalklands, thought to be capable of bearing a population density, using neolithic techniques, of 10 people per square kilometre. It is likely that the true figure for 3000 BC lies somewhere between, given that large areas are likely to have gone out of production because they were worn out.[7]

Various global estimates are available. Burgess suggested that the population of Britain in 2500 BC was around 500,000; this is higher than earlier estimates, to fit the large labour forces needed for the large-scale monuments being built at that time.[8] But the population had been virtually double that in 3000 BC. Steady population increase during the fourth millennium meant that there were around 900,000 people living in Britain in 3000 BC, but this was immediately followed by a population collapse to around 500,000 by 2900 BC.[9] This is the most vivid expression of the great unrecorded crisis that overtook Britain in 3000 BC.

Colin Renfrew attempted a belated neolithic census of Orkney. He used the tombs on Rousay, which he assumed were all in use at the same time, to give a figure of 260. The population of Rousay in 1790 was 770, and fell to about one-third of this to the neolithic level of 237 by 1961. Renfrew floated the hypothesis that one could take the pre-Industrial Revolution populations (around 1800) of the other islands in the group and divide them by three to provide approximations of the neolithic population. He tested the hypothesis on Eday, confirmed that the method worked,[10] and went on to calculate a total population for Orkney of 6,000.

Whether that figure is right or not, the assumptions Renfrew made about the relationship between size of monument and size of community are unjustified. Medium-sized chamber tombs such as Quanterness are thought to have absorbed about 10,000 man-hours of labour, the fine stone circle at Stenness about 40,000 man-hours and the nearby Ring of Brodgar 80,000 man-hours. Maes Howe, the most ambitious project undertaken on Orkney in the neolithic, cost in the region of 80,000–100,000 man-hours. Renfrew argued from this a stepping-up of social organization, and the gathering of a proportionally larger work-force, implying a welding together of several Orcadian bands into a larger social group for the

Maes Howe, one of the greatest architectural masterpieces of ancient Europe. The view back towards the entrance passage (and the midwinter sunset) from the spacious tomb chamber, 4.6m square. The tall 'buttresses' to left and right were probably standing stones that stood on the site before the tomb was built round them.

communal project.[11] While this *may* have happened, the same monuments could have been built by a smaller work-force working on them for longer. If competition among neighbouring communities drove the monument-building programme on to ever more ambitious projects,[12] ambition may have caused communities that were not increasing in size to work harder and longer in order to outdo their neighbours. The argument that spectacular monuments prove that a centralizing tendency involving communities ten times larger was at work is not overwhelming. And if the argument does not convince for Orkney, it does not for Wessex either, nor for anywhere in between.

THE NATURE OF SOCIETY

Communities in the early neolithic, 4000 BC to 3000 BC, were mostly small-scale, autonomous and equal in status with one another. Each community consisted of a homestead or a hamlet, occupied by perhaps one extended family, a social unit that had endured for thousands of years;[13] there were scarcely any villages, let alone towns. Indeed many of these 'band' communities were little changed from the mesolithic groups who were their ancestors, with the single exception that they had bigmen or headmen, who unobtrusively and without any apparent authority, held the tribe together. The village leader of Papua New Guinea qualifies for his position by his personality, not by any hereditary right; he is confident, original, a man of ambition and initiative. He is expected to chair discussions, to arbitrate, to act as foreman. He is the sort of figure likely to emerge in British neolithic society in the fourth millennium, taking it from the level of band organization to that of tribal organization.[14]

In some areas the settlements were uniformly spaced; other factors permitting, the band was likely to settle in the middle of the landscape it exploited, so that relatively short journeys were required to reach all the resources. It was not hostility or unsociability that caused this 'repulsion' of settlements, though the maximal spacing would certainly have reduced friction if disputes ever arose about access to resources. Another sign of this egalitarian or 'nascent' society is that there is no hierarchy of places that might suggest a socio-political hierarchy.[15]

Some prehistorians believe there was a rigid authoritarian structure with strong centralized control by chiefs and/or shamans. Some prehistorians see the scale of the communal monumental projects appearing from 3000 BC onwards as evidence of huge labour forces pressed into service by powerful leaders: Silbury Hill (it was said) required 1,500 people to work on it for 5 years, 18 million man-hours in all.[16] There are two problems with this. One is that it assumes the work was done in a short period and therefore required a huge work-force, yet we have no way of telling whether Silbury was built quickly or slowly. It looks as if Silbury was built all in one go,[17] but that means only that the work was continuous, not rapid. The other problem is that it is assumed that people have to be *made* to work, but if a whole society is enthused by an ideology, as I believe the nature of the monuments shows, coordination is all that is needed – not powerful leadership at all.

Society was intensely conservative and traditional, fanatically and unshakeably rooted in the past, and seemingly uniform over large areas, to judge from the remarkable uniformity of, say, long barrow architecture. Some prehistorians argue that this shows that people lived in fear of displeasing the gods or ancestors, and that this fear effectively constrained every aspect of society. While that may be so, it is equally possible to infer from the same evidence a society in which everyone was positively swept along by a common ideology. The smallness of the scale of society made living outside it unthinkable, and heretical views, whether religious, social or political, were probably rarely expressed. Fear need not have played any part in it.

The evolution of society (after Jensen 1982, 127)

Morton Fried's terminology (1967)	Elman Service's terminology (1971)
Egalitarian society	Band organization
Ranked society [Britain 3000 BC?]	Tribal organization [Britain 3000 BC?]
Stratified society	Chiefdom organization
State society	State organization

In a small-scale egalitarian society there are invariably religious specialists. Even the simplest societies have their shamans, unusual people with a particular insight into spiritual matters, or maybe just a flair for superstition, and they take on the role of 'wise man' or 'wise woman', signalling special places, special times, instigating monument-building and presiding at religious ceremonies.[18] The shaman would have had supporters in the community, but there was no organized priesthood.

Even while the segmentary society prevailed, there were significant regional differences. The small-scale, family/farmstead communities typical of the fourth millennium continued in the east, while in the west, notably in Wessex, something more complex was emerging in the late neolithic. Around 3000 BC profound changes in the nature of society were under way. At least some groups became larger; there was a clear development of quality variation; valuable artefacts began to be made; and a few very high-status centres began to appear, as did symbols of social division.[19] One of the most striking features was the divergence in status between men and women. In 3500 BC men and women enjoyed equal status. By 3000 BC men enjoyed a status twice or three times as great as that of women.[20] Children had low status in 3500 BC and slightly lower status in 3000 BC, so I propose a four-tier status-split: children, women and adolescents of both sexes, men, and bigmen,[21] though in practice it is not usually possible to identify bigmen in the archaeological record. During the tribal period ranking began to develop; by 3000 BC the egalitarian society of the mesolithic and early neolithic had become a ranked society.[22] Ranking meant that not only were there variations in status, but also limitations on access to status. Coveted, highly valued objects – first stone axes, then amber, then jet, then gold – could only be acquired with difficulty and at great cost, and they gave access to status.[23]

The nature of society changed at the millennium. In the 1970s Colin Renfrew argued for the evolution of a chiefdom society in Wessex during the fourth and third millennia, leading to a more or less unified tribal confederation encompassing the whole of the Wessex chalklands by the time the sarsen monument at Stonehenge was built at the end of the third millennium.[24] The role of the chief would have been a development from that of the bigman. He would have hosted the 'moka', or big display feasts, planned and organized the large-scale communal labour projects, led diplomatic and political initiatives, kept the peace and, if necessary, instigated feuding against enemies. The big difference between chiefs and bigmen was that chiefs usually acquired their positions by inheritance, and as a result acquired a certain numen as magic people, royalty in effect and eventually *in fact*, in a way that bigmen did not. So one major change implicit in Colin Renfrew's picture is the birth of kingship, an important steering principle in Britain's development from that time onwards.

At the same time the role of shaman developed towards that of priest. The task of designing and organizing the more complex monuments now being built implies a group of religious specialists rather than just one person. With supporters, acolytes and novices, trainee priests, around him, the priest might pass on a more developed body of spiritual knowledge. Whether this amounted to a formal priesthood is still, to

Wessex 3500 BC – 3000 BC

The Wessex chalklands were apparently divided into five major territories: the Dorset Downs, Cranborne Chase, West Salisbury Plain, East Salisbury Plain and the Marlborough Downs. These are inferred from the clusters of long barrows and the locations of causewayed enclosures. It is not clear whether Mendip in the west and the Southern Cotswolds in the north-west made two further territories; there are no obvious central places. Various attempts were made in the 1970s and 1980s to draw 'frontiers', as here, based on the assumption that the causewayed enclosures were geographically as well as culturally central. The map nevertheless shows that some enclosures were at the edges of these territories, or at least the edges of their core areas. Did the two enclosures on the chalk scarp south of Windmill Hill, Rybury and Knap Hill, perhaps serve the people living in the adjacent Vale of Pewsey?

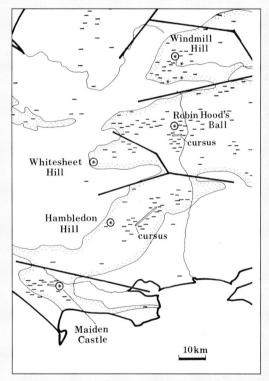

Wessex 3500–3000 BC. The named sites are major causewayed enclosures. Dash = long barrow; solid black line = possible boundary between tribal territories, assuming enclosures were geometrically central; small dotted area in the west = Carboniferous Limestone; large dotted area in the centre = Chalk. The map implies that the Wessex chalklands had evolved into five large tribal territories.

Wessex 3000 BC– 2500 BC

On a local scale there were significant changes around 3000 BC; old centres were replaced by new ones a few miles away. Windmill Hill was supplanted by Avebury, Robin Hood's Ball by Stonehenge, the Dorset Cursus by Knowlton Circles, Maiden Castle by Mount Pleasant and Maumbury Rings. But on a regional scale the pattern remained broadly similar.

Colin Burgess (1980, 171–5) calculated that the (late neolithic) population of each territory was 3,000–8,000, which would have supplied an ample labour pool for communal projects, more than adequate to provide the 18 million man-hours required to build Silbury Hill. The 30 million man-hours Burgess estimates for the sarsen monument at Stonehenge would have stretched the East Salisbury Plain community to the limit, and herein lies a powerful argument for a paramount chief commanding all the labour force of Wessex from 2400 BC onwards. A difficulty is that some of the big projects, such as the Dorset Cursus, were built well before this, at a time when society was simpler.

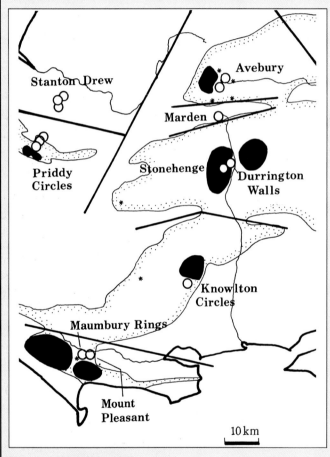

Wessex 3000–2500 BC. The superhenge territories. The circles represent large henges or stone circles. The round barrow clusters developed close to these ceremonial centres. The asterisks represent the old causewayed enclosures.

The ceremonial monuments did not necessarily represent everyday social, secular foci, or even centres of population, so the territories and their 'frontiers' remain elusive. Ever-alert to all the possibilities, Renfrew himself noted seven different possible spatial relationships between 'life space' and 'death space' in a landscape, and we cannot be absolutely certain which of these applied in neolithic Wessex (after Burgess 1980, Renfrew 1973 and 1981).

my mind, very doubtful and I prefer to think of less formal witch-doctor figures. As both society and its monumental projects became more complex, some sort of division of responsibility may have begun to develop.[25]

Colin Renfrew's interpretation of the ceremonial landscape of Wessex can be successfully extended to other parts of Britain.[26] In the Upper Thames Valley the fourth-millennium causewayed enclosure at Abingdon gave way to the third-millennium Big Rings henge at Dorchester-on-Thames. In the Chilterns the Maiden Bower causewayed enclosure was replaced by Waulud's Bank. Other major ceremonial foci developed in the Mendips (the Priddy Circles), at Kilmartin in Argyll and at Thornborough in Yorkshire.

Attractive though it is, Renfrew's idea of a chiefdom society emerging in mid-neolithic Wessex may be a piece of cultural chauvinism, a reading back into prehistory of the social structures of more recent times. Ideas such as chiefly authority, frontiers and even territories may have had no currency in this pre-state situation. Activities of élite groups and individuals in prehistory may not have operated across areas in the way that they came to in the historic period; they may have been very local in some ways, such as the organization of food supply, yet very far-reaching in others, such as the acquisition of prestige goods. Another objection is that we now see the neolithic way of life as depending rather less on sedentary cereal cultivation than we did in the 1970s. People were more mobile. There is no doubt that Avebury was a high-status structure in 3000 BC and that it was intended to demonstrate high status, but there is no evidence that it was intended to stress the importance of a particular leader; the emphasis seems to have been on advertising group identity.[27] The pull of power centres such as Avebury and Stonehenge may have had something to do with blood lines or clans, or with certain specialist activities; Burl has argued persuasively that stone circles in Cumbria performed a particular function in relation to the axe trade.

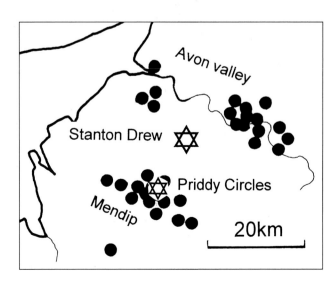

Monuments and settlements in Somerset. The settlements form three distinct clusters, round Bath, the mouth of the Avon and the Mendips. The Priddy Circles were built in the midst of the Mendip cluster. The Stanton Drew ceremonial centre was in an unsettled area, perhaps serving all three settlement clusters.

In a non-state system there may have been chiefs or bigmen but they were not commanders or tyrants. If they had been, the monuments would have been completed. The story of Stonehenge is one of continual discussion, modification and periodic large-scale changes of mind: these are not the characteristics of rule by dictators. We are looking at something very like the inverse of a feudal medieval European society. Chiefs were not there to command, and people were under no obligation to obey their chiefs. The real seat of power was not the residence of the chief, but instead the holy place identified by common consent or earmarked by the local priest. The religious élite, however organized or disorganized, in some way interpreted or divined what was required in the way of designing or modifying or decommissioning a monument and, to judge from ethnographic parallels, this would then have been agreed by the whole community in a discussion chaired by the bigman. People exercised authority over their chiefs, rather than the other way round.

We may have been guilty of temporal chauvinism in attempting to identify sharply defined political territories along modern lines. Whether or not enclosures or tombs are used as central places, there is no reason to suppose that the groups who built them exercised a rigorous control over particular areas, excluding outsiders. The territories-and-frontiers model is probably not appropriate to the small-scale societies and low population densities of the time; it is mainly competition for resources that causes frontier zones to crystallize into hard boundaries – and that would come later. It is likely that tombs, henges and stone circles were expressions of the social identity of the local groups, and the communal labour input involved would reinforce that expression. On the other hand, we know that people crossed Britain with raw materials and artefacts and to do so, other than by sea, would have involved walking across hundreds of different band territories. This suggests a fairly relaxed attitude to territory and there was doubtless a hospitality obligation on the part of the host group. There were no doubt agreed codes of conduct for correct behaviour inside other people's territories. We can imagine complex chains of social relationships that cut across the landscape divisions suggested by the monuments, relationships that were continually negotiated and oiled by gift exchanges.[28]

The only real frontiers would have been the shoreline and the horizon, and people regularly crossed both of these. They were permeable boundaries. And with mobility, the boundary between earth and heaven, the horizon itself, becomes a shifting boundary. So a fluid, soft-focus network of boundaries would be likely.

The iron age territories in Wales were loosely based on bronze age territories,[29] and possibly these in turn originated in the neolithic. Wales was very sparsely populated, with a thin scatter of farmsteads; no settlements larger than a couple of houses have yet been found. Some areas were nevertheless more intensively settled than others, and when neolithic finds of every kind are mapped, a pattern of clusters becomes visible, at Walton, Hay-on-Wye, Newport, Rhondda, Barry, Porthcawl, the Pembroke peninsula, Prestatyn, Conwy and the Menai coast of Anglesey. Sparse though the neolithic activity in Wales was, there was at least one concentration in each of the iron age territories. Glamorgan, which in the iron age became the land of the Silures, had four of these clusters; Gwynedd, the land of the Ordovices, had two; Powys, the land of the Cornovii, had one (Walton-Hindwell); Dyfed, the land of the Demetae, had one (Pembroke); the land of the Deceangli had one (Prestatyn). The pattern of settlement in Wales suggests that the much later tribal territories of the iron age may already have begun to take shape.

CHAPTER SIX

WAYS AND MEANS

ROADS

Since time out of mind people had found their way from place to place by long-enduring and well-remembered paths. Some tracks had become busy thoroughfares with people carrying bundles of stone axe-heads, pottery and other commodities long distances overland. Not for nothing does the plantain make itself known in the pollen record now, the humble plantain that grows on tracks and earthen roads, because it will withstand being trampled upon. From this time forward Britain had a fully developed system of paths and roads.[1]

Many of the paths originated as animal tracks. The larger animals were migratory and had long before established their own routes through the wildwood. Wild cattle moved seasonally between the upland moors of southern Scotland and the pastures along the coasts of the Solway Firth; they did the same in Wales, ambling down from summer pastures in central Wales to winter along the coast of Cardigan Bay.[2] Animal tracks converge on points of difficulty, such as narrow defiles or fording-places on rivers, fanning out in between to make a broad zone of braiding alternative paths. And people did the same. Well before 3000 BC people were sharing or borrowing many of these natural routeways, even to the point of adopting the skeins of alternative paths. Since hunting was still an important part of the neolithic way of life, people would have had more than one motive for following the animal tracks. In some areas dense undergrowth below the woodland canopy would have made travel difficult. In places where deer, wild boar and wild cattle had cleared pathways through the undergrowth to make their own way, people would naturally follow.[3]

Travel was a long-established human habit, even if most resources could be obtained locally. Two thousand years earlier people in Fifeshire are known to have followed paths up to 20km long through the landscape, some involving crossing wide rivers.[4] In southern England people may have used the western part of the Pilgrims' Way to transport Portland chert for toolstone from Dorset to Surrey.[5] In the neolithic too

The Rollright Stones, a circle of seventy-seven blocks of weathered limestone arranged in a true circle 31m in diameter, may have been built on an important cross-country route.

there was long-distance travel; people living in north Wales, southern Scotland and Wessex had access to Whitby jet, which they used for belt sliders, proving that they had long-distance overland contact with the Yorkshire Wolds group.[6]

Until the 1950s it was widely accepted that long-distance scarp-crest trackways like the Pilgrims' Way had their origin as neolithic roads. This was based in part on tradition, in part on an assumption that neolithic people preferred to live on high ground, where the remains of their barrows are still to be seen; the main roads naturally followed the populated ridges. But during the past fifty years more and more evidence has come to light showing that people lived on low ground as well. In 1940 the Jurassic Way was claimed as a prehistoric road because of the concentration of prehistoric sites close to it, but since then increasing numbers of sites have been discovered well away from it. In fact the Jurassic Way is now seen as *avoiding* the most densely populated parts of prehistoric Northamptonshire.[7]

Similarly, scholarly interest in the Icknield Way as a prehistoric highway attracted evidence in support of that assumption, but it is now clear that there are many prehistoric sites well away from the trackway,[8] and this might appear to argue against the Icknield Way's status as a prehistoric track.

It has also been argued that scarp-crest trackways that might have been expected to lead to important places actually did not. The Icknield Way leads south-westwards along the Chiltern escarpment, continuing across the Goring gap in the Thames valley to become the Ridgeway over the Berkshire and Marlborough Downs, leading *almost* to Avebury. Almost but not quite. As it approaches Avebury, the prehistoric highway swings south to miss the great henge by 2 miles. Christopher Taylor argues that the lowland routes in the area followed by modern roads and farm tracks are more likely to have been used in antiquity than the Ridgeway.[9]

But these arguments need not defeat tradition. In a later period Anglo-Saxon minor settlements were often located away from major roads, which were used by armies – and armies were predatory and dangerous, whether hostile or hungry. The fact that many middle to late neolithic foci were on low ground, like Avebury, Marden, Mount Pleasant or Waulud's Bank, does not preclude the use of higher ridge-top routes for cross-country communication.

If we look at a medium-scale map of the ridge-top routes in southern England, they do appear to converge, in a fairly purposeful way, even allowing for accidents of geology and landscape, on the high-status monuments in Wessex. It looks to me as if

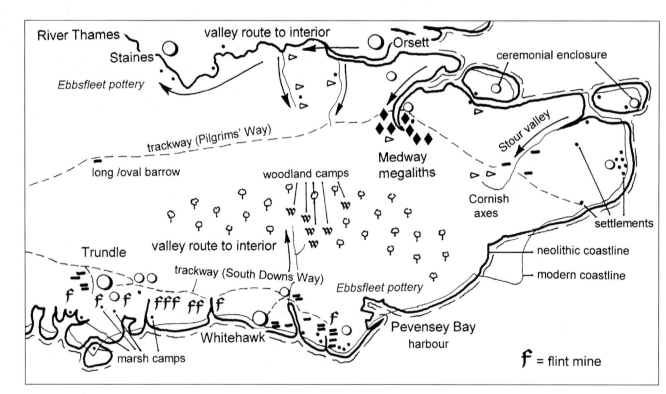

South-east England was a strongly differentiated landscape, but with locales connected by ridgeways (dashed), valley routes (arrows) and bay-hopping sea routes. Dots represent settlements, circles ceremonial enclosures.

Icknield Way

Over 400 neolithic stone tools found in East Anglia (Cambridgeshire, Norfolk, Suffolk and Essex) originated outside the region. The origin of some could not be traced, but 7 came from Northern Ireland (Tievebulliagh), 16 from Leicestershire (Charnwood Forest), 20 from Wales, 41 from Northumberland (Great Whin Sill), 60 from Cornwall and the largest number of all, 90, from Great Langdale in the Lake District.

Obviously this does not prove that neolithic people travelled long distances to trade or exchange commodities, because the movement of stone tools could be the result of many local transactions involving only short walks. The geographical distribution of the foreign axes in East Anglia nevertheless does hint at the routes by which they were transported.

There is a strong concentration of imported axes

Findspots of Great Langdale axes (*filled circles*) in East Anglia. The pattern suggests arrival by sea, then distribution via the Great Ouse valley and Icknield Way, as well as some coastwise trading. The few far-travelled Irish axes that have been found (*filled lozenges*) fall into the same pattern (after Parker Pearson 1993).

along the south-eastern edge of the Fens, confined between the fen edge and the Icknield Way. Since the Icknield Way ends on the north Norfolk coast, axes from Northumberland and even the Lake District could have been brought from the Tyne by boat to that point, then carried south over land along the trackway. The Icknield Way marks the eastern edge of the main concentration of finds. The Great Ouse and the River Cam mark the western edge, and I suggest that this water route south from the Wash was also used. Cornish and Welsh axes could have arrived from the opposite direction along the Icknield Way.

Round the Suffolk and Essex estuaries there is another concentration of foreign axes, which must have been brought in by sea. The East Anglian evidence points to the use of coastwise sea routes, as well as rivers and long-distance trackways. It also confirms that neolithic people preferred living on low ground.

the traditional scarp-crest trackways really were used in the neolithic. They minimized the need for river crossings; they avoided the wet, miry clays that would have been impassable in winter; and they were easy to navigate; following a ridge is easy, and the thin woodland cover would have made it easy to see where you were. Often the track braided to make at least two alternative routes, one along the crest of the escarpment, which would have been dry under foot even in winter and easy to navigate, and another along the scarp foot, which would have been dry enough in summer and would have obviated the climb up on to the ridge after each river crossing.[10] The argument against the Ridgeway is not convincing. The Ridgeway veers away 2 miles short of Avebury because of the physique of the landscape: it has to follow the crest of the escarpment. It is fairly clear that spur tracks led down from the Ridgeway into Avebury: the country lane that still leads to the east entrance of the henge, which later became the Anglo-Saxon Herepath, and the West Kennet Avenue that leads from the Sanctuary up on the Ridgeway.

These spur tracks functioned in very much the same way as the feeder roads that lead into modern British cities from various points along tangential motorways, such as those leading into Northampton from junctions 15, 15a and 16 on the M1; meanwhile, the M1 continues northwards to skirt Leicester (junctions 21 and 22), just as the Ridgeway continued on its way southwards, to skim past the Knap Hill causewayed enclosure and the Marden superhenge.

Almost certainly there would have been many lowland road routes besides the scarp-foot tracks, but these are now undetectable and undatable under later developments

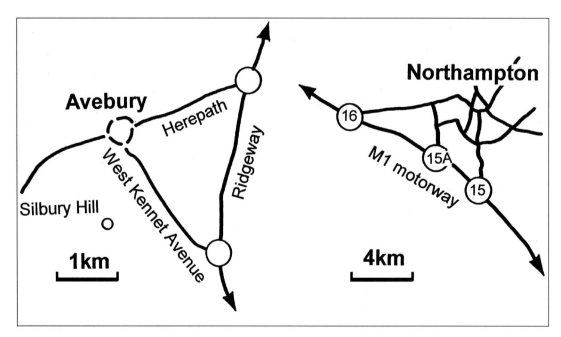

Neolithic and modern road systems compared: Avebury then and Northampton now.

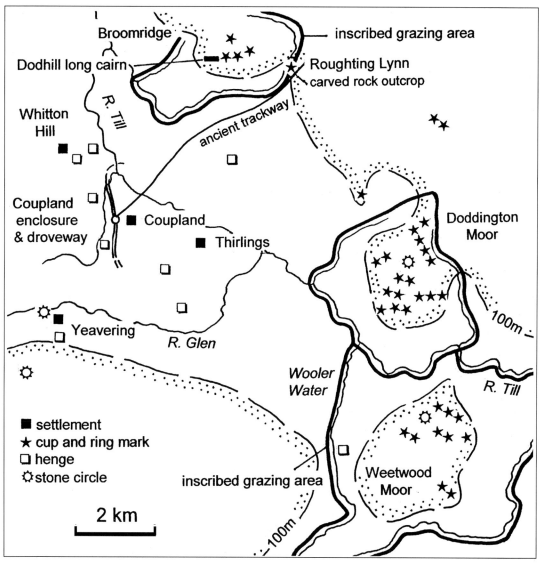

Neolithic Northumberland: the Milfield 'Avenue' or droveway and its surroundings. Rock carvings were markers for grazing territories on the hills. The henges and settlements were on the lower ground.

such as the A roads that we now accept without thinking as the natural routes across the landscape.[11] Some sections of the Pilgrims' Way are still country lanes and farm tracks, but some, as modern walkers discover to their horror, are occupied by busy roads such as the A31.

Ceremonial monuments often imply lines of movement through the landscape. The West Kennet Avenue linking Avebury with the Ridgeway has already been mentioned. In the Milfield Basin in Northumberland an earthen avenue passes right through the Coupland Enclosure, in one entrance and out of the other, which tells us how people moved through the henge. An apparently modern track leads north-eastwards from the Coupland Enclosure, crosses the River Till, then climbs the hillside to the cup-

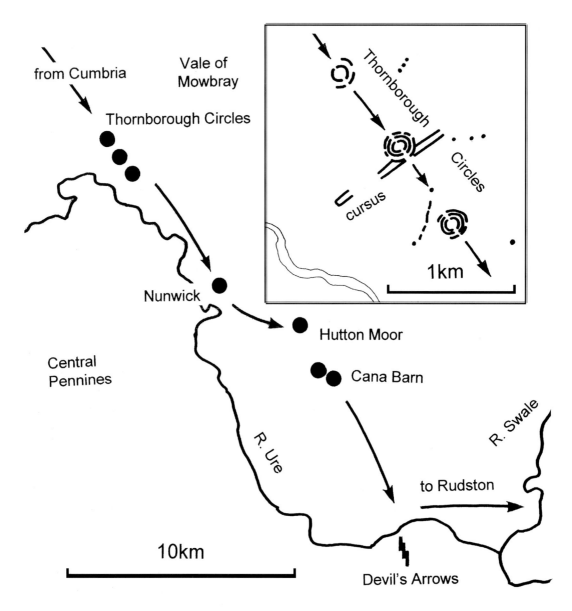

A sanctified axe trade route? The line of monuments in the Ure valley, east of the Pennines (after Harding 2000b).

and-ring mark carved on the rock at Roughting Lynn, at about 100 metres. This 6km-long track follows the natural route from the valley floor henge up to the Broomridge, the inscribed moorland grazing area signposted by the cup-and-ring mark, and is therefore probably neolithic in origin.[12]

Arrangements of monuments in lines imply either that people walked from one monument to another in sequence or that the monuments were erected beside a thoroughfare used for some other purpose. In the Ure valley in Yorkshire the three Thornborough Circles were laid out in a line that, when projected well to the south-south-east, passed close to three more henges, Nunwick, Hutton and Cana Barn, and then the Devil's Arrows, three stones standing where the line crosses the River Ure. The whole linear complex is 17 kilometres long. The Thornborough Circles lie at the break-of-slope between the level landscape of the broad valley floors of the Ure and Swale to the east and the hill country to the west. This is a natural location for a (dry) valley-side route. We also know that axes were carried from the Lake District across to the Yorkshire Wolds, and the Ure valley offers the easiest route across the Pennines, so it is extremely likely that axe traders passed the line of henges.[13] The likeliest route for axe traders from Great Langdale was east-south-eastwards via Ambleside, Windermere, Kendal and Sedbergh, following the line of the modern A591, A684 and A6108, then up Garsdale, over Garsdale Head into Wensleydale, and taking the easy walk down Wensleydale to the Ure's emergence into the lowlands. Significantly, the Thornborough Circles mark this important exit point where the road entered an entirely new landscape. The major ceremonial centre at Rudston lies due east of the Devil's Arrows, and these three megaliths in turn stand very close to the Ure–Swale confluence, deliberately located to mark another important node in the communications network.[14] The monuments may therefore have been visited by pilgrims from far afield. Pilgrims seek an unusually intense religious experience in an environment far removed from their everyday world, in a place where they may in safety cross over into the realm of the transcendent.[15] It is significant that the henges are similar to one another, and it is characteristic of pilgrimage routes that the shrines along the way replicate each other, rather like the Stations of the Cross in a Catholic church, each offering a literal rite of passage.

The tracks discussed so far have been inferred rather than proved, and it is in their nature that, directly at any rate, they defy dating. There is nevertheless one group of tracks that do survive in the archaeological record, and *can* be radiocarbon dated – the trackways of the Somerset Levels. Because they were built, and built of wood, they can be both excavated and dated.

These carefully engineered walkways across the marshland were made to connect the dry 'islands' of Burtle, West Hay and Meare with the higher ground to north and south, the Wedmore Ridge and the Polden Hills.[16] The tracks were made of a variety of different wood. The structures were often a metre wide, but some, like the Sweet Track, provided as a walkway only a slippery plank 25 centimetres wide. They were easily and quickly made – a dozen people could have made 2 kilometres of trackway in a day – though the felling and preparation of the timber would have taken longer.

Many ancient roads can be inferred with some confidence. The high henge bank at Avebury has four distinct entrance gaps, two of which (west and south) had megalithic avenues leading to them, very obviously processional approach routes. The other two (north and east) did not, but they must also have been points of access. The east entrance has only a farm track of very local importance leading to it today. In the eighteenth century it had a more important route leading to it, the Bath Road; earlier still it was a Saxon herepath. It seems to me almost certain that this same route was in use in 3000 BC,[17] in part to act as a spur link between Avebury and the Ridgeway for

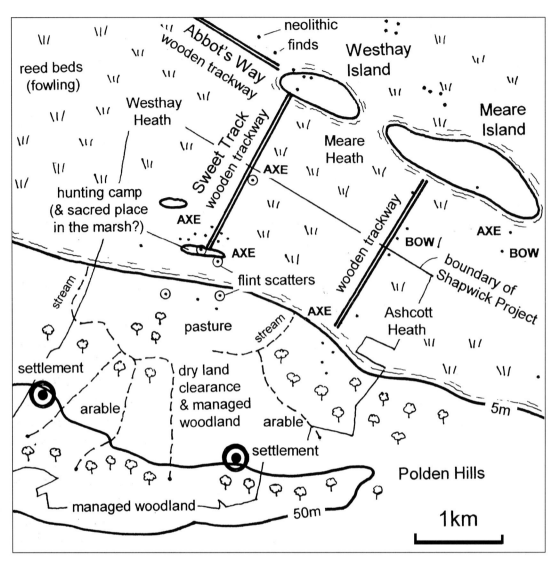

A neolithic landscape in the Somerset Levels (based on the findings of the Shapwick Project and other sources).

people arriving from the north-east, in part to provide access to the sarsen fields immediately to the east of the Ridgeway. The stones used in the building of Avebury were very likely dragged in along this road, which looks today very much as it did then.

The architectural kinship between monuments a long way apart shows that people must have travelled long distances; it was the only way ideas could move. Dorchester's Big Rings has similarities with the North Yorkshire henges; the Whispering Knights portal dolmen has relations in Wales; Rollright nearby has affinities with stone circles in Cumbria.[18] The Grooved Ware assemblage shows that there was long-distance communication of ideas; the same special pottery was used in ceremonial centres as far apart as Wessex and Orkney. In a similar way the same design of herringbone drystone masonry was used in tombs as far apart as Midhowe on Rousay and Tinkinswood in the Cotswolds.[19] There was contact, therefore there must have been travel.

There were very few horses in Britain, and those few were wild. Travel was on foot, though perhaps not everything was carried on foot. The solid, single-piece wheel had been invented and used for several centuries in 3000 BC. The wheel is known from Uruk in the Near East as early as 3500 BC and wagons were shown on pots in Poland at about the same date. Wagon-ruts with a gauge of 1.0–1.2 metres were made by wagons at Flintbek in Germany; the waving bottoms of the ruts prove that they were made not by sledges but by wobbling wheels. These too have been radiocarbon dated to 3500 BC. The earliest wheeled vehicles seem to have been four-wheeled carts pulled along by a pole and yoke. Maybe people pulled them along; more likely oxen were used.[20] It is curious that the wheeled wagon appeared right across Europe and the Near East at about the same time, implying that, once it had been invented, its potential was seen immediately; the attractions and advantages of the wheel were apparently inescapable. People saw the wheel – and *had* to have it.

The radiocarbon dates tell us that everybody wanted the wheel as soon as it was available, but we cannot be sure what they wanted it for. Contrary to the popular image of the stone age, the wheel existed before most of the megaliths, but it can have solved none of the major technical engineering problems involved in megalith-building, because there were no metal bearings and without those even the most stoutly made wooden wheels would have broken up under the weight of a megalith. On the other hand, when a team of oxen was harnessed to a megalith on a sledge, non-load-bearing wheeled bogies could have been used to guide and separate the ropes, and stop them snagging the oxen's legs; the trolley would also have helped to distribute the oxen's pull more evenly.[21] I assume that although the carts were not used for shifting megaliths, they would have been routinely used for transporting harvested crops and possibly some manufactured goods, such as pottery and baskets.

Using roads for long-distance travel involved crossing streams and rivers. In many places the water was shallow enough for people to ford, but elsewhere ferries were certainly needed. There were probably ferries across the Ouse, Adur and Arun, where the South Downs Way crossed these southward-flowing rivers, whereas the Cuckmere, wider and shallower than now, would have been fordable at Alfriston. A major crossing existed on the Humber, very close to the modern Humber Bridge, where substantial remains of boats, laying-up platforms and even a winch have survived from 2000 BC. These remains of a sophisticated and well-organized ferry service suggest that ferries had operated at the site for hundreds of years before that. A similar ferry probably operated across the Severn estuary, again not far from the northern modern bridge. The Humber boats in use in 2000 BC were complex plankboats 17 metres long. At other sites dugout canoes were used; a well-preserved one was found recently on the foreshore of Strangford Lough, proving that logboats were not just used on the safe waters of rivers and lakes but in salt-water estuaries too.[22]

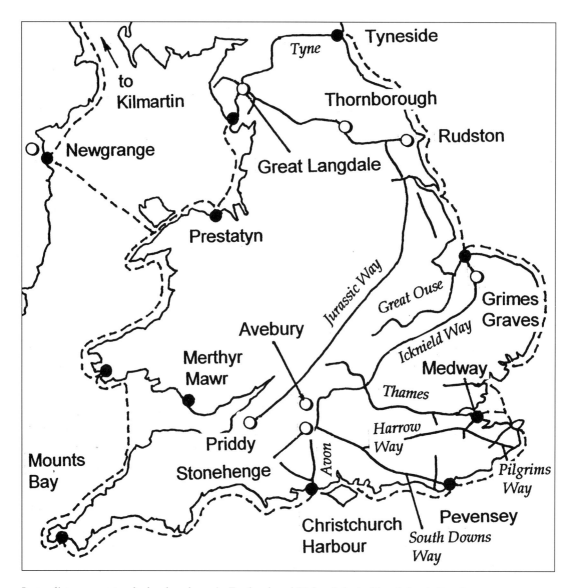

Long-distance routes, by land and sea, in England and Wales. Selected key inland sites shown as open circles. Ports shown as filled circles.

The dugouts and rafts found at eighteen sites in the northernmost reach of the Trent floodplain (near Gainsborough and Scunthorpe) and the Vale of Ancholme to the east have so far proved to be iron age – the famous Brigg 'raft' dates from 650 BC – but the concentration of neolithic settlements along the sides of these floodplains suggests to me that there were neolithic ferries across the Trent and Ancholme as well, perhaps linking segments of a road route that connected the Doncaster area with the south coast of the Humber round Immingham, a route now followed by the M18–M180.[23]

Skinframe boats are likely to have been made, given the availability of both animal hides and the technology for perforating and sewing them together; since any number of hides may be sewn together, these boats may have been as much as 20 or 30 metres long, catering not only for estuary crossings but for plying on the open sea. Most of this sea-going navigation was bay-hopping; people preferred to keep within sight of land, as navigation depended mainly on recognizing seamarks. Bays were also natural harbours and therefore became ports. Mounts Bay, Christchurch Harbour, Pevensey Bay and the estuaries of the Thames, Medway, Blackwater, Stour and Orwell all functioned as importing and entrepot ports, as did the Tyne, the Humber and the Wash. The complete pattern was a complex web made up of all the different kinds of communication – local and long-distance usage of ridgeways and lowland road routes, specialized timber trackways in fenland areas, dugouts and plank-boats across rivers, composite boats and skinframe boats on the open sea. The overall pattern is once again startlingly evolved. Simple ideas were combined and developed to produce a result that surprises us with its elaborateness and ambition.

POTTERY

Many archaeologists use the style of the pottery they find as a way of inferring a site's date and cultural affinities. If pottery can be proved to be 'foreign', it can be an indicator of communication and transport. Often it has proved to be more complicated than that sounds. For instance, if similar bowls are found in two widely separated places, we may not be sure whether the bowls themselves were transported from the one place to the other, or to both from a third, or if it was only the *designs* for the bowls that travelled. But first let us look at the way the pottery was made – the first to be made in Britain.

We take the round shape of pottery for granted because it is almost universal, but that is because it is the shape automatically produced by a wheel rotating the clay between the potter's hands. Before the introduction of the potter's wheel other shapes were possible, yet the rounded shape was still preferred, probably because it imitated containers already in existence, made of other materials. Textile bags and osier baskets used for carrying and storing food almost certainly preceded the introduction of pottery, and they are easier to make into rounded forms than anything with flat sides. The decoration on some Grooved Ware pots deliberately imitates the weave of a rush or basketwork container. Before pottery, liquids were held in leather bags; when filled, they swelled into rounded shapes. Again, some of the pottery decoration imitates the perforations round the neck that were needed to thread a thong through a leather bag, make it secure and allow it to be hung up.[24]

Making pottery was an intensely personal activity. With modern scientific analysis it is sometimes possible to trace a pot back to a particular house, even to a particular hearth.[25] The pots were simply made. Clay dug from the ground was kneaded to soften it and make it workable, then it was pressed into sheets from which the vessel was assembled. Experiment shows that clay rolls flattened into ribbons 4–5cm wide would have been easy to use, but the clay needed to be left to dry out after adding just

Grooved Ware pottery, showing how the rich decorative style imitated basketwork. (After Chris Jones in Parker Pearson, 1993)

one such ribbon or it was impossible to maintain the shape. The drying-out took up to a day, so making a medium-sized vessel might take a week, more in damp weather. The work had to be done piecemeal, so it would have fitted easily around other domestic work, and it seems more likely that it was carried out by women than men for that reason, though probably not exclusively so, just as in many societies today. A turntable of some kind made building the walls of the vessel easier; this might be a rush mat, a wooden plaque or a small stone slab.[26] When the shape was complete, the seams were removed by patting the walls between fingers and knuckles. The potter wet her fingers and rubbed them over the surface to give a smooth leathery finish. On Orkney Unstan Ware was burnished with a bone tool to make the surface shiny and impermeable; as yet there were no glazes. Some wares were plain, others decorated by dragging a bone splinter across the clay ('incised decoration') or pushing fingernails, bird bones or whipped cord into it ('impressed decoration').

Some of the special Grooved Ware vessels were given extra appliqué ornaments made of rolls of clay, often in ribs or cordons ('relief decoration').[27] Different potters, even those living next door to one another, used their own preferred recipes for making Grooved Ware vessels, much as people do when cooking meals.[28]

Then the pottery was fired. At some settlement sites people managed to stoke up fires hot enough to fire pottery.[29] Over most of Britain there was plenty of firewood available to keep kiln-fires burning for days if necessary. On Orkney, where a great deal of pottery was made, there cannot have been enough wood for this purpose, but experiments with dried seaweed have shown that it is a very successful substitute, and once the fire is established layers of damp seaweed are effective in sealing the fire in. Elsewhere, turf clamps were probably used to seal the fire. Immediately after firing, the pottery was dowsed with milk to reduce porosity and give a stable, waxy finish.[30]

The earliest style to emerge in Britain was Grimston–Lyles Hill Ware, named after sites in Yorkshire and Northern Ireland, but it was the norm over much of Britain in the early neolithic until 3000 BC. It developed in 4600 BC out of the Michelsberg style imported across the North Sea from the north European mainland. Decoration would have given the pottery a tribal identity, an ethnicity, that might have limited its usefulness as a commodity for exchange. Anonymous plain wares suited the expansion phase of the neolithic way of life, when there was more mobility, and they were exchanged across considerable distances.[31] Grimston–Lyles Hill pottery was round-bottomed, plain and finely made. In the south-west of Britain a different style emerged around 4100 BC as a result of a quite separate European influence from the south, across the English Channel. This, the Chasséen ceramic tradition of north-west France, was a European influence that was maintained until 3000 BC.[32] Like Grimston, the 'Hembury' style of the south-west was undecorated but included some distinctive globular bowls with big curving lugs that were perforated for threading carrying or hanging thongs. These bowls were of finer fabric and more carefully made than a lot of bronze age pottery. A sub-type of Hembury was the special fine red ware made on the Lizard in Cornwall. Some of this was sent to Wessex, but the distribution of the Lizard Ware – and Hembury Ware as a whole – was very restricted; the name 'South-Western' is very appropriate for this pottery type.

The Abingdon style was shorter-lived, around 3800 to 3200 BC, and was used in central and south-east England. Like the other 'South-Eastern' styles, Abingdon had no continental forerunners, and I assume that they all evolved out of the initial plain wares. Windmill Hill and Whitehawk styles, for instance, appear to be developed from Hembury, Mildenhall from Grimston. Abingdon Ware consisted of round-based bowls with a band of outside decoration between rim and shoulder. Some distinct regional styles were appearing as 3000 BC approached. There are similarities between the styles of pottery called Abingdon, Windmill Hill, Ebbsfleet, Mildenhall and Broome Heath, but generally they are found where they were used, in distinct areas.[33]

The main middle and late neolithic pottery tradition was the Peterborough style, beginning (earlier than once thought) in 3400 BC.[34] It developed out of the Grimston tradition and started as a regional style in the Lower Thames valley, beginning with Ebbsfleet bowls (coarse, heavy, round-based vessels with a well-marked shoulder); they had impressed whipped cord decorations inside and outside the rim and became more and more widespread, extending from Dorset to Yorkshire by 3300 BC. The Mortlake style, developing from 3000 BC to 2700 BC, was more profusely ornamented, with close patterning of bird-bone or fingernail impressions covering the outside of the bowl. They also had strongly outward-turning rims and deep necks, which may have been designed to take a hanging thong.[35] The bird-bone pattern seems to have been particularly popular in Wales.[36]

Grooved Ware appeared at the peak of the development of plain and decorated wares in 3000 BC.[37] The chronology of Grooved Ware has been much discussed. Current thinking places its *floruit* at 2900–2100 BC (according to Garwood) or 3100–2900 BC (according to Brindley). There is also a problem in that the older Unstan Ware overlaps with Grooved Ware in the period 3300–3000 BC, leading some archaeologists to infer two different cultures.[38] Colin Renfrew reminds us that since calendar dates from 3300 and 3000 BC rest in a fold in the radiocarbon conversion graph they are indistinguishable.[39] Derek Simpson nevertheless believes that the earliest Grooved Ware in England and Wales is that found at Kings Barrow Ridge, close to Stonehenge, and that it dates from 3500 BC.[40] I prefer Renfrew's interpretation, which is that in Orkney Grooved Ware appeared in 3000 BC, having developed out of Unstan Ware during the preceding three hundred years.[41] The alternative idea, that for several centuries two entirely separate cultures existed side by side in the Orkney islands, is hardly credible. John Hedges' careful mapping of the two respective culture areas reveals four cultural zones – Grooved Ware in Sanday, Unstan Ware in Westray, Eday, Stronsay, Rousay and Shapinsay, then Grooved Ware in Mainland and then Unstan Ware again in Burray and South Ronaldsay – a distribution pattern that does not convince Renfrew or me.[42] One key fact that is often overlooked is that the fabrics of these two supposedly distinct types of pottery are petrologically identical; they were made of the same clay. Grooved Ware also succeeds Unstan Ware in a stratified context at Pool, Sanday.[43]

This strikingly new and original style of pottery is often found in use side by side with Peterborough Ware pottery. Grooved Ware has a simple bucket, barrel or flowerpot shape with a flat base. Smaller vessels 10cm high and 10cm in diameter are probably drinking cups. The ornamentation is sometimes very elaborate: incised grooves in geometric designs, sometimes with relief ornament in ribs or cordons, create an effect of sumptuous richness. Grooved Ware was a prestige commodity, an object of desire. Indeed, 80 per cent of the Grooved Ware in Yorkshire has been found concentrated in under 1 per cent of the land area, and that lies within 5 kilometres of the Rudston Monolith, an important tribal focus at the centre of a ceremonial complex.

Grooved Ware was the 'Sunday-best' pottery in 3000 BC. Its specialness is shown by its presence at high-status sites throughout Britain and its concentration near great monuments. Though original, the style had roots in the art of the passage graves and, whatever that art meant, it was kept alive in portable form for several centuries longer on this very special pottery.[44] The fact that it was flat-based shows that there were suitable flat surfaces for it to stand on and this in turn suggests furniture with level surfaces: tables, shelves, cupboards. Some of the most distinctive features of the houses at Skara Brae are the monumental stone dressers that dominate the living space: these dressers with shelves are where the Grooved Ware vessels were displayed.[45]

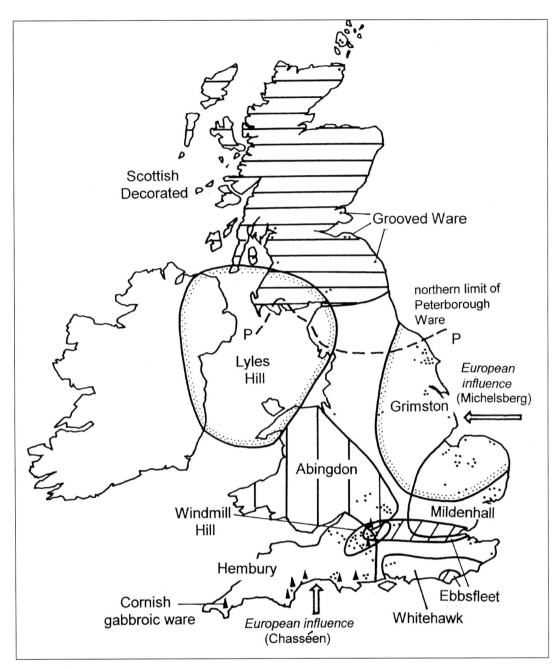

Pottery styles.

The Grooved Ware used in Ireland and North Wales is decorated with the circles and spirals seen in passage grave art; that used in England is decorated mainly with straight lines. The Grooved Ware used in Orkney is decorated with both, as if emphasizing yet again that Orkney was the source of the style.[46] Grooved Ware makes its first appearance in England at Stonehenge, with some startlingly early radiocarbon dates for three sites within a mile of Stonehenge itself. The Stonehenge people had to have this new high-status style as soon as it became available.[47]

The spread of Lizard Ware across into Wessex is much more easily explained as a trading operation in finished pottery. The pattern of finds shows coastwise trade along the Channel to Christchurch Harbour, then up the Avon – a similar enterprise to the shipment of Cornish axe-heads, and very possibly in the hands of the same people in the same boats. But it is also possible that the transfer of pottery was incidental to the shipment of some other commodity, such as salt, which had to be carried to Wessex in some form of container.[48] Grooved Ware, on the other hand, was apparently shipped for its own sake. The origin of Grooved Ware in Orkney and its almost immediate introduction into high-status sites hundreds of kilometres away in England implies the initiation of an ambitious trading operation between Orkney and Wessex.[49] The Orcadians held themselves in high esteem around 3000 BC, to judge by the evidence of the highly ambitious Maes Howe–Brodgar–Stenness ceremonial complex, and this may be explained in part by the prestige gained from the booming trade in the new Orcadian pottery style. Another possibility is that high-status groups in England wanted pottery from Orkney simply because it was associated with a very special community – in other words the pots were akin to pilgrimage souvenirs.

Most Grooved Ware is found close to the coast and in river valleys in southern Britain, with concentrations along the Stour and the Avon, the rivers that converge on Christchurch Harbour, the Kennet and Thames, the Stour, Orwell and Blackwater estuaries, and the Fens. These all imply delivery by sea to conspicuous natural harbours on the south and east coasts of England, and transport from there up river valleys and overland to ceremonial centres such as Mount Pleasant and Durrington Walls. Other major foci that were Grooved Ware clients include Rudston, Dover and Deal, the Peak District and Thornborough Circles, these last two well inland.[50]

Very small amounts of Grooved Ware found their way into Wales. Three sites on Anglesey have produced fragments of it; the rest are at ceremonial sites close to what is now the border with England – which seems, even then, to have represented some kind of status divide.[51]

But were people actually carrying Grooved Ware pots the hundreds of kilometres involved? Or was it the idea, the design concept, that travelled? People from Wessex, for example, travelled to Orkney, saw the pottery and, for whatever reason, decided that they must have it for themselves. They memorized the shapes and ornamental designs; more likely they drew them. Then they returned home and commissioned their own potters to make pseudo-Grooved Ware from their descriptions and sketches. Another possibility is that itinerant potters went from region to region making Grooved Ware to the customers' specifications. The fact that there are quite strong regional differences supports either of these alternative hypotheses. The *art* came from Orkney, even if the pots themselves did not, just as the Orcadian potters seem to have acquired their design ideas from the passage grave art of the Boyne valley.

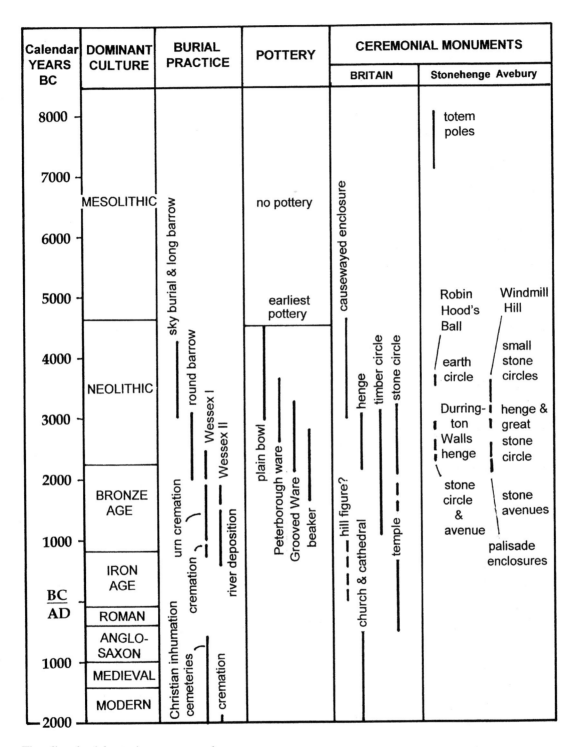

Time line: burial practice, pottery and monuments.

A SENSE OF PLACE

The controversies surrounding Grooved Ware highlight one of the key issues about the neolithic – travel. How did people conceive of the extraordinary journeys they undertook? How did they know where they were going? How did they find their way? It seems unlikely that they had maps, and there is little to suggest that they even thought in cartographic terms. The nearest approximation to a neolithic map that has been acknowledged in Europe is carved on a rock outcrop in central Italy. It shows the detailed layout of a village, complete with houses, gardens, paths – and even people and livestock, as seen from the high vantage point of the rock outcrop where the map-maker was standing; so even this was more a view of the locale from above than a map.[52] Exploring neolithic concepts of geography, of space, of place, of *other* places, of distance and direction, can tell us much about the neolithic way of thinking.

The evidence that raw materials, finished goods and ideas were transported over short, medium and long distances is already before us. Designs for Grooved Ware were transmitted, by sea and over land, the entire length of Britain. Stone axes – not the designs but incontrovertibly the axes themselves – were occasionally carried equally long distances. There is other evidence besides, such as the Whitby jet that found its way across to North Wales for belt sliders, the rock for the drystone walling at the West Kennet long barrow that was carried from the Cotswolds.[52] As we saw earlier, this willingness to move materials great distances was not new to the neolithic. Two thousand years earlier chert was carried east from Dorset to Surrey and flint was taken west from the Wiltshire Downs to the Mendip caves.[53] Nor was this a British eccentricity; the same sort of thing was happening all over Europe. Dolerite from Plussulien in Brittany was quarried in huge quantities in the late neolithic and traded widely across France and as far afield as southern England and the lower Rhone valley. Similarly, the distinctive butter-coloured chert from Grand Pressigny in the Loire basin near Poitiers was traded upriver to the south and south-east, down the tributaries of the Loire to Brittany and overland to the north-east into the Paris basin.[54]

Tracing the scatters of finds enables us to reconstruct trade routes with some confidence. The axe exchange system shows that there were two early neolithic distribution networks, one taking Cumbrian axes south-eastwards, the other taking Cornish axes north-eastwards. The two met on the eastern margins of the Fens, and stimulated the development of flint mining at nearby Grime's Graves in the middle to late neolithic. The simultaneous transfer of flint axes northwards and westwards from the chalklands of south-east England may have given the Windmill Hill–Avebury complex its very special role. Windmill Hill and Avebury were the last monumental sites before the flintless lands of the Severn valley and Wales; the enclosures may have been a major focus for exchanging flints – another node in the network. Again, a comparison with France can help us. The great megalithic complex at Carnac in southern Brittany lies at the interface of two distribution networks: Plussulien dolerite from the north and Grand Pressigny chert from the south.[55]

On a local level band groups made at least seasonal visits to their nearest ceremonial centres. Most communities had a family shrine-tomb, where informal contact could be made with the world of the ancestors at any time; this was the long barrow or chambered tomb on the hilltop just a kilometre from the settlement, sometimes closer. For most there were also seasonal visits to a higher order ceremonial centre where they would meet members of other bands, exchange news, livestock and artefacts, take part in religious and other ceremonies, arrange marriages and enter into other commitments. This was the causewayed enclosure, the henge, the stone circle. The people living at the farmstead of Stonehall on Orkney would have made relatively frequent visits to the Cuween chamber tomb, just 200 metres away from their house, and rather less frequent – perhaps quarterly – visits to the grand ritual focus made by the Stones of Stenness and the Ring of Brodgar, 7 kilometres away.

But such journeys were still short, and we know people undertook much longer expeditions. There were pilgrimages to distant ceremonial centres – to major henge complexes and stone circles made special by past events or by remarkable architecture, or just by being at nodal points in the communications system and therefore much visited and celebrated. These were places for special religious

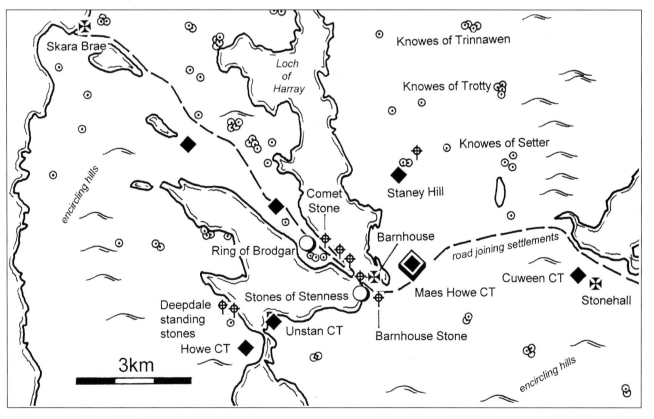

Orkney, perhaps the most impressive neolithic landscape in Britain. Black diamonds = chambered tombs; dot-within-circles = burial mounds; circle-and-crosses = standing stones.

activities, places far removed from the realities of the travellers' everyday experiences. They were also places where prized objects were exchanged, at least by those who could afford them or whose existing status was high enough to warrant an extravagant gift.

The landscape was already steeped in associations with events of the recent and long distant past and therefore played a major part in recording and shaping history and in shaping a sense of the past. Parts of it were the domain of the living, parts were the domain of the ancestors, peopled by spirits, defining myths. Places were given names, and that process of name-giving domesticated them and integrated them into the pattern of human experience; named hills and named rivers became part of the extended family.[56]

A macrocosmic, cellular view of landscapes prevailed. It was only what you could see from the ground when you were standing in a place or walking round it that gave it its geographical identity. The identity of a place was bounded by the local horizon and characterized by the shape and distance of that horizon. At Stanton Drew in Somerset, hills hem in the stone circles, giving the place a small, confined, safe and homely feel. At Stonehenge the open Plain throws the local horizon far back and allows long-distance views extending many kilometres, providing good sightlines for astronomical observation; this gives the henge a far less safe, more exposed, 'outdoor' feeling and a sense of cosmic ambition. The Castlerigg stone circle stands on a low convex ridge, surrounded on three sides by glacially eroded valleys, beyond which are the high and wildly dramatic mountains of Cumbria; this site has the feeling of being raised up on show in a stage set, a kind of natural altar in a natural abbey, a perfect location for religious ceremony.

People interacted with their local landscape on economic, social, political and spiritual levels, although they would not have thought of separating their responses in this way. The environment immediately surrounding the settlement was seen as part of the community, living and ancestral, material and spiritual. People probably conceived of places they visited, their neighbours' local landscapes, in the same cellular way, as locales, as basins, wooded valleys or sandy shorelines, rather than as points on a map. Subdued and rather characterless locales must have acquired their distinctive identity from the built monuments; it was they that became the defining points. Inevitably, though, visitors would see the landscape unit in a less informed way than the people who lived in it. They would be less aware of the meaning of the way a ceremonial monument sat in the landscape, perhaps completely unaware of the special interior qualities of the monument. I think it is likely that only the Orcadians would have known that on the winter solstice at Maes Howe the setting sun shone magically down the entrance passage right into the tomb's heart.

Mystical secrets like that were shibboleths that differentiated outsiders from insiders, strengthening the tribal bonds. Some megalithic art was open to public view, some hidden inside tomb chambers, some only seen by the tomb builders. So very few knew the whole story, and therein lay the key to individual status.[57]

Hindwell – a major ceremonial focus in Wales

A spectacular enclosure, a huge oval of tall posts, was created at Hindwell at the centre of the Walton basin surrounded by the moorlands of Radnor Forest. It seems no one lived round the edge, on the hills; everyone lived on the fertile low ground, most of them right in the centre, the area shown in the map, on a central spinal ridge. Although low, this commanded views across the whole basin and it had been the natural choice for a settlement site for over a thousand years.

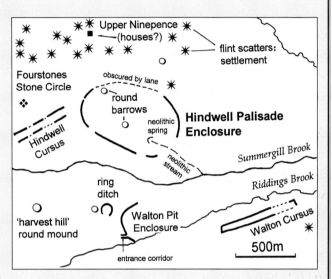

The people at Hindwell built round houses 5–15m in diameter, each with a central hearth. On lower ground to the south they built their monuments: two cursus monuments near streams, then a palisade enclosure marking off the narrow spur between the Summergill and Riddings Brooks. A round barrow and a large mound of Silbury type were added near the Walton Enclosure.

A neolithic landscape in Powys. At Hindwell people lived close to a major ceremonial centre (developed from Gibson 2000).

North of the Summergill Brook, on the lower ground below the settlement, the inhabitants built a small stone circle and a huge enclosure made of close-set oak posts nearly a metre thick and probably 7m tall. The posts had first been scorched to weather-proof them, then left to disintegrate in position, as was often the neolithic way.

Its story rooted in the middle stone age and reaching on into the bronze age, Hindwell was a major ceremonial complex rivalling Avebury.

Fourstones stone circle.

Those special named locales or landscape nodes were linked by paths, movements and narratives, so that the landscape became a story, embedded in the communal experience, full of human significance.[58] And people certainly walked around each locality to experience it. Silbury and Avebury are only just visible from one another. They can only be experienced today by moving round the landscape in a particular way, and the construction of the stone avenues emphasizes that this is what neolithic people did too. The earth and stone avenue added several centuries later at Stonehenge shows that people moved around that ritual landscape in a particular way too.

Neolithic people inherited an interest in paths from their forebears. Hunter-gatherers are interested in the landscape in specific ways: in the places where food may be found, in the locations of their hunting camps and in the routes that connect them together.[59] Each track has a past, a history and a mythology, born out of untold generations of human usage; just to walk it is to be told stories of yesterday and of the remote ancestral past. The tracks had become permanently visible narratives of a community's activities and values, by this time deeply entrenched in the British psyche.[60] That nostalgic, backward-looking love of landscape, supposed to be quintessentially 'English', was already well developed.

The way to the family shrine-tomb did not need remembering – it was inborn, instilled, second nature – and the path to the ceremonial centre was the same. Journeys that took people further afield, outside their territory, would have been memorized as lists of landmarks, shrines and temples, paths and perils, people to be met and befriended, people to be avoided, reliable ferries, difficult fords. No doubt the people who undertook the longest journeys learnt these itineraries by rote, probably as lists in chanted verse, perhaps even in song. Non-literate societies have their own ways of preserving important information, chief among which is oral tradition. No doubt elders who had undertaken epic journeys recited the itineraries so that the young could learn them, interweaving colourful anecdote and picturesque landscape detail to make them more entertaining, adding linguistic tricks like rhyme, alliteration or metre to make them easier to remember. Here, we stumble on the invention of poetry, and the composition of the first sagas.

Landscape was looked at in one way, lived in in another, moved across in yet another; people's thoughts, memories and dreams probably gave it another, mythic dimension too. Most journeys were short and motivated by basic needs like food production. The informality of these movements is beautifully summed up for us by the still-surviving footprints of neolithic people on the tidal mudflats at Formby in Lancashire. In 3000 BC this was an expanse of creeks and lagoons at the mouth of the Mersey, a place where people came to hunt and fish. Women and children picked their way carefully among the lagoons collecting shrimps and shellfish, while men headed swiftly out to the estuary, every so often darting sideways in pursuit of a deer or an ox.[61]

GEOGRAPHY AS ITINERARIES

People learnt their way across the landscape by memorizing a series of paths. It was probably only familiar and comprehensively visible landscapes that were taken in their totality as areas, such as the band territories, and they might be seen whole from a raised vantage point beside the ancestral long barrow – and of course the microcosmic landscapes bounded by the banks of ceremonial enclosures. For longer journeys people had to memorize long sequences of landmarks.

Itineraries were used as a method of navigating in sixteenth-century waggoners' (seamen's manuals). Portolan maps exaggerated coastal features: headlands were made more prominent and estuaries offering shelter were widened. Reefs and shoals were conspicuously marked. Ports and other coastal towns were boldly named so that the coastline turned into a list of named river mouths, promontories and hazards, an itinerary written on a map. Something like this would have been memorized by neolithic travellers, taught by rote to the young and passed from generation to generation, so that a web of linear routes became well known and well used, both coastal and cross-country.

There must have been an awareness of approximate distance, expressed in terms of days travelled, not miles, kilometres or any megalithic equivalent, just as in the Alps today walks are signed with the number of hours to the next village. Near Davos once, long ago, I thought I might walk over a mountain ridge to a village in the next valley. I knew it was not far horizontally, because I had a map, but I was put off by the daunting 'funf stunde' the locals knew it would take. The time a journey takes is often still the key consideration.

The itinerary approach to travelling flourished in the middle ages and was still widely used in the seventeenth and eighteenth centuries.[62] We still use itineraries. The London Tube map is a classic topological map. The relative positions of the stations along the various

One of the finely shaped Stones of Stenness. From the very beginning the stone circles were prominent landmarks and therefore waymarks.

lines are shown, but not the distances between them; all you need to know on the Underground is how many more stops there are until the one where you get off. Once you are on the train, only your particular itinerary is visible above the window opposite your seat, because only that itinerary is available during your journey. The map breaks down if you attempt to work out how far Russell Square on the Piccadilly Line is from St Paul's on the Central Line. You can tell neither distance nor direction, because of the way in which the map has been constructed.

The neolithic concept of the world beyond the horizon must have been very much like these topological maps. Lines across the landscape, straight or tortuous, would have been carefully learnt but areal knowledge was not available; there was no medium within which it could have been amassed. It is very unlikely that someone living near Stonehenge could have had any idea how far away, in a straight line, the Preseli Hills were, or in which direction. A vague general sense that they lay to the west or north-west would be all that was possible.[63]

For the longest journeys people may have relied on local pilots for guidance past particular hazards. Inshore fishermen in Cornwall today develop a total knowledge of their own stretch of coastline, which they regard as part of their village. It would have been well worth any neolithic traveller's while to tap into local knowledge of this kind, and some sort of system of pilotage may have been available to negotiate difficult coasts in short stretches, changing pilots every 5 miles.[64]

CHAPTER SEVEN

The Touchstones

THE AXE

The stone axes that people were using in 3000 BC were tools of a type that had
been in use for thousands of years. The axes of the earlier hunter-gatherers
were rough-hewn, but neolithic axes were often highly polished. The later
axes were also skilfully hafted in stout wooden handles. A hole was drilled through the
thicker end of the handle and the axe-head driven halfway through it to make a
simple cross-shaped tool.[1] Sometimes the axe-head was fitted into the end of a hooked
handle with a swept-back head; this was probably designed as a shock absorber.
Normally the wooden handles decayed, but a well-preserved one was found at the
Etton causewayed enclosure. The design is clearly shown in a stone carving at Gavrinis,
Brittany, where the ceremonial context shows that the axe was not just a tool but had a
powerful symbolic value too, like Thor's hammer. Some contemporary Breton images
show the axe associated with the goddess, the terrible death-dealing mother. At an
everyday level, people used it to fell or ring trees, to clear the wildwood and make a
new landscape. Changing the landscape was one of the greatest and most far-reaching
neolithic ideas. The all-important axe was central to it; it is not surprising that it
became a central symbol, weighty and sharp-edged with meaning.

Some axes show signs of wear, and even reshaping. Some were never used at all,
but were laid with reverence in special places. Many *could* not have been used; some
were miniatures, too small to be used, and made of chalk, of all things. Some were
made of jadeite, so thin and fragile that they would have shattered if anyone had
tried to use them, yet they were imported from the Alps at great cost and in
significant numbers – seventy of them have been found in Britain. They seem to have
been valued for the magical protection they bestowed, and were sometimes buried as
foundation offerings.[2]

The supernatural quality attributed to axes helps to explain a curious feature of the
axe quarries and factories from which they came. They are often in high, inaccessible

places, when it would have been easy to get stone of similar quality from lower sites. Some of the Great Langdale quarries were on a high, dangerous, near-vertical face. Why, when similar stone was available nearby on a gentler slope? Were the miners unsystematic and ignorant? Were they perhaps farmers from neighbouring lowlands who only quarried the stone part-time and therefore unthinkingly followed the tracks of earlier miners? Perhaps, but it is also possible that there was something special about that particular place that had nothing to do with petrology.

Something similar is seen in Sussex, where flint mines working from 4000 to 3000 BC are all on windy hilltops: Church Hill, Harrow Hill, Blackpatch Hill and Windover Hill. It may be that the flint seams were traceable on the flanks of the hills, and this gave a useful indication of the depth of shaft that would need to be dropped from the summit. In other words, the neolithic miners were acquiring knowledge of geology. This same principle was applicable to many of the igneous and metamorphic source-rocks, which also tended to occur in bands. It is easy to understand why the miners were less interested in flint already exposed at the surface, as this was frost-damaged, whereas the tabular flint buried many metres underground, blanketed and insulated by the overlying layers of chalk, remained in continuous undamaged slabs, ideal for making a variety of large flint tools. It is also possible that the higher sites were less thickly wooded and thus easier to develop.

The quarry sites were often perched between earth and heaven, or between earth, heaven and sea, commanding impressive views, and they may have had spiritual significance attributed to them on that account.[3] The dolerite axe factory of Le Pinacle on Jersey had a spectacular location, a distinctive rock formation overlooking a coastal plain. The idea that the prominence of the landmark made the place and the objects originating there sacred can be transferred to other factories. Tievebulliagh,

---

The birth of the 'stone age'

The idea of a stone age seems the most natural thing in the world to us now, but it was invented as recently as the nineteenth century. When William Cunnington, who died in 1810, was unable to interpret the finds from all the barrows he excavated, he was advised by the Revd Thomas Leman of Bath that 'three great eras' could be distinguished 'in the arms of offence found in your barrows', and he identified the three ages of bone-and-stone, bronze and iron. Leman was offering him the three-age idea, but Cunnington took no notice. Nor did anyone else. It was not until Christian Thomsen, the Museum Curator in Copenhagen, published the three-age theory in 1836 that it took off.

It was three decades later still that Sir John Lubbock, in his *Pre-Historic Times* of 1865, divided the Stone Age in two, coining terms for the old and new stone ages that we have been using ever since: Palaeolithic and Neolithic.

Pike o' Stickle, Preseli and Creag na Caillich at Killin all have spectacular sites. All are raised, exposed, highly visible, command distant views and possess a mythic quality that suggests that they may have been regarded as special places, even before the extraction and exporting of axes began. Hilltops are sacred in many cultures because they are places where earth touches sky – peak sanctuaries like Mount Juktas on Minoan Crete spring to mind – so it is a short step to interpreting the hilltop axe factories as sacred sites where the stone itself was deemed to possess special qualities.[4]

If all people wanted was a stone axe to cut down trees, they could in most areas have contented themselves with an axe made out of local rock; in Wessex there was an ample supply of axe-flint, for example. But people in Wales wanted flint axes that had come from far away in Sussex, and people in Sussex wanted dolerite and other igneous axes that had come from distant Wales. The *distances*

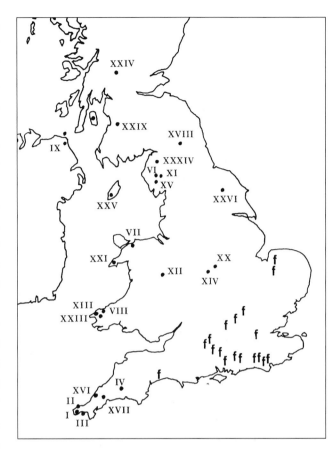

The axe factories: f = flint mine, VI = Great Langdale.

they had travelled added to their value and their talismanic strength. Hence the appeal of jadeite axes from the Alps. Axes from Tievebulliagh in Northern Ireland were transported as far afield as Shetland, Rudston and Kent, though most were used locally.[5] Presumably axes used within a short distance of the factory were recognized as local, and axes that were exotic were recognized as foreign, but we have no way of knowing whether people had any sense of the exact origin of exotic axes,[6] whether a man chopping down a tree in Sussex with a Great Langdale axe had any awareness that it had come from Cumbria.

FLINT AXES AND FLINT MINES

Next to water and wood, flint is one of the longest-serving resources in Britain. By 3000 BC it had been in constant use for over half a million years.[7] This was not just to make axes to fell trees and open land for farming but, as we have seen, a development with a spiritual, symbolic value all its own. The flint mines, which survive in today's landscape as scatters of conical pits separated by grassy cones of chalk rubble, form some of the oldest earthworks visible in the English landscape, as well as the earliest evidence we have of organized mineral extraction. The oldest are in the South Downs at Findon near Worthing, where mines were operating on Church Hill as early as 4100 BC.

A recent survey suggests that only a dozen extraction sites were involved, a surprisingly small number given the huge extent of the chalk outcrop, the volume of flint axes produced and the island-wide demand for toolstone. I think Barber and Topping may have been over-enthusiastic in their rejection of so many previously claimed sites; I believe there are good reasons for reinstating Windover Hill in East Sussex as a neolithic mine.[8]

A line of eleven mines runs from Windover Hill in the South Downs westwards across the rolling chalk lands to Durrington beside Stonehenge. Two further sites lie well to the north, in Norfolk: Buckenham Toft and the major industrial area of Grime's Graves.

Large areas of chalk landscape in the north of England escaped the attention of neolithic flint miners, a fact which needs exploring. The northern chalk is denser, which may have been a deterrent, though it did not stop people digging pits, post-holes and quarry ditches for barrows or cursus monuments. The northern flint also tends to splinter rather than break cleanly. Whatever the reason, northern flint was not the neolithic stone of choice. Only 5 per cent of the flint axes found in Yorkshire were made of stone from the Wolds: the other 95 per cent were imported from the south of England.

Even within the south there are significant variations. The Cissbury and Church Hill miners exploited superior seams of nodular flint,[9] while the Blackpatch and Harrow Hill mines exploited inferior seams.[10] This can only be explained in one way: the topographic position of the second pair of sites, next to Church Hill and Cissbury, was deemed more important than the quality of the flint.

The South Downs flint mines have dramatic sites at the heads of steep slopes. In the centuries leading up to 3000 BC, they stood in grassy clearings in damp woodland. They were probably all visible from adjacent lowlands, where the communities who mined the flint were living. In an all-over-green early neolithic landscape, the bright stabs of freshly dug chalk stood out with startling clarity. The mines were often false-crested. As the long barrows, built at the same time, were also false-crested, it must be assumed that people placed mines on the shoulders rather than the summits of hills deliberately, knowing that this would make them visible from nearby lowlands. As if to emphasize the point for us, neolithic barrow builders often built their long barrows close to flint mines, as at Martin's Clump, Easton Down and Windover Hill.

The scale of the flint mining operation has sometimes been exaggerated. This is partly because by the end of its life the cratered landscape of a flint mine may extend along 400 metres of hillside, and partly because before the days of radiocarbon chronology it was assumed that the neolithic was very short, beginning in 2000 BC and ending in 1500 BC. Radiocarbon dating has stretched the neolithic to four times that length; the new 'long' chronology allows plenty of time for shafts to be opened, worked and backfilled without calling into play a high intensity of activity. Shafts were

3 metres

Flint mine on Harrow Hill in the South Downs. There are galleries on two levels, following two seams of flint.

probably dug at a rate of only one a year at Grime's Graves, as at the other, older, sites. The geographical scale of the flint mining industry was also small, even compared with what was going on in contemporary mainland Europe.[11] The largest English flint-mining complex covered 16 hectares, which is only a quarter of the size of the big Polish flint mines.

The mining technique was orderly and methodical, often with successive shafts opened in rows along the contours. Miners used wooden ladders to reach the galleries; in some mines they made elaborate stairways with joists socketed into the shaft walls. The shafts may have been fitted with conical roofs to keep the rain out. Gnaw-marks on antler picks show that voles were running about in the galleries, and the likeliest way for voles to reach the foot of the shaft alive is by running down some kind of staircase. Rope marks on the walls show that miners hauled flint up in baskets or bags on ropes. Probably only ten or twenty people worked each mine, half of them quarrying in the galleries, the other half transporting the flint to the surface. As soon as the mine was exhausted it was backfilled, to prevent livestock and children from falling down the shafts; a young girl met her death at Cissbury in what appears to be one such accident, and her family buried her where she fell.

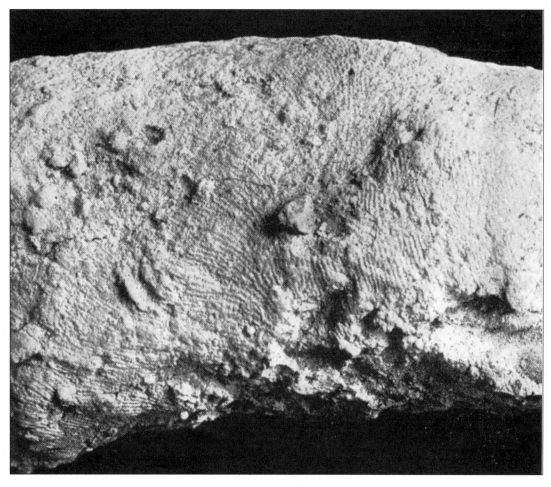

The hand-print of a flint-miner. This antler-pick from Grime's Graves became coated with wet chalk mud during use and now preserves the hand-print of one of the miners.

How people organized the mining operation is still unclear. I think it unlikely that teams of peripatetic specialist miners toured the country, or that people living near the mines worked in them to the exclusion of other work, like nineteenth-century coal miners, or that travellers from far afield visited the mines whenever they liked to collect the toolstone they needed; although there are some variations in working methods, for example between Harrow Hill and nearby Blackpatch, the way the mines were worked is far too orderly and systematic for that.[12] It is more likely that the local people opened a new shaft every few years and dug the flint out when their other work allowed, rather like the traditional summer hop-picking in Kent. It was probably the people living on the coastal plain at Worthing who controlled the mining and therefore the trade in flint axes from 4100 BC until 3000 BC, by which time Cissbury was at the end of its productive life and Easton Down across in Wiltshire was gaining supremacy; at this time the first shafts were being opened in the Breckland, and it was Grime's Graves, with its 360 deep shafts descending 12 metres, that would come to dominate the flint trade in the late neolithic.[13] 3000 BC was a pivotal moment in the flint axe trade, as in so many other activities.

Whichever community controlled the axe trade must have acquired extra special status, supplying as it did much of England and Wales. It must be highly significant that in the downland block where the early neolithic flint mines were located (between Arundel and Portslade) there were no ceremonial monuments at all.[14] Possibly the community that worked the flint had too little time for monument building; possibly they were honoured guests at the causewayed enclosures in the downland to east and west. Whatever the dynamics, the 'Worthing people' eventually lost their pivotal position; in about 3000 BC control shifted to Salisbury Plain. After the mining was over, the Worthing people were to build a cluster of four or five small henges within that same area, whereas henges were not built at all to east or west – possibly a reflection of their continuing special status.[15]

One of the galleries in Canon Greenwell's Pit at Grime's Graves. A piece of the target seam can be seen in the centre, projecting from the base of the chalk pillar. Flint slabs were prised up from the floor with antler picks.

We must not lose sight of the special nature of all the circumstances associated with the flint mining. The special site qualities many of the mines possess – high, conspicuous, commanding dramatic views, close to and possibly attracting monuments – show that the axes had special, magical properties derived from the place of origin. Some of the axes travelled long distances, hundreds of kilometres, and the geographical scale of this movement in Britain was by no means exceptional. In France Grand Pressigny flint found its way east to the Rhone valley and north to the Pas de Calais.[16] Axes from the Krzemionki mines in Poland have been found 400 kilometres away on the Baltic coast.[17] Possibly the colour and texture of the flint spoke to its users of the place it came from, but how many people would have been able to make that connection we cannot tell. The Polish flint was distinctively striped and visually very striking. The Grand Pressigny flint was a rich honey colour, not unlike copper, and that association may explain why, not long after 3000 BC, very large flint blades started to appear, probably in imitative response to the appearance of copper daggers from south-eastern Europe. Perhaps characteristically, the colour the British favoured for their toolstone was a dull steely grey.[18]

Owning a stone axe brought status, proof of membership. It was a sign of wealth, of the capacity to give hospitality and exchange gifts. It was probably also a symbolic unifier of people and earth. The handing on of axes from person to person, from community to community, gave form and definition to relationships. Handing axes on to others was one of the many highly significant acts of social bonding that took place at the enclosures.

NON-FLINT STONE AXES

Across Britain as a whole there were four distinct stone axe provinces. In south-east England most axe-heads were made of flint; in south-west England most were made of coarse-grained igneous rock; in the Scottish Highlands most were made of metamorphic rock. The fourth province was easily the largest, covering southern Scotland, Wales and northern and central England; there most of the axe-heads were made of fine-grained igneous rocks. The percentage of fine-grained igneous axes was highest around the sources, so we find that in the Pennines and the Midlands at least 50 per cent of the axes are fine-grained, whereas in Cumbria the percentage is 80 or more.[19]

Again, taking Britain as a whole, three places in particular produced most of the axes: Cumbria, the South Downs and Grime's Graves. There were two dominant exchange networks: one was along the south coast of England from Cornwall to the Thames and East Anglian estuaries, the other across the Pennines from Cumbria to the Yorkshire Wolds and the Fens.[20] Grime's Graves is at the boundary between the two exchange systems, evidently intended for production for some distant market, but it may have been geared to manufacturing disc-shaped knives as much as axes. Knives were especially common in the Yorkshire Wolds, and if it could be proved that Grime's

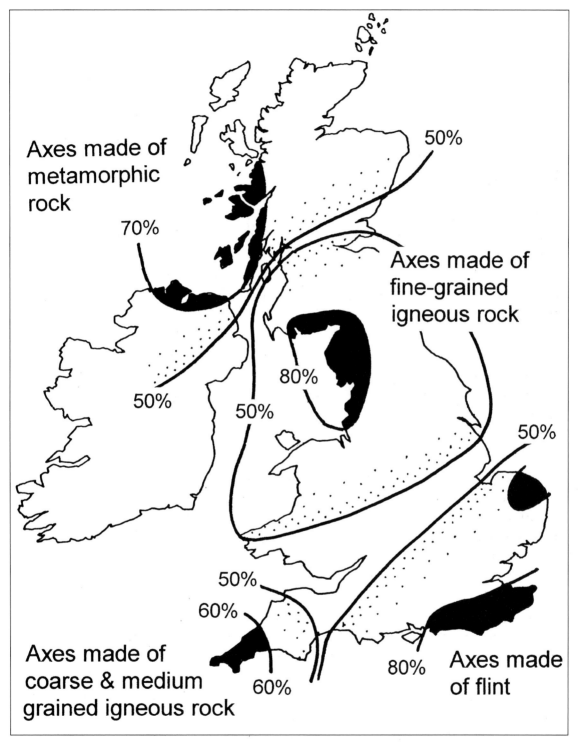

Axes made of
metamorphic
rock

70%

50%

50%

50%

80%

Axes made of
fine-grained
igneous rock

50%

50%

50%

50%

60%

Axes made of
coarse & medium
grained igneous rock

60%

80%

Axes made
of flint

Stone axe provinces. The black areas are the main axe production areas (after Pitts 1996).

The Grime's Graves goddess, left as an offering in the gallery of a flint mine. Religious belief saturated people's everyday lives.

Graves was supplying them, it would support the idea that the site was trading to the north as well as to the south, linking together the two great exchange systems at the point where they overlapped.[21]

Because igneous rock is petrologically distinct, tools made from it can be traced more easily back to their origin. We know that twenty-two non-flint solid rock sources existed on the mainland of Britain, a couple in the English Midlands, the rest in the hard rock regions of the north and west.

The biggest Welsh axe factory was Graig Lwyd at Penmaenmawr, an impressive headland. Mynydd Rhiw, with its equally dramatic location on the western tip of the Lleyn Peninsula, is smaller but unique in Britain in having no known surface outcrop. The hornfels (metamorphosed shale) had to be mined through a layer of glacial deposits 3m thick, which raises the interesting, and as yet unanswered, question: if it was nowhere visible on the surface, how did the miners know it was there? The four pits are arranged in a line across the slope; each was dug in turn and then methodically filled with the upcast from the next. The roughing-out process was farmed out to 'finishers' who worked in various places up to 50 km away from the mine; they gave the axes their final though unpolished form.[22]

The distribution pattern of stone axes has been closely studied for a century and is thought to be well understood. Stone axes were produced at twenty different centres in Western Britain, but only eight of them have been positively identified; there is still much to discover. Great Langdale axes were used locally within Cumbria, but also produced on a scale that allowed them to be exchanged much further afield.[23] Something between 45,000 and 75,000 axes were produced on that mountainside alone.[24] Studies of hammerstones suggest that two distinct groups of people went up to Great Langdale to work the stone.[25] Trails of Cumbrian axes leading westwards along the northern shore of the Solway Firth, north-westwards up the Annan valley, following the A74(M) towards Glasgow, and eastwards along the Tyne valley to Newcastle and Blyth show the routes the axe traders plodded along with their backpacks. But the north was already well provided with igneous toolstone and the main direction of exchange was towards the south-east. Large quantities of Cumbrian axes were taken to the Yorkshire Wolds, Lincolnshire and the Fenland edge by sea,

The Langdale axe factories (asterisks). The hatched area represents the outcrop of bedded tuffs and Wrengill andesite. The unhatched band looping round Scafell Pike is the outcrop of hornstone. The industry went on at quite high altitudes, as the contours show.

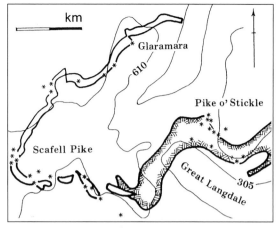

Axe factories and trade routes (dashed lines) in Cumbria.

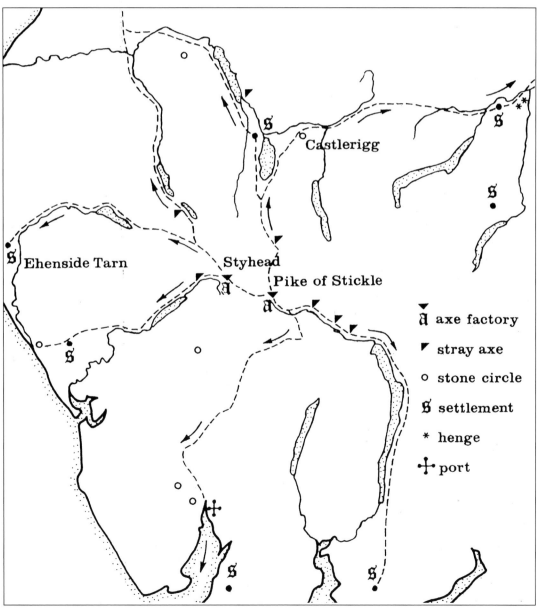

with boats taking consignments south from Tyneside along the North Sea coast to Bridlington, the Humber and the Wash, and by land, crossing the Pennines by one of two routes – the Garsdale–Wensleydale route mentioned earlier (the A684) or the more southerly Ribblesdale–Airedale route via Settle, Skipton and Shipley (A65–A650). An extra customer province to the south, in the Thames valley, was most likely used by traders travelling by boat along the North Sea coast.[26]

In a similar way we can reconstruct the routes traders followed from other rock sources to other destinations. The scatter of Cornish axes along the south coast of England shows how they were transported by bay-hopping navigators and dropped off at a sequence of conspicuous natural harbours: Christchurch Harbour, Pevensey Bay and the Medway, Thames and Essex estuaries.[27]

The pattern of use and exchange within Wales was intricate, with locally made axes from five different sources in use everywhere. Graig Lwyd was the biggest Welsh factory, producing 75 per cent of the axes used in North Wales; some reached the Peak District, Yorkshire and the English Midlands. Mining began at Graig Lwyd and Mynydd Rhiw very early (4000 BC), and may even have been begun by mesolithic hunters.[28] There were three axe factories in the Preseli Hills in Pembrokeshire and one in central Wales, at Hyssington. These supplied locally made axes which were in use alongside imported axes. In Gwynedd and Anglesey the locally made Graig Lwyd axes predominate; they are also common in central and south-west Wales and spread across in significant numbers to the English Midlands and Peak District. The pattern in Wales was further complicated by the importation of axes from Cumbria to the north, the English chalklands to the east and Cornwall to the south-west.[29]

Trade relationships between producer and consumer provinces existed for other commodities as well, though the locations were different. In the years following 3000 BC the main concentration of belt sliders made of jet was in the Yorkshire Wolds, which we can think of as the producer province. There were lesser concentrations of belt sliders in Southern Scotland, Snowdonia and Wessex, three customer provinces supplied by the producers in the Yorkshire Wolds.[30]

The axe exchange networks expanded and changed through time. Towards 3000 BC there was a marked increase in the value people put on exotic axes. They became more desirable, but this was nothing to do with the practical usefulness of the axes; invariably there was perfectly serviceable toolstone available in the customer region and imports were economically unnecessary.[31] The axes were probably exchanged in significant transactions such as dowries or bride-wealth, and were both offered and sought as objects of high value. It is assumed that the expansion in distribution was driven by demand from the customers, not by the energy of the producers. It was at this time that groups in Britain, and especially in southern England, began to form links and alliances with more distant communities conducting their lives in different ways. The acquisition of exotic axes was but one symptom of that change; they were drawing on a whole fund of new ideas as well as artefacts that would affect every aspect of their lives. This opening up of previously closed social networks may have led on to

Stone axe production and consumption in England and Wales. Dot-within-circle = axe factory; arrow = axe trade route; shaded area = concentration of exotic axes, and therefore axe consumption area. Note that all the consumption areas in the south and east focus on fine natural harbours (Developed from Cummins 1980).

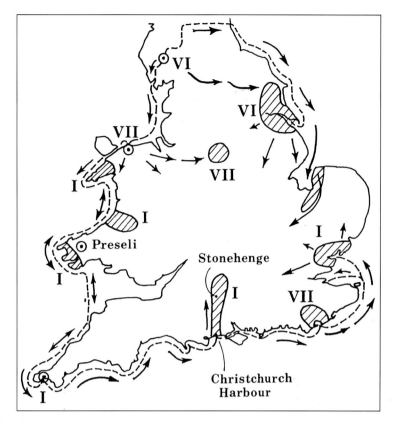

the major process of social differentiation that was to give the late neolithic period its character.[32] Objects that could confer status became desirable, and more and more different types of status-conferring objects were being made. It is therefore very strange that the Great Langdale axe factory appears to have closed down around 3000 BC,[33] although it is possible that axes continued to be produced for some time after that from the very large quantities of waste (including discarded rough-outs), without any new quarrying being necessary.

Axes moved across country by way of a multitude of short-distance movements, by individuals exchanging axes for other objects at local territorial boundaries. Some were transported over long distances in large consignments, perhaps by sea, and then traded piecemeal.[34] When we look at the distribution of each type of exotic axe in terms of ratios with local axes, high densities in at least two areas emerge: the source area close to the factory and a customer area that is in some cases a very long distance from the factory. In each case the customer area is centred on a fine natural harbour, which is good evidence that consignments of axes arrived by sea. They were shipped along the coast in a series of short voyages from bay to bay, rarely losing sight of land, bay-hopping long distances round Britain.

This evidence of organized sea-borne transport of consignments of axes is reinforced by other evidence. Caches of local and foreign axes at two sites in Wales, one on the north coast at Prestatyn and one on the south coast at Merthyr Mawr Warren, look like depots of axes awaiting export.[35] With the distinctive seamark of the northern end of the Clwydian Range rising behind it, and the lowlands of the Vale of Clwyd and Dee estuary on each side to west and east, Prestatyn would have been an easy location for navigators in the Irish Sea to find. Concentrations of Cumbrian axes in Clwyd show that axes were indeed transferred across the water and landed at Prestatyn for distribution inland.

The sea was a major medium of communication, just as it had been for thousands of years. By 3000 BC the Atlantic seaways were in regular use for transporting axes, raw materials – and ideas. It was by sea that ideas about megalithic architecture travelled. It was by sea that communities were bonded to other, sometimes surprisingly distant, communities by ceremonial gift exchanges. In Polynesia the Kula Ring bound the peoples of many widely separated island communities together in a complex socio-economic web; something similar evolved among the communities surrounding the Irish and Celtic Seas – an enduring system of giving and accepting, a system of obligation with highly developed rules that all the participating communities understood.[36] This neolithic Ring is all but invisible archaeologically, yet the distribution of exotic axes hints very strongly at it. The axes are the hard, skeletal remains of the Ring; the information, ideas and feelings of duty, friendship and obligation that went with them are the long-perished flesh. And that Ring may have

Dyffryn Ardudwy chambered cairn, Gwynedd. The smaller, older, chambered cairn shown here is a portal dolmen.

nested within a still larger Ring. If all this seems unlikely, remember that one of the axes deposited in the reed-beds beside the Sweet Track well before 3000 BC came all the way from the Alps.[37]

Once the consignments of exotic axes were unloaded on to the harbour beaches, they were carried inland – but how? The wheel was available in Europe generally at this time, and it is possible that people made carts, waggons or wheelbarrows for transporting stone axes. Baskets could have been used. The remains of some baskets have been found, and the decoration on some pottery suggests basket work. A cord-ornamented bowl from the Ballykeel portal dolmen could represent a type of hemispherical basket. Zones of vertical marks may represent the alder rods, while zones of horizontal marks could represent rush-string courses; the three lugs could represent basket 'handles' used for threading carrying straps so that the weight would hang on the shoulders.[38] But it would have been very arduous carrying a consignment of axes in a basket.

I think it more likely they were carried in wooden-framed leather or basketwork backpacks.[39] The frame of the Iceman's backpack was made of a 2m-long hazel rod bent round into a horseshoe and fixed together with a couple of wooden boards 40cm long. This firm frame kept the backpack in shape on the traveller's back, exactly like a modern rucksack. The axeheads were almost certainly wrapped in leaves, grass or moss – prehistoric bubble-wrap – to stop them moving about and abrading one another as the trader walked, and to stop them damaging the pannier or digging into the trader's back. It is easy to imagine the traders walking along with practised, measured step, stooped and bulky figures, wrapped up against all weathers, leaning intently forward to balance the weight of the stone, travelling purposefully across the countryside in small groups for safety and company, for all the world like a scene from Tolkien.

The axes are virtually indestructible, and we have to remind ourselves that there were lots of commodities that have long since perished but would have formed part of the gift-exchange network. That may have included raw materials, marriage partners, pottery, food, labour.

The earth circles of the early neolithic were places where many axes were either deliberately deposited or accidentally dropped – it is hard to be sure which – and this has led some to speculate that the enclosures were centres of trading in axes. There is evidence that flint axes were actually made at the Maiden Castle causewayed enclosure.[40] It is probably no coincidence that in Sussex and Wessex the causewayed enclosures went out of use at about the same time that the flint mines closed down.[41] Aubrey Burl has made the parallel proposal that stone circles were trading stations in the axe trade, and it may be that causewayed enclosures, henges and stone circles were all used intermittently as meeting-places for the exchange of axes.[42] But this leads us into a new area of enquiry – the great neolithic monuments. Whatever were they *for*?

CHAPTER EIGHT

THE CASTLES OF ETERNITY

Britain, 3000 BC. A rural landscape, green with sweeps of pasture and arable fields that look to us more like gardens. Beyond the gardens and meadows are swathes of ancient forest and ever-growing areas of scrub and new woodland creeping across abandoned fields. It is still a woodland world.

Here and there the greenness is sharply punctuated by new buildings, pale, raw and startling against the green,[1] some a dazzling white, many of them strikingly large and permanent-looking against the modest and often flimsy architecture of the farmsteads and seasonal hunting camps. These bone-white buildings are temple-tombs, not so much for the dead as for the ubiquitous ceremonies relating to death, rebirth and the all-important cycles of fertility. They are there to obliterate the distinctions between the living and newly dead, to reassure the living that they will one day be folded into the embrace of their ancestors; they are there to show people that their ancestors legitimize their use of the land, to remind people of death itself, to commemorate the mythic time scale, the over-arching past that consumes the present. They were to be, and succeeded in being, enduring monuments, not to individuals but to a more inclusive idea of humanity.

For nearly a thousand years giant collective tombs had been built in a great arc right across the Atlantic fringe of Europe, from Scandinavia in the north-east to Portugal in the south-west. They were not built in the heart of continental Europe, where the inhabitants of the longhouses buried their dead in earthen graves, much like modern Christian burials.

LONG BARROWS AND MORTUARY ENCLOSURES

Curiously, the lowland people of eastern Britain borrowed the (full-length) European longhouse idea as the prototype design for their collective tombs, the earthen long barrows.[2] We are used to seeing long barrows as soft green mounds melting into green downland, but when they were new – and for decades afterwards – they were sharply defined with deep bounding ditches and blinding chalk-white domes visible for many miles. Their visibility, and that of the high-sited chamber tombs in other regions too, shows that they were meant to make a visual impact and do far more than house the dead. A very small mound would have sufficed to cover the handful of burials, which are invariably tucked anonymously under one end of the long barrow. The mounds must have had some other function as well; indeed some long barrows had no burials beneath them at all.

Calculations based on the human remains found in long barrows, which were built relatively infrequently over a long period, seem to suggest that there were only 250 people living in southern Britain at any particular time.[3] Obviously there were many more than that, so we might wonder what happened to the bodies of the thousands of other people who lived and died at that time. The answer is probably to be found in the neolithic practice of sky-burial. Instead of bodies being disposed of all in one go as they are today, in the neolithic at least some were treated to a two-tier rite. First, they were laid out in the open air in special compounds for birds, rodents and insects to devour and for decomposition of the flesh to take its course. Some of the bones found entombed at Wayland's Smithy and Parc le Breos had been gnawed by rodents while the flesh was still on them. Bones found inside the Skendleby long barrow in Lincolnshire had snails' eggs laid on them, which shows that they had been in the open air at some stage. Tooth marks on the bones show that several different species of scavenger were at work. In a partly open, partly wooded environment rich in scavengers, the destruction of corpses would have been quick. A human body can be reduced almost to a skeleton in as little as a month; within a year the skeleton can be completely disarticulated.[4] An experiment with a sky-buried pig showed that flies and maggots can destroy all the flesh within a matter of days. Sky-burial turns out to have been an exceptionally efficient way of defleshing a corpse.[5]

The bones in some tombs show evidence of sorting – skulls in one compartment, long bones in another – and this would only have been possible after all the flesh had gone and the skeletons had become disarticulated.[6] The sorting seems to have little to do with social status, except on the simplest level. Sometimes the bones of men were separated from those of women, and old from young, but there was no distinction according to class. Some see this as evidence that early neolithic society was inhibited, that mortuary ritual was designed to conceal distinctions among the living;[7] it may rather be that social distinctions did not exist, either in death or in life.[8]

The process of defleshing was sometimes assisted.[9] If for some reason the flesh did not fall away fast enough, people sliced off such flesh as remained; cut marks on some of the bones prove that butchering like this did take place. It is hard to imagine still-grieving family members doing this, but it seems they did, or perhaps a neighbour did it for them. The wooden chamber in the Haddenham long barrow near Cambridge contained the remains of five or six people. One corpse was missing its head. Another consisted of head, neck and arms only, as if someone had taken hold of the corpse under the armpits and pulled until the shoulder girdle parted company from the rest of the rotting body. One arm had a cut mark where the muscle was sliced off above the elbow.[10] People were evidently ready to handle half-rotted bodies, and there is evidence that this handling occurred repeatedly. Whether people generally were less squeamish than we are it is not possible to tell, but it looks as though they were. It may be that the responsibility to do this work was assigned to a particular person, family or group within the community. Ghoulish though all this may sound, a very similar defleshing prior to final burial used to be practised in Greece, and it continued until relatively recently.

Often in southern England mortuary enclosures were rectangular and bounded by fences, ditches or banks, to mark them out as special taboo places, though with the cawing of carrion and the strong smell of decaying flesh people would scarcely have needed warning off. Some of the enclosures had structures within them, such as rectangular mortuary houses or raised platforms for sky-burials, sometimes hung with ox-hides, and entrances embellished with arcs of totem poles. The Skendleby long barrow (built in 3140 BC) was fitted with a curving façade made of posts. This was exaggerated by extending it 2 metres beyond the post-built side walls of the barrow. The façade's curved shape emphasizes its role as a cyclorama against which important

Fussell's Lodge long barrow. A partial reconstruction of the mortuary house (left), porch (right) and façade. The mortuary house is shown 'under construction', but it may well have been in a state of collapse by the time the façade and porch were built.

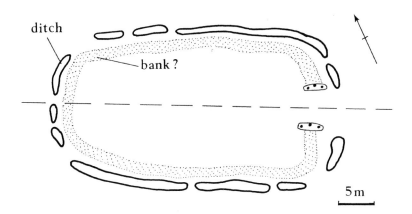

Mortuary enclosure on Normanton Down. The gate was faced with horizontal planks, perhaps to stop the bank material from collapsing into the entrance (after Vatcher 1961).

rituals were played out. This development begins to define a forecourt area. The Giants' Hills façade has no entrance gap left in it, so there seems to have been no intention of reopening or re-entering the barrow once it was built. The curved wall of solid timber seems to symbolize the separation of the world of the dead from that of the living, like the curtain at a crematorium. In front of it, the living performed their ceremonies, ate their funeral feasts, pleaded for the intercession of the ancestors, showed their solidarity with the past. Behind it, the sleeping ancestors listened, validated, supported.

The mortuary enclosures were often converted into barrows. At Wor Barrow a rectangular enclosure 26m long was built on the site first, bounded by a palisade wall, and several corpses were laid out in it before the barrow itself was heaped up on top. The wooden structures with their decaying corpses were left in place, occasionally set on fire first, before being buried under tonnes of rubble and soil. From the small numbers of bones in the barrows, I can only assume that most bodies were left to disintegrate in the mortuary enclosures. There are seldom any grave goods in the tombs, so there is no reason to assume that the dead treated in this special way were members of a ruling élite – and there is no other evidence for believing that such an élite existed in 3000 BC. It may be that when the time came to make a long barrow, however that momentous decision was made, a collection of human body parts was gathered together for inclusion in the barrow, and maybe it did not matter whose they were – or how many.

As well as being burial places, the tombs were territorial markers, representing a claim on the farmland they overlooked. They were large enough to be conspicuous, 2–3m high and often 30–90m long: four long barrows are over 150m long. Probably the entombed grandparents were part of that claim, and their spirits mediated in the otherworld on behalf of the living.[11] Like the medieval parish church, the neolithic tomb was an important landmark, a social and religious focus, a place for family burials, a place for praying and wishing, a place where the bond with the past could be renewed and a larger sense of time re-established. Just by being there, in an otherwise

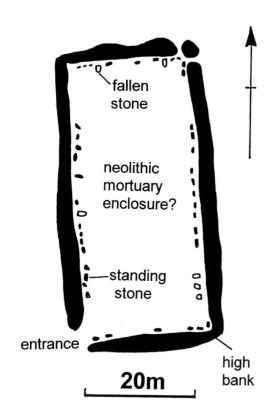

fallen
stone

neolithic
mortuary
enclosure?

standing
stone

entrance

high
bank

20m

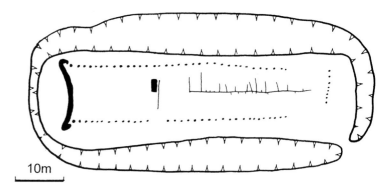

10m

Above: Giants' Hills long barrow, Lincolnshire. The black crescent is the foundation trench for the south-east façade. Two rows of fence-posts (dots) were made to retain the mound material, which was thrown up from a big surrounding quarry ditch.

Left: King Arthur's Hall, a megalithic mortuary enclosure – a rare survival on Bodmin Moor, Cornwall.

Street House. A reconstruction of the mortuary house, hidden behind a screening façade. Compare with the illustration on page 107, something similar in stone (after Scott 1992).

fairly undifferentiated landscape, neolithic tombs played a major role in defining place. Suddenly there were conspicuous man-made markers punctuating the landscape, giving it a startling, man-made definition – and once the markers were there the place could never again be seen in the same way. Not only were there imposing built objects in the landscape, drawing the eye, but the areas round them were also by implication redefined: they might be sanctified by proximity to the tomb, and become foci for pilgrimage or forbidden places overhung by taboos. They might have paths leading to them, or away from them towards other foci.[12]

Drawing inferences from the distribution of long barrows is risky, because so many have been destroyed by ploughing, but from the survivors in lowland England it is possible to make some cautious observations. To begin with, they form distinct clusters, as in the Avebury area, the West Sussex Downs north of Chichester and the East Sussex Downs east of Brighton. The remarkable concentration of long barrows round Avebury may reflect that site's great importance as a centre.

The locations favoured for tombs was a matter of local preference. In many regions they were built on the margins of the farmland, sometimes, as far as we can make out, on the very boundary of the territory. In Orkney the smaller, and some prehistorians think older, tombs were placed out on the marginal land, so that the ancestors commanded panoramic views of their territories, and the living working in the fields below might look up and be reassured by the presence of the ancestors watching over them from the boundary between earth and sky. A very similar pattern is seen in south-east England, where long barrows were invariably built high up, but false-crested so that they were not just visible from the farmland below but conspicuous on the skyline. Most

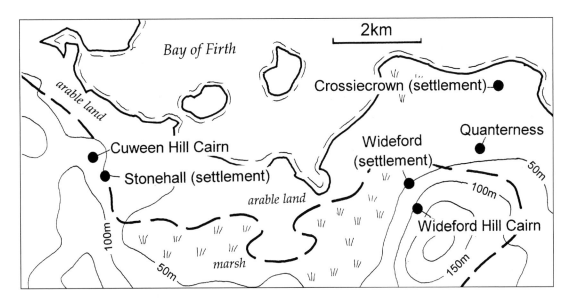

Siting of Orkney chamber tombs. Three settlements round Wideford Hill and their family tombs. In each case the tomb was built on higher ground, just a few tens of metres up the slope and to the right from the farmstead (after Downes and Richards 2000).

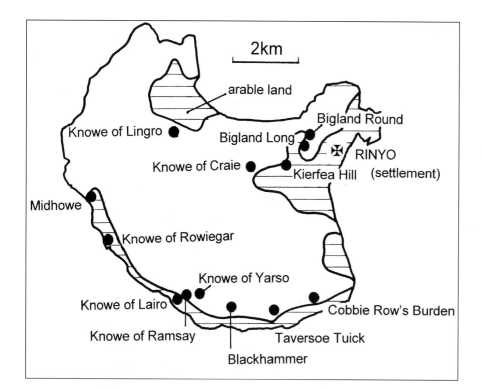

Siting of chamber tombs on Rousay. The tombs are on the edge of, or just above, the productive farmland (shaded) (after Renfrew 1973).

Nutbane, a mortuary building. The cult-house is flanked by totem poles and provides access to a small mortuary enclosure. The scene is probably representative of the first phase of use at many of the English long barrow sites.

remain conspicuous, even in their weathered-
down and grass-grown state, half their original
height and dark with vegetation. The chamber
tombs in the Cotswolds, such as Nympsfield and
Hetty Pegler's Tump, were similarly built high
up and conspicuous, but facing out into the
Severn valley although their settlements and
farmlands were probably located in the dip
slope valleys on the other side of the hill.[13]

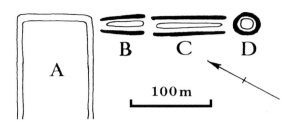

The north-eastern end of the Dorset
Cursus (A). Long barrow C was added to
long barrow B to turn it into a bank
barrow. Barrow D is a later round barrow
built on the same axis. Neolithic and
bronze age barrow builders were fond of
developing linear cemeteries in this way.

On Cranborne Chase, a topographically
featureless area virtually devoid of settlement, a
special sacred landscape of intervisible earthen
long barrows was created, with the Dorset
Cursus, a special earthwork corridor, marked out to connect selected long barrows.
The physical geography of Cranborne Chase was unchallenging; it was the man-made
features that became the defining points and gave it excitement. The landscape was
formally structured as a conduit for ancestral bones en route for the 'death island' of
Hambledon Hill.[14] It has been suggested that long barrows in southern England
generally were built in unoccupied land, well away from the farmsteads. Out on the
territorial boundaries, they were evocative places, where people might feel they were
on the brink of the world where the ancestors lived on. The same has been suggested
for the causewayed enclosures, and it is probably no coincidence that long barrows –
and later round barrows too – often stand close to enclosures.[15]

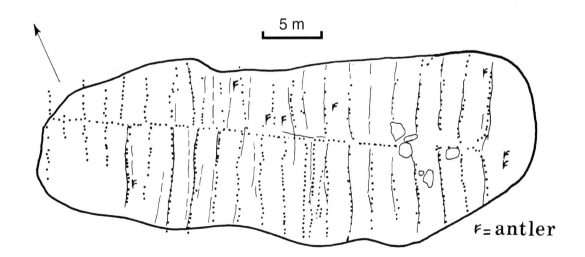

South Street long barrow. The two flanking ditches are off the plan, top and bottom. The pattern of
stake-holes (black dots) and hurdles (lines) can be seen in the neolithic land surface beneath the mound.
The bays between the hurdles are thought to represent work stints. The workers deliberately buried their
antler picks in the growing mound. This long barrow had no human burials in it at all.

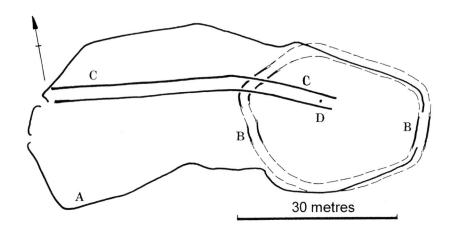

Maiden Castle. A = inner rampart of the iron age fort; B = ditches of the neolithic causewayed enclosure (built 3500 BC); C = ditches of the Long Mound, a bank barrow built in 3200 BC; D = ritual burials.

In the Midlands there was a different pattern; long barrows were frequently built in low-lying positions on the floors of river valleys, on farmland and not far from settlements. Some of the Wessex long barrows follow this pattern too; the South Street barrow near Avebury was built on low-lying land that had previously been ploughed.[16]

In the years leading up to the demise of the long barrow, the builders shifted towards greater monumentality, as if they were itching to make some new and grander statement and struggled to utter it through a type of structure that was inadequate to the need. Soon they would create entirely new monuments – henges, superhenges and great round barrows – but before they launched into these new types they attempted to aggrandize the old. They added a tail to the Pentridge long barrow to make it twice as long; they re-dug the side ditches of Wor Barrow and a couple of other Wessex long barrows to make the mounds higher. They even experimented with building a couple of gigantic long barrows called bank barrows – one at North Stoke and another at Maiden Castle.[17]

CHAMBER TOMBS

The Cotswold-Severn chambered tombs were long barrows with stone chambers, an in-between type of tomb. They were usually built in commanding positions, but not always. Parc le Breos in Gower stands in the bottom of a dry valley and is visible from nowhere except close at hand. Its location may be connected to the local topography, as in the neolithic it stood beside a spring, and it is possible that the interest in springs and streams that is now thought of as 'Celtic', although it was clearly a bronze age preoccupation, may after all have its origins earlier still, in the neolithic. A short distance up the valley Cathole Cave contains palaeolithic, mesolithic, beaker and bronze age deposits, though curiously nothing from the neolithic; the place may nevertheless have had mythic associations in the neolithic that were strong enough to override other considerations.[18] In south-west Wales generally, chamber tombs were

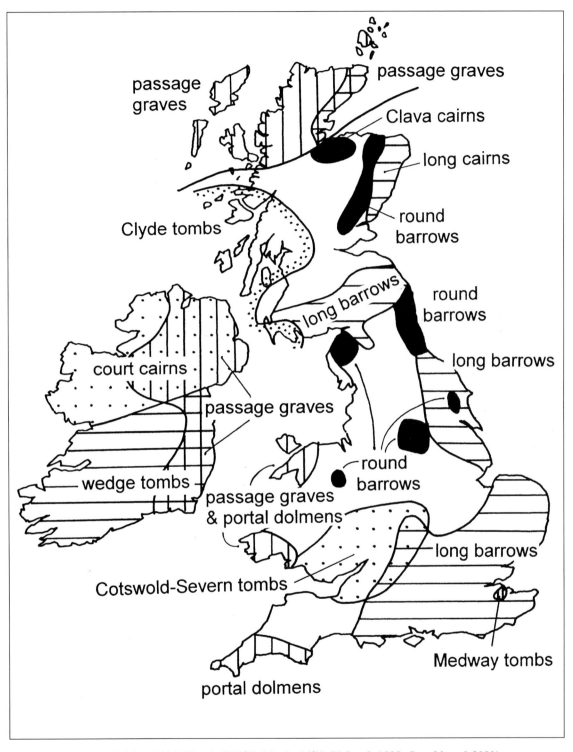

Tomb types (after Ashbee 1984, Henshall 1970, Manby 1970, Richards 1992, Oswald *et al.* 2001).

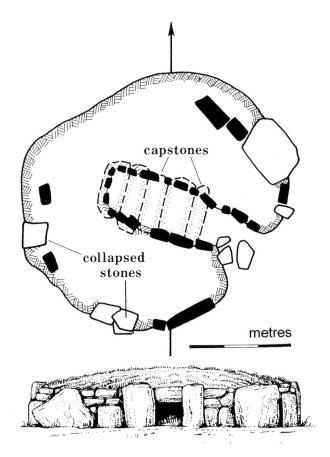

Pennance entrance grave: plan and reconstruction.

capstones

collapsed stones

metres

designed to draw attention to specific places that were already imbued with cosmological significance; they were points along pathways of movement across the landscape.[19] In the Black Mountains chamber tombs were more conspicuous, with views that gave a focus on rivers, hills and spurs.

The stone tombs of the north and west of Britain were sometimes superficially like the earthen long barrows. The difference was that they were hollow vaults; built of stone, they could sustain hollow chambers. These burial chambers were often connected to the world of the living by an entrance passage, though this had to have some sealing mechanism. Just as today we talk of coming to terms with loss and bereavement as 'closure', so too in 3000 BC people needed to close a door on death. Midhowe is the most spectacular stalled cairn on Rousay in Orkney. Under its long rectangular cairn lay an impressive chamber built of drystone walling, probably originally roofed with huge sandstone flags that long afterwards were looted to make the iron age broch nearby. The Midhowe entrance passage was fitted with double blocking: two separate drystone walls that had to be dismantled each time people wanted to enter the tomb, probably only when another family member died and had been sky-buried for a time.

Chamber tombs depended on the availability of building stone and there was plenty in the hard rock highlands. There were no suitable stones for building tomb chambers in the chalk and clay lands of southern and eastern England. In some cases timber chambers may have been made, but it is difficult to distinguish the remains of such a structure from those of a barrow raised over the site of a free-standing timber mortuary building. But there was more to chamber tombs than mere geological empowerment. The shores of the Irish Sea cradled a new culture – the culture of the passage grave builders. The passage grave was imported from Brittany to the Boyne

Plas Newydd burial chamber, Anglesey. The covering mound has completely gone. The massive capstone is a metre thick – pure showing off.

Trethevy Quoit in Cornwall.

valley and Anglesey, then spread outwards from those two foci, radiating westwards across Ireland and southwards through Wales to the English West Country.[20] Builders made the passage graves extra special by adding carved art work. The beautiful coiling spirals they carved in the passages and chambers found their way even to Orkney. The transmission of the idea says much for the navigability of the western seaways and the unexpected willingness of people to travel long distances.

Portal dolmens developed out of the passage graves and diffused over the Irish Sea province. Many portal dolmens were built in Ireland and a few on the eastern seaboard of the Irish–Celtic Sea, in Anglesey, Snowdonia, Dyfed and Cornwall. The portal dolmen is a streamlined version of a passage grave, a précis with a single chamber. The fact that portal dolmens and passage graves are diffused across the same province suggests that the seaways remained in use throughout this period.

For a long time prehistorians have assumed that building monuments went with farming. The idea was that farming created a closer bond between people and the land that sustained them; that in turn led to the building of ancestral tombs and later other monuments, to emphasize the land legacy. If that is the whole truth, there should be no monuments pre-dating 4500 BC – the beginning of agriculture – but there *are* some that are earlier.

When two of the line of posts in the Stonehenge car park produced radiocarbon dates of 8275 and 7000 BC,[21] most Stonehenge commentators were silent on the matter: some said the samples must have been contaminated. Now that a third post in the row has been dated to 7450 BC, [22] it is no longer possible to dismiss the radiocarbon dates as 'mistaken'. The Stonehenge car park was a mesolithic focus of some kind, and it cannot be regarded as a coincidence that the site was seen as special in the ninth, eighth, fourth, third and second millennia BC. Some prehistorians still fight a rearguard action, arguing that the mesolithic posts were raised so long before the other phases that they cannot have anything to do with Stonehenge, but the fact is that there was a substantial ceremonial structure consisting of a line of free-standing totem poles in a woodland clearing only a stone's throw from the site of the circles of earth, timber and stone.[23] It is possible that other features of the time regarded as distinctly neolithic are equally an inheritance from the mesolithic. It has been suggested that the axe factories were, after all, instigated by earlier communities with a hunter-gatherer background. Careful mapping in north-east Yorkshire has shown mesolithic–neolithic

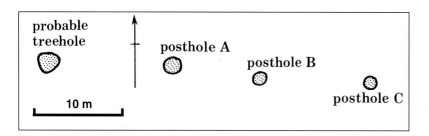

The line of totem poles dating from the earliest phase of Stonehenge, 7500 BC.

The post-passage and conjectured roundhouse at the centre of Stonehenge: a partial reconstruction of what seems to have been a ceremonial foyer.

continuity, indicating that at no fewer than twelve locations neolithic people occupied mesolithic sites.[24] Even in 3000 BC there was a legacy from the past.

In a wooded environment any late mesolithic monuments – tombs, even – would very likely have been made of wood, the material closest to hand; this perished and passed out of the archaeological record. By the time people came to build the large stone structures of the neolithic, the landscape was becoming deforested, nudging them to build in stone rather than timber, although this argument cannot be pressed too far as a great deal of forest survived. Such timber as was used survived usually because it had barrow material heaped over it later, like the Haddenham wooden burial chamber, or was deposited in a wet low-lying site, like the Etton enclosure. Neolithic communities often systematically replaced timber ritual structures with stone ones as a metaphor, to emphasize that a place once used by the living was now dedicated to the dead; folklore is full of stories of people 'turned to stone'. Turning a wooden monument to stone was a way of making it into a moongate to the world of the ancestors, just as a living human being turns into a stony skeleton as he or she enters the world of the dead. A great many mesolithic centres must have been coastal, and the rising sea level would have submerged them, and either destroyed them or made them impossible to find.[25]

On balance, I think it is possible that there *were* mesolithic monuments in Britain, other than Stonehenge, and that they were made of timber, but we will be very lucky indeed if we find any trace of them. It has even been suggested that the huge shell

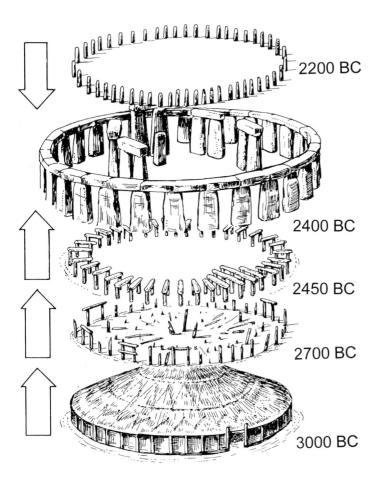

2200 BC

2400 BC

2450 BC

2700 BC

3000 BC

Continuity at Stonehenge. In time, timber turned to stone.

middens found on the Atlantic coasts functioned as communal monuments; they had human burials tucked into them, after all, just like the neolithic long barrows.

The distribution of mesolithic cemeteries suggests another link between middle and new stone ages. These early cemeteries in Portugal, Brittany and southern Sweden were created by communities to whom family trees and territorial claims were emerging as important. It was precisely these areas that would become the cradles of early neolithic monument-building cultures.[26]

Looked at in another way, farming did not always prompt people to build big family monuments. The earliest farmers in mainland Europe did not build them. Maybe we can explain the difference in terms of settlement pattern. In central and eastern Europe people lived in substantial villages where there may have been shrines that were not specially related to burial; the social structure was such that death and burial need not be emphasized. On the Atlantic fringe, including Britain, people lived in very small scattered communities which may have needed some kind of landscape focus, and it was the family tomb that became that focus. Dispersed across the landscape, people wanted a focus that was both visible and permanent to supply some symbol of security and continuity.[27]

There is a hint of ceremonial burials on an ambitious scale at an early site near St Albans. Here a scorched logboat contained a disarticulated and decomposed corpse together with a couple of wooden boxes. It foreshadowed key characteristics of neolithic burial practice – a two-stage funerary rite, sky-burial, earth burial, cremation and boat burial – and it is surprising that this happened as early as 4700 BC, right at the end of the mesolithic, before farming was under way.

Certainly agriculture and a more sedentary lifestyle would have made people in the neolithic more conscious that they were taking nature over, not just passing through the landscape but forming a partnership with it. The *idea* of appropriating nature was even more important than the reality. Before 3000 BC there is not very much evidence for large-scale human impact on the landscape, so the economic impact of agriculture was probably limited. The neolithic was less a distinctive economy than a distinctive set of social relations and beliefs built round a series of binary oppositions (us and them, in and out, culture and nature, tame and wild, made and unmade, life and death).[28] Often the monuments are the earliest sign of a neolithic mindset. Monuments were themselves being used to transform the landscape, in advance of tilling and other agricultural techniques, to redefine the world. Monuments were often a declaration of what was to be rather than a consolidation of what had been achieved: not a commemoration but a promise. Barrows, stones, avenues and enclosures marked out the land, redefining the world and saying what it would do.[29]

In particular, the neolithic preoccupation with tomb-building speaks of a heightened awareness of the social significance of death. Death was a threat to the continuity of society, which was in its turn important in determining the usership of land. People devised elaborate mortuary ceremonies in an attempt to create an impression that they were bringing nature under control. People took their dead through a series of rites of passage from living to newly dead, to decaying and disintegrating, and finally to investiture as an ancestor. They took their loved ones from integration through disintegration to reintegration. What happened physically to the body at each stage was symbolic of these transformations.[30] The persistence of the mortuary ritual, albeit with all sorts of local variations, across very large areas shows that an overriding set of beliefs prevailed right across north-west Europe; there were rules, at least governing the death rites, that had to be followed. A point that has yet to be explained is the uneven distribution of the tombs. Perhaps some areas were regarded as ancestral homelands, others not; perhaps they were only built in areas where there was active competition for land; perhaps they were felt to be necessary where migrants were setting up colonies.[31] This last seems to me the best way of explaining the tight cluster of megalithic monuments along the shore of the Medway estuary in Kent, where colonists seem to have arrived by sea from the west of Britain.

Tombs were built to several very distinct regional designs. The fact that they were often composite in character shows that people moved about, looked at tombs built by neighbours or even by groups living far afield, and copied the features they liked.[32] The external shape of the rectangular or trapeze-shaped earthen long barrows of eastern and southern England was clearly based on the external appearance of the central European longhouse. This idea, that houses for the dead were based on houses for the living, even if not the local living, is a fruitful one and works well in other areas. The round tombs of the north were similar in shape to the round houses of the hunter-gatherers. The Loch Olabhat crannog was kidney-shaped, with a bowed front curving in towards the entrance. This shape is repeated in many a stone tomb, and it may be (as some have suggested) that the crannog was built in imitation of a tomb.[33] but it seems more likely to me that it was the other way round – the tombs were imitating the form of a domestic enclosure that was probably very common; in other words, the kidney-shaped tombs were built to resemble an entire homestead rather than just a house. But still the metaphor was 'home'.

Two big Orkney tombs, Quoyness and Quanterness, were built to the same plan and in the same materials as an Orcadian stone house. One of the houses at Barnhouse is identical in layout to the tombs: a rectangular room with an entrance passage leading into the middle of one of the long sides and six symmetrically arranged rectangular bed recesses.[34] Here, the architectural metaphor is taken a significant step further – in Orkney people were not just making *houses* for the dead, but *beds* for them too. The Orcadians passed from home to tomb, from bed to cist, from sleep to death. Even the simple cist burials, no more than stone boxes made out of four slabs planted in the ground, were references to the stone box-beds that were standard furniture in Orkney houses at Barnhouse and Skara Brae.

There has been a recent tendency to draw attention to differences between the architecture of long barrows and that of longhouses. In particular, it is pointed out that the mortuary structures concealed inside barrows are quite *un*like neolithic houses. Paul Ashbee's idealized reconstruction of Fussell's Lodge long barrow as a solid longhouse with a pitched roof is seen as an exaggeration.[35] Ironically, evidence is now appearing in support of the Ashbee idea, from an unlikely location. A search for a suspected neolithic village on the island of Westray led to the discovery of a major chambered tomb. This consists of a mound 21m across covering a large (7 × 4.5m) burial chamber, the largest ever found in Britain and dating from 3000 BC. The

The Fussell's Lodge long barrow when complete (after Ashbee 1966). The resemblance to a European longhouse seems to have been intentional.

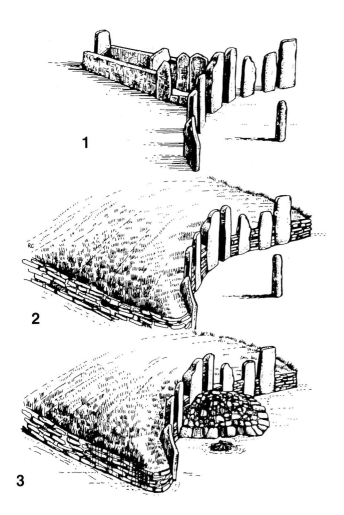

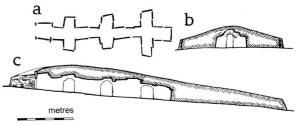

Stoney Littleton, a Cotswold–Severn chambered tomb. The transepted tomb chambers in plan (a); the burial mound as a whole in cross-section (b) and long profile (c).

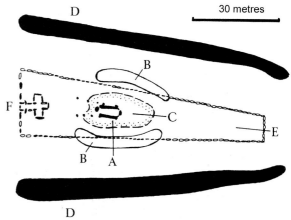

Wayland's Smithy, a two-phase long barrow. A = mortuary building; B = quarry ditches of Period 1; C = small long barrow of Period 1; D = quarry ditches of Period 2; E = large long barrow of Period 2; F = burial chambers and façade at southern end of Period 2 monument. At first sight the later barrow seems to override the earlier barrow without regard for it, but some care was taken to make its sides parallel with the converging lines of stones and posts forming the early mortuary structure.

Cairnholy in Galloway. The building sequence at a Clyde chamber tomb. 1 = The megaliths of a burial chamber and façade are raised. 2 = A drystone wall is raised as a kerb for a covering long mound. The forecourt is used for rituals including fires. 3 = After several centuries of use the tomb's doorway is finally sealed up.

chamber is near-rectangular, with bowed sides and rounded corners, very like the well-known neolithic houses at Knap of Howar, not far away on Papa Westray. The huge burial chamber was meant to look just like a house. Human fingers and toes found close by suggest a sky-burial site next to the tomb. A family lived in a house; the same family lived on in the family tomb.[36]

Often the mortuary structures under burial mounds were simple timber boxes defined at each end by the two halves of a split tree driven into the ground, such as Wayland's Smithy, Giants' Hills 2 and Haddenham. They appear to have had plank roofs that could be lifted off so that body parts could be fished out for recirculation and fresh bodies put in.[37] To the east, often beyond a blind entrance, a ceremonial façade was raised, a line of totem poles, sometimes straight, sometimes curving, defining an area where the living might meet to commune with the dead. The forecourt was the scene of meetings, meals and fires.[38] When the time came for the mortuary structure to be closed for ever, it was sometimes set on fire before earth and rubble from two long quarry ditches were thrown on top. Only the forecourt remained accessible; the living might still visit. Indeed, at some Cotswold-Severn tombs the living went on burying the dead in the forecourts.[39]

The Cotswold-Severn chambered tombs found on each side of the Severn valley were an in-between type of tomb, with the external form of the earthen long barrow taken from the lands to the east and south combined with the internal arrangement of stone chambers borrowed from the lands to the west and north. The uprights of the stone chambers and entrance passage were built first, then the area that would become the mound was marked out with lightweight fences as sets of paired rectangular cells arranged along the tomb's long axis. This was apparently a way of subdividing the non-specialist work of assembling the cairn material; probably one family or even one person took on the responsibility for filling a section from the adjacent quarry ditch. The practice was borrowed from the builders of the earthen long barrows, where the mounds were sometimes formally partitioned by hurdles. Unlike the long barrows, the Cotswold-Severn tombs had a drystone wall built round the edge, giving the whole monument a neat rectangular outline.[40]

In 3000 BC traditions were being mixed in this way all over Britain; it was a time of reaching out and taking in new ideas. Although we have no documents from the neolithic, we can begin to see the monuments themselves as a kind of text; like travel books, they burst with references to other monuments, other people and their customs, other places.[41]

North and west of the Cotswold-Severn tombs, entrance graves were built. These were developed from the basic cist (stone box) idea, but in the most exciting way. The leading edges of the tall flanking stones made a kind of porch or doorway and held aloft a massive sloping capstone, worn like a broad-brimmed hat pushed to the back of the head. They were surrounded, possibly covered, by a cairn; this does not usually survive as the entrance graves stand on agricultural land and the smaller stones have been cleared.[42]

Many of the tombs visible in 3000 BC were not recently built; they had been standing long enough to need modifying. Some had begun as timber mortuary enclosures or shrines and were now covered by long barrows; some had begun as one, two or three small round tombs and were now expanded into a much larger long barrow. Dyffryn Ardudwy near Barmouth is a fine example, where two small stone entrance graves were turned into a trapeze-shaped long mound; the pebble cairn has subsequently spread, once more uncovering the two beautiful little stone chambers. It was not so much that ideas of tomb architecture were changing, rather that people were getting ideas from further afield and grafting them into their monuments – and

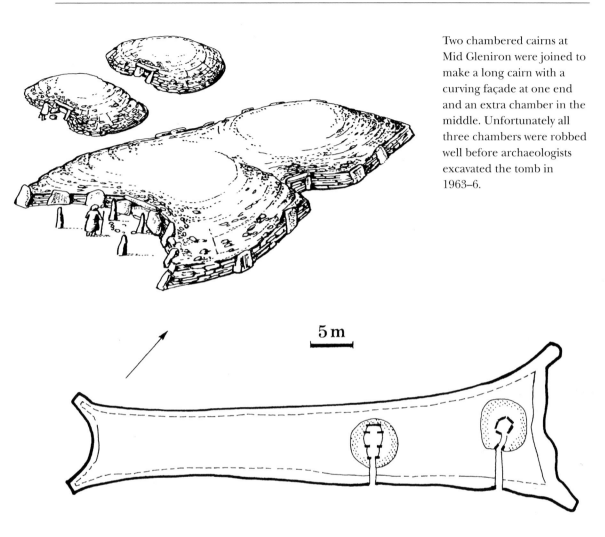

Two chambered cairns at Mid Gleniron were joined to make a long cairn with a curving façade at one end and an extra chamber in the middle. Unfortunately all three chambers were robbed well before archaeologists excavated the tomb in 1963–6.

5 m

Camster Long cairn in Caithness. Two early round chambered cairns were converted into a fine long cairn with, unusually, a curved façade at each end (Henshall 1963).

exactly the same thing was happening on the European mainland too.[43] Occasionally an old monument was completely replaced. The stalled cairn at Howe on Orkney was levelled and a thin layer of clay spread across the foundations before a brand-new monument was built, a Maes Howe-type cairn, on exactly the same site.[44]

One curious adaptation was the addition of 'tails' to old monuments. Some heel-shaped and circular cairns in the north were given extensions to bring them more in line, both literally and metaphorically, with the long barrow tradition.[45]

Further north, at Barclodiad in Anglesey and Calderstones in Liverpool, we see the passage grave idea that was shared by the Boyne valley across the Irish Sea and ultimately imported from Brittany.[46] The same idea was adopted in Orkney too.

Their meanings were also subtly reinforced when people deposited certain items, substances or products in them. Often antler picks were carefully placed on the floors of enclosure ditches, as at Avebury. A century ago it was thought these were merely discarded tools, thrown down because they were worn out, but the positioning is often methodical, significant. They were offerings, not rubbish. Certain objects could be left only in certain places. It is not clear what the meanings might have been, but some reinforcement of the magical quality of the place was evidently intended. It was to emphasize the nature of the place, to intensify its individuality. Even in this, people were giving the world sharper definition, greater differentiation, making every part of it special.

In 3000 BC these tombs were standing, splendidly complete and already established since no one could remember when, in the timeless landscape of the ancestors. But change was in the air. The last long barrows were built in 3000 BC, and poor specimens they were too: the dog-end of a great tradition, a truncated form called the oval barrow.[47]

SINGLE GRAVES, INDIVIDUAL BURIALS

In Yorkshire a new style of burial rite began, this time under large round barrows. The burials were still collective, but the crouched corpses were buried intact, replacing the old long barrows with their disarticulated bones. This implies that either there was no preliminary sky-burial or the period of sky-burial was brief enough for the bodies to remain articulated. The most spectacular example was Duggleby Howe in the Yorkshire Wolds, where many bodies were buried in a crouched position in a large pit and a huge covering mound raised over them. Five hundred years later another layer of mound material was added, making it even bigger, and forty-three cremations were tucked into it. The barrow is impressive enough in itself, but air photos have revealed that it stands in the middle of an enormous enclosure, an earth circle over 10 hectares in area.[48]

The cairn at Whitegrounds near Malton in Yorkshire began in 3800 BC as an entrance grave under an oval cairn. It initially contained the remains of three decapitated people, a man, a woman and a child, their heads buried in a separate heap. Seven hundred years later a big earthen round barrow with a kerb and central single grave was raised over the entrance grave; it housed one man with a polished flint axe and a jet slider.[49] Duggleby Howe, not far away, was begun as a single grave, although it ended up containing a horde of people. By the late neolithic, not just individual people but whole people were being buried. This shows a significant change in attitudes, not just to the worth of individual people, but to the nature of death, its significance to the community, and possibly to concepts such as the nature of land tenure and entitlement to territory.

The emphasis was shifting from collective to individual burial. Not everyone was given this special treatment, and most corpses were still left to disintegrate in the mortuary enclosures. The handful of people given single burial may have been randomly chosen to represent the community, or they may have been regarded as important individuals, perhaps because their personal qualities made them the best equipped to intercede with the ancestors – chosen intermediaries.

The change marks the emergence of a more hierarchical, competitive and stratified society. The strategic placing of whole people in the landscape marks a very significant moment, when individual people began to matter, when literally self-conscious people, people like us, self-contained and self-aware, began to emerge.[50]

In Norfolk between 3200 and 3000 BC people sealed up their old collective tombs and opened a whole new tradition of individual burials in round barrows that they built close at hand;[51] the henges at Arminghall and Markshall near Norwich became the focus of a large round barrow cemetery. Stonehenge too gathered round barrows around it, though organized in an unusual way. At first sight the landscape here seems to be spattered randomly with round barrows, but statistical analysis shows that there are especially large numbers of barrows 1km and 2.0–2.3km away from Stonehenge. The barrows form two loose rings, the inner incorporating the Normanton Down Group and the Old and New King Barrows, the outer incorporating the Winterbourne Stoke, Lake, Wilsford and Durrington Down groups.[52] The cemeteries respect the gentle undulations of the topography; wherever possible they stand on the crests of ridges from which Stonehenge may be seen. An exception is on the north side of Stonehenge, where the cursus cuts right across the landscape, and that major processional way had to be avoided by the barrow builders.

In some places natural mounds were treated as surrogate barrows; at Longham in Norfolk a natural hillock left over from the Ice Age had several late neolithic burials in beakers inserted into it. People were consciously tying the funerary landscape into the natural landscape.

All the old long barrows, including the long cairns of the Cotswold-Severn tradition, were sealed up. The living were putting a clear boundary between themselves and the ancestors, making blockings of timber, stone and earth that would be a door on death. The mortuary deposit from this time on became more separate from the world of the living than before. Access to the knowledge of who was and who was not inside the tombs may have become more than ever the exclusive preserve of a special shamanic group.[53] The energy committed not only to building tombs but to refining their design, shows a brooding preoccupation with the relationship between the living and the dead. People continually negotiated a reciprocity between the two worlds. My impression is that the fundamental ambition was to remain in a state of suspension, floating between the two worlds, to walk the tightrope, and lock together time present and time past for time future. The ancient Egyptians were building their first pyramid at this moment. Their houses and palaces lasted for a short time and could be renewed or replaced when necessary, but their tombs, which they called their 'castles of eternity', were built to last for ever.[54] This same interplay between the short time-scale of individual human lives and the longer time-scale of the life of the community can be seen in contemporary tomb- and temple-building in Britain, where the houses came and went but the monuments were designed to last for ever. The tombs were the castles of eternity. They belonged to the time of the ancestors.

CHAPTER NINE

LINES AND CIRCLES ON THE LANDSCAPE

I f people were punctuating the landscape with tombs that brought the eye to a halt like full stops and exclamation marks, they were also making larger, linear, marks that divided the landscape up into chapters.

CURSUS MONUMENTS

In 3000 BC the cursus monuments were already made. These long narrow enclosures with parallel sides marked by ditches and banks were apparently modelled on mortuary enclosures but were much bigger in scale, broader and longer. There are other reasons for assuming a connection with burial rites: the longer ones often lead to a long barrow. Often they are straight-sided and oriented north-west to south-east or north-east to south-west, the solar orientations that were built into some of the tombs, though there may have been shifts of emphasis between lunar and solar orientations around 3000 BC. One section of the Dorchester Cursus was aligned on the midsummer minor moonrise, another on the midsummer sunset.

The area just inside the south-western end of the Dorset Cursus was levelled, apparently to make a gathering place. From it, observers looked north-eastwards along the cursus to a long barrow (Gussage St Michael III) conspicuously silhouetted on the skyline. The rising moon at its southernmost position in 3000 BC would have appeared in the notch between the barrow and the right-hand cursus bank. While to us such an alignment might seem a pointless curiosity, neolithic people may well have regarded the moon as a deity associated with death, and that conceptually linked the lunar observations and the processional visits to the long barrows which the cursus physically linked together.

There are two cursus monuments close to Stonehenge. The Greater Cursus is slightly bent, and appears to have been laid out in three stages. The eastern section, ending at a long barrow, forms an alignment with the Cuckoo Stone (a fallen monolith), the site of the later Woodhenge and a major bend in the River Avon; it

A neolithic landscape on Cranborne Chase. The Dorset Cursus passed through a landscape thick with long barrows and mortuary enclosures. It joined eight long barrows and separated an area of settlements to the north-west from the major ceremonial centre at Knowlton to the south-east (after Johnson 1999 and other sources).

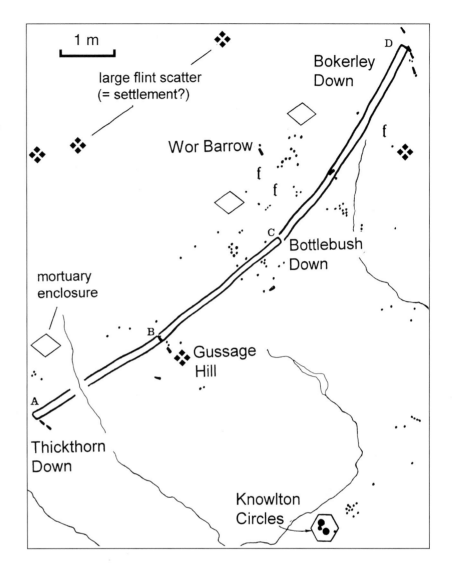

may be a coincidence that the line points to the place where the sun rises at the equinoxes. The two processional ways near Stonehenge are a reminder that they sometimes occur in groups; there are four at Rudston and as many as five (though very small) at Goldington in Bedfordshire.

The Dorset Cursus is an extraordinary anomaly. The largest monumental avenue by far, it wanders with deceptive informality across the landscape from south-west to north-east. The middle section is thought to have been built first, and aligned on the midwinter sunset; the setting sun slid from view behind a long barrow that had been deliberately incorporated into the cursus terminus. Later the Dorset Cursus was extended both to the south-west and to the north-east. Now ploughed down, the chalk banks once stood 2 metres high. The spacious interior was maintained as pasture, but it ran between woods and crossed three chalk valleys, and it was not possible to see from one end to the other. Moving along inside the cursus must have been rather like

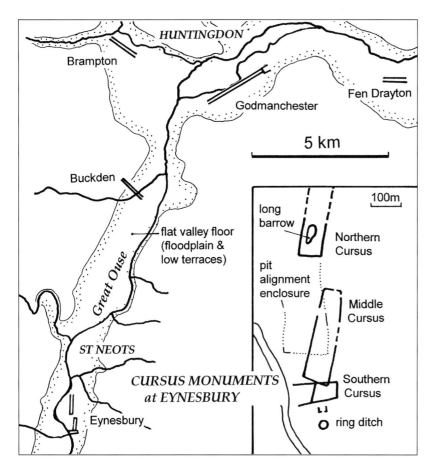

The lower reach of the Great Ouse, a sacred river that attracted cursus monuments (after Last 1999 and Malim 1999).

travelling along a white-walled road and it is generally assumed, rightly I think, that the cursus was used for ceremonial processions connected with funerary rituals.

Cursus monuments both large and small are found right across southern Britain.[1] One on the floor of the Great Ouse valley at Godmanchester ran in a straight line connecting an earlier box-shaped enclosure to the river bank, and there is surely some profound religious significance in the link with water. The early enclosure is unlike anything seen anywhere else, a huge trapeze-shaped stadium 350m long and 230m across, marked on three sides by a ditch. Within the ditch twenty-four posts stood at regular intervals round the perimeter, and several of them are thought to mark solstice or equinox positions of the sun and moon.

The connection with water is repeated at site after site in the middle reach of the Great Ouse valley. Seven cursus monuments were laid out across the level gravel terraces, brushing past the river or leading to it; five more have been found further upstream, near Bedford. Here we catch sight of the Great Ouse as a 5000-year-old sacred river, a British Ganges.

Some cursus monuments are associated with henges. At Stonehenge it almost looks as if the cursus was a forerunner of the earth circle, and Stonehenge to some extent replaced it. But, even after its original function lapsed, once the monument was built and visible it would inevitably have continued to play some part in the way people responded to the landscape for centuries to come. Some archaeologists think the Greater Cursus made a sacred boundary, that the area to the north of the cursus was regarded as different from the area where Stonehenge itself stood. But it is hard to be sure, as the relationships between henge, cursus and landscape at other sites are not the same. A peculiarity of the Greater Cursus is that it stops some distance short of the River Avon, apparently to ensure that the two ends were intervisible. The priorities were not always the same.

The earth lines at Maxey, 1.6km long and 60m apart, lead to a crossing place on the River Welland. They bend slightly in the middle, where a large henge 130m in diameter was later built right across them – apparently to replace them. The arrangement reminds me of the stone setting at Avebury, where, in the final design, a sinuous avenue leads up to and then away from the Great Circle. It was the same concept – in stone at Avebury, in earth at Maxey – but the chronological order was different: at Avebury the circle came first and the avenue second, at Maxey it was the other way round.

At Rudston the four cursus monuments cluster round the monolith, not the henge, which lies some distance away to the north – another variation on the pattern of earth circle, earth lines and stones. The cursus monuments connect with a sacred stream again and converge on a point marked by the Rudston Monolith, which stands on a

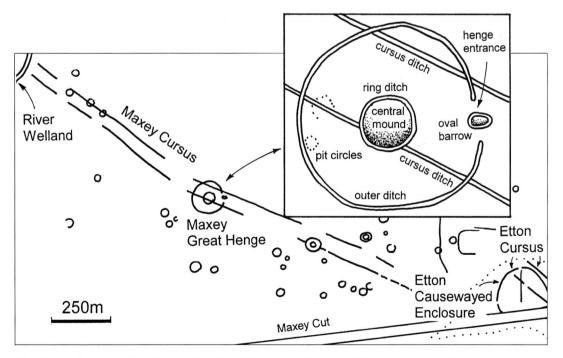

The Maxey ceremonial landscape. The dotted lines show how neolithic stream channels surrounded the Etton causewayed enclosure.

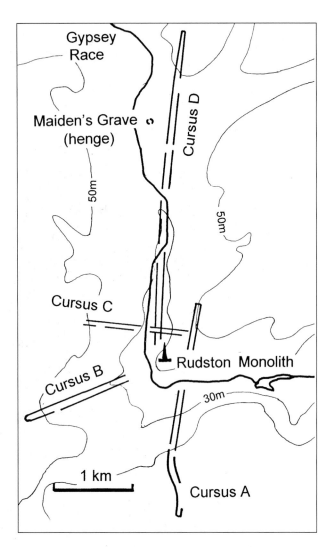

Rudston, the great ceremonial centre in the Yorkshire Wolds (after Harding 1999).

major bend in the Gypsey Race, the only river in the Wolds. That insistent association with a sacred stream may even be telling us that some human remains were cast into rivers, and maybe the later prehistoric practice of river burial had already started. Each cursus terminal at Rudston exactly marks the local horizon when viewed from the opposite terminal: the terminals are intervisible.[2] Quite why that should be is unclear, but it tells us two very important things: that each cursus was designed to fit into the landscape in a very precise way, and that for some reason people positioned themselves at one end and while they were there looked very carefully at the other. The far end touched the horizon. This suggests to some that the cursus was made to mark and observe significant astronomical events – or it may be that it was simply a pathway into the sky, a way to reach the otherworld.

Sometimes the cursus crossed marshy ground, streams and even rivers; this would have obstructed any procession, especially in winter. Perhaps the cursus was a space where young men were tested, in the sight of the ancestors, by being made to race from one end to the other, getting a ducking in marsh or stream along the way, especially at the end. This could explain the emphasis on the two ends of the cursus; they were the starting and finishing points of a life-changing contest. Finds of arrowheads at some sites imply that archery may also have featured in the test.[3]

These mysterious lines were major defining features of ceremonial landscapes in Britain in 3000 BC. Line and circle, cursus and henge. The very forms of the monuments seem to reflect the two fundamental forms in primitive dance: the Indian-file processional dance and the Ring o' Roses round dance. They held some profound religious significance, like the star of David or the cross and crescent of later religions, though it is unlikely that we shall ever understand their full meaning. But the repetition of line and circle shows how fundamental they were to the belief system.

1 The Stanydale 'temple', looking in from the entrance. The sill indicates where a wooden inner door once hung. In the middle are two stone-packed holes for posts (which were spruce); these held the ridge pole. At the back are six wall recesses, which some interpret as shrines, but they may equally well have been domestic storage cupboards. (*Mick Sharp*)

2 Quoyness chamber tomb, Sanday, Orkney. Its exterior clearly shows the internal structure, which consists of three well-made concentric drystone revetment walls. The innermost wall, at the top of the picture, encases the burial chambers. It may be that these walls were intended to remain visible, in which case Quoyness would have looked like a small ziggurat. (*Mick Sharp*)

3 The wonderful tomb chamber at Quoyness, showing the narrowing (corbelling) of the chamber to its full original height of 4 metres. The three small doorways lead to side chambers, of which there are six altogether. (*Mick Sharp*)

4 Knap of Howar, Papa Westray, Orkney. A well-preserved stone house. The building on the right is thought to be the house, that on the left the barn, added later. (*Mick Sharp*)

5 Midhowe stalled cairn, Rousay, Orkney. The view is from the innermost stall back towards the entrance. The side walls survive to a height of 2.5 metres and do not oversail. The ceiling was probably made of big flagstones which were removed, I suspect, in the iron age to build the nearby broch. Human remains were placed on and under low stone benches lining the twelve stalled compartments, each consisting of two facing cells. This big and impressive monument is 32 metres long. (*Mick Sharp*)

6 Skara Brae, Mainland Orkney. A view into House 7 from the doorway, showing the hearth, seat and dresser. Note the shallow recess in the wall above the dresser; it seems to have been carefully made for aesthetic rather than practical reasons. (*Mick Sharp*)

7 Skara Brae. The main underground passageway, roofed and paved with slabs of stone. The doorways into the houses lead off this passage with its drystone walls. (*Mick Sharp*)

8 Barnhouse. The newly discovered village near the Stones of Stenness. (*Mick Sharp*)

9 Camster Long, a very fine (restored) 60m-long cairn in Caithness, seen from the north-eastern end. In the foreground is one of two projections from the mound which made the 'horns' of a forecourt. To the left is the discreet entrance to one of two small passage graves under the cairn; it leads to a chamber only 2 metres across. (*Mick Sharp*)

10 Callanish, Lewis. One of the finest and most imposing ancient monuments in the British Isles, this stone circle has thirteen stones arranged in a circle only 11 metres in diameter. The central stone is almost 5 metres tall and set into the edge of a small chamber tomb; the uprights of its passage and chamber can be seen immediately to the left of the tall stone. A cross-shaped arrangement of stone rows converges on the stone circle. A stone avenue runs northwards for 82 metres. The shorter stone rows to east, west and south were probably intended to be avenues but were never finished. The scale of the monument has only recently been realised. Until 1857 the lower half of it was drowned in peat. The landowner, Sir James Matheson, ordered its removal, which doubled the height of the stones overnight. (*Mick Sharp*)

11 Rock art at Ormaig, Kilmartin, Argyll. Many of the symbols are the simple cup-marks seen at many other sites. The unusual symbol here is the cup-mark surrounded by eight or twelve smaller cup-marks, in turn surrounded by a circle. Is this intended to represent a stone circle within a henge, or something more abstract? Is the overall design a text, a map or just a sequence of separate statements? (*Mick Sharp*)

12 Machrie Moor, Isle of Arran, a remarkable concentration of megaliths. A stone of one stone circle, fluted by natural weathering, stands in the foreground. Another stone circle can be seen in the background with some of the tallest circle-stones in Britain. There are six stone circles in this area. (*Mick Sharp*)

13 Pike o' Stickle, overlooking the Great Langdale valley in Cumbria. The greenstone was quarried from the crag at the top of the picture, and worked into rough-outs for axe-heads on the scree immediately below. (*Mick Sharp*)

14 Mayburgh henge, near Penrith, Cumbria, looking across the single entrance on the east side. Originally two pairs of portal stones stood in this entrance, just as at Stonehenge. The single standing stone on the left is the sole survivor of a setting of four stones at the centre of the enclosure. The surrounding bank, 65m across, is made of river cobbles. The River Eden itself is close by, to the right. Mayburgh, King Arthur's Round Table and the Little Round Table should be thought of as a triad of henges, not unlike Thornborough. Mayburgh, the largest of the three, was the centrepiece of a major ceremonial centre. (*Mick Sharp*)

15 The Devil's Arrows, Boroughbridge, North Yorkshire. The three gritstone monoliths form a line leading to a ford on the River Ure. The crossing-place has guided communications right up to the present day; heavy goods vehicles race past on the A1(M) while the Devil's Arrows perform their silent traffic duty. The foreground (northern) stone is 5.5 metres high; the other two are 6.5 and 7 metres. In antiquity there were other features here, including a fourth stone. (*Mick Sharp*)

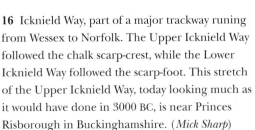

16 Icknield Way, part of a major trackway runing from Wessex to Norfolk. The Upper Icknield Way followed the chalk scarp-crest, while the Lower Icknield Way followed the scarp-foot. This stretch of the Upper Icknield Way, today looking much as it would have done in 3000 BC, is near Princes Risborough in Buckinghamshire. (*Mick Sharp*)

17 Wayland's Smithy long barrow. The magnificent façade consists of six sarsen monoliths, three on each side of the tomb entrance. The gaps were carefully filled with drystone masonry, a characteristic neolithic feature. The resulting façade is one of the finest pieces of megalithic architecture in Britain. Behind it, the 55m-long chalk mound tapers, and the quarry ditches converge, to make the monument appear even longer from the forecourt end. (*Mick Sharp*)

18 Stony valley, near Avebury, Wiltshire. The sarsen field in this and neighbouring valleys is the source of the Avebury megaliths, and probably the Stonehenge megaliths too. The large stone nearest the top of the picture appears to have been hauled some of the way towards Avebury, then abandoned. (*Mick Sharp*)

19 A polishing stone (or polissoir) on Overton Down, 3 kilometres east of Avebury. This stone has been grooved and polished by people polishing harder stones on it. It is in effect a neolithic workbench for producing finely finished stone axes. (*Mick Sharp*)

20 Silbury Hill, near Avebury, Wiltshire. This is the largest man-made mound in prehistoric Europe, but its purpose is still a mystery. Recent work suggests that the terrace visible near the top was part of a spiral road to the summit. As well as helping in the building process, this would have made ceremonial processions to the summit platform possible. (*Mick Sharp*)

21 Knap Hill, Wiltshire. The well-preserved earthworks of this causewayed enclosure show up impressively on the skyline, seen here from the Ridgeway to the north-west. Two of the five entrances can be seen. It was built in 3450 BC, though pottery was still being dropped on the site as late as 2200 BC. (*Mick Sharp*)

22 Stoney Littleton long cairn, near Bath. The beautiful arched doorway made of Blue Lias stands at the centre of an incurved forecourt. One of the jambs carries a large ammonite; its spiral shell was probably seen as a natural expression of passage grave art. The drystone walling of contrasting cream Jurassic limestone was restored by the nineteenth-century excavator the Revd John Skinner, who loved the tomb but despaired of his drunken parishioners, and later committed suicide. (*Mick Sharp*)

EARTH CIRCLES

Around 3000 BC people felt compelled to rethink their ancient round enclosures.[4] They went on making banks and ditches enclosing precincts about 120m across, but incorporated changes that must have carried heavy symbolic significance.

The old causewayed enclosures are only roughly circular, with the bank inside the ditch as if to keep something out, and with many pseudo-entrances across the ditch; some have two or three loops of ditches and banks, apparently reflecting attempts to make the enclosures bigger and more imposing; usually there are no traces of structures inside the enclosure. The new monuments, the henges, are more exactly circular in plan, with the bank outside the ditch as if to keep something in, and (usually) with just one or two entrances – Avebury is exceptional in having four. Often there were post circles, sometimes stone circles and other structures, within. The monument builders were making a bid for greater formality and grandeur; some of the new enclosures were very imposing. But we cannot be certain that the two types of enclosure were used in similar ways.

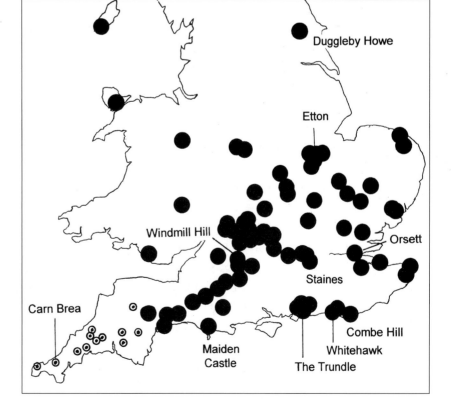

Causewayed enclosures in Britain (filled black circles). The small dots within circles are fortified tor enclosures. Nearly all the causewayed enclosures were created in south-east England, which is consistent with the importation of the idea from mainland Europe (after Oswald and Barber 2001).

The European origins of causewayed enclosures

The idea of enclosing a special area for communal use with an interrupted ditch (i.e. a ditch with gaps in it) came from the European mainland. The ancient Britons borrowed it and changed it to reflect their own society, their own customs. By the end of the Linear Pottery culture all the characteristics of neolithic causewayed enclosures were in place in the agricultural landscape, together with all the variations from place to place that archaeologists have found so hard to explain in Britain. Some enclosures had interrupted ditches (= true causewayed enclosures) and some had

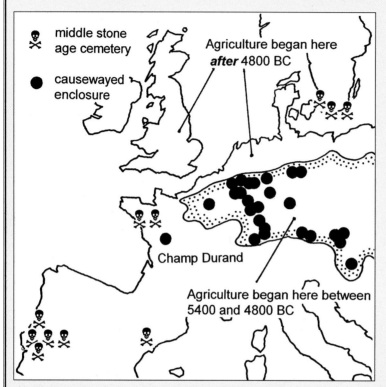

The European origins of two British neolithic monuments, causewayed enclosures and formal 'monumental' burials. The area of early agriculture also marks the extent of Linear Pottery settlement (after Clark 1977, Ammerman and Cavalli-Sforza 1984, Luning 1988, Bradley 1992 and other sources).

uninterrupted ditches (= proto-henges); some had settlements inside them, some not; some are one hectare in area, some several hectares.

By the end of the Linear Pottery culture, the plan of the causewayed enclosure was more or less standardized, with one, two or three circuits of ditch and bank – only a few had palisades as well – and the enclosures were to be found scattered across a large area from central France right across southern Germany and into Poland. There are conspicuous gaps – none have been found in the Netherlands – but more are being discovered all the time. Nearly all of them were created in the area where agriculture began between 5400 and 4800 BC.

In Europe the enclosures were gradually transformed into series of earthworks with an emphasis on the entrances, which were sometimes aligned on cardinal compass points, sometimes on significant astronomical events.

Here we have some points in common with earth circles in Britain. Avebury's four entrances are to north, south, east and west. Stonehenge's main ceremonial entrance is towards the midsummer sunrise. On the whole the larger enclosures seem to have been, or doubled as, settlements, while the smaller enclosures were reserved for ritual, more like the henges of the late neolithic in Britain.

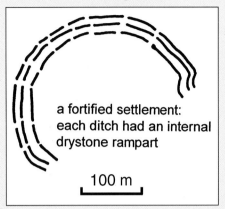

a fortified settlement: each ditch had an internal drystone rampart

100 m

Champ Durand, a causewayed enclosure on the European mainland.

Champ Durand was the westernmost enclosure, bordering a coastal marsh west of Poitiers. In its opening phase it had a ceremonial and funerary use. Skeletons have been found in its ditches. In a second phase it was remodelled and elaborated into a kind of citadel with three concentric stone walls rising above substantial ditches, not unlike dark age Cadbury. The entrances had substantial wooden gates and one entrance at least had a drystone tower guarding it. Champ Durand seems to have housed a large number of people and appears to be an early precursor of the hill-forts of the iron age.

In the 1970s the causewayed enclosures were regarded as foci, and archaeologists borrowed a term from geographers to describe them – central places. They were territorial centres where a particular tribal group congregated from time to time. Treating them as centres meant that territorial boundaries might be inferred from their location; another geographical technique, Thiessen polygons, could be applied to find the likeliest course of the frontiers – halfway between each centre and the next. In this way prehistorians mapped entire socio-political landscapes, but it was obvious even at the time that in some areas the technique did not work.[5] One problem with spatial analysis is that we do not have the complete distribution pattern. In 1950 thirteen causewayed enclosures were known; by 2000 there were seventy, and the number seems set to rise.

Recent environmental studies show that Windmill Hill, Maiden Castle, Knap Hill and some of the Sussex enclosures were surrounded by woodland. That means they must have been laid out on marginal land, away from the land cleared for agriculture, away from the settlements. The enclosures were sacred places deliberately positioned on the wilderness edge, liminal places where the forces of the natural world might be tapped. This is not unlike the pattern in iron age Gaul, where major religious sanctuaries were deliberately located on the tribal boundaries, places that were physically and spiritually dangerous.[6] Windmill Hill and Rybury lay on the edges of

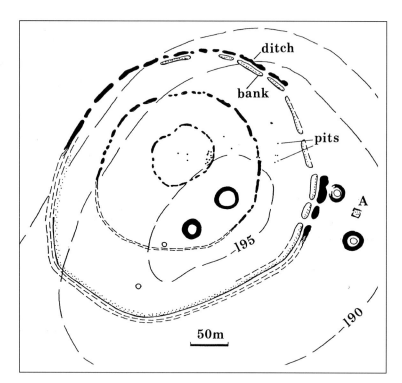

Windmill Hill causewayed enclosure, centred 100m away from the hilltop, showing that it was intended to be seen from the low ground to the north-west, and not from Avebury, which lies to the east (after Piggott 1954). A is a neolithic cult-house.

concentrations of long barrows, which reinforces the idea that the earth circles marked the end of the made world and the beginning of the wilderness.[7] In Sussex it may be that the earth circles were created one by one, starting in the west and ending in the east as the neolithic revolution crept eastwards through the South Downs, in which case Combe Hill, the easternmost enclosure, must have been the last to be built. The western ditches at Combe Hill contain objects redolent of the tamed, domestic landscape that lay, fully visible from this vantage point, to the west. The eastern ditches contain objects that suggest the limits of forest clearance, the wilderness that lay in the Wealden vale to the east.[8] The enclosures were begun as single or double circuits of ditches, then some of them were fitted with extra rings outside – a third or a fourth – probably as a mark of status. In Sussex, The Trundle and Whitehawk became pre-eminent in this way, developing into virtual fortresses.

Hambledon Hill carries an unusual trio of enclosures.[9] The main central enclosure was used as a cemetery. On the ditch floor human remains were carefully placed at intervals: rotting heads and partially disintegrated bodies. The bones of the lower torso (backbone, pelvis and thigh-bone) were in several places found together, presumably because they were still held together by strong muscle attachments. This enclosure was used for sky-burial, the exposure of human bodies immediately after death, to be picked clean by carrion. Once most of the flesh had gone, the body parts could be picked up, carried around and used in rituals. People seem to have had no problem with handling rotting human bodies. As the excavator, Roger Mercer, says, Hambledon Hill was a vast, reeking cemetery.

Two Sussex causewayed enclosures. A = Combe Hill, near Eastbourne. B = Whitehawk in Brighton, a high-status multi-ring enclosure with a gated ceremonial entrance to the north-west. b = bank, d = ditch.

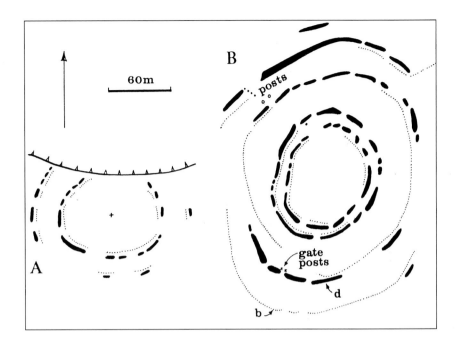

The Abingdon enclosure too may have been a cemetery for sky-burial. Only 100 metres to the east of the enclosure's centre a long barrow was built and the two were evidently in use, side by side, at the same time.[10]

The causewayed enclosures varied a lot, even to the extent of some being up on hilltops, like Windmill Hill, Crickley Hill, Bury Hill and Offham, and others down on low ground. One – Etton near Maxey – was built right down on a low terrace, though this was only in use for a decade, perhaps because it was waterlogged much of the time.[11] Its water-born magic was channelled up on to the low island of Maxey by the cursus and eventually, when the cursus was 'finished', down to wetlands again beside the River Welland.

It is interesting that high-altitude enclosures tend to have widely spaced ditches, while low-altitude enclosures have closely spaced ditches. Some enclosures were low status, marked by a single bounding ditch and bank; others were raised in status by having a second or third circuit added. It is even possible to distinguish four regional groups, which may reflect distinct culture areas: Sussex, Wessex, the Thames valley, and the Midlands and East Anglia.[12] Some were deliberately paired (Rybury and Knap Hill, and the two at Fornham All Saints), which may mean that for some reason an old enclosure had to be replaced.[13]

This practice of pairing or replacing may have been more widespread than we have thought; the well-known stone circle known as Long Meg and Her Daughters was built alongside, and actually touching, an older but until recently unnoticed large earthen enclosure, which the stone circle evidently replaced.[14] The stone ring is a flattened circle, with the flattened side built up against the earth enclosure; in other words, we can now see that there is a simple practical explanation for the flattening of the Long

Meg circle; the elaborate pseudo-mathematical explanations offered in the 1960s turn out to be redundant.[15]

By 3000 BC no new causewayed enclosures were being built, and the existing enclosures were falling out of use. Briar Hill at Northampton was not maintained after 3200 BC, though it was still visited; the old enclosures at Abingdon and Maiden Castle were both abandoned in 3200, after being in use for seven hundred years.[16]

People shifted their attention to a new type of enclosure – the henge. It was in 3100 BC that the earliest henges were created, the enclosures at Barford and Llandegai.[17] At Maxey the rather sketchy cursus that connected the old Etton enclosure with the River Welland was itself decisively replaced by a big henge built right across it.

Avebury is unusual in being a very early, very large henge, and the first by a long way of the Wessex 'superhenges': the other superhenges – Marden, Mount Pleasant and Durrington Walls – seem to be Avebury imitations made several hundred years later. Avebury is a colossus. It may be that its extraordinary size – 427 metres in diameter, with a circumference of more than a kilometre and an area of 11.5 hectares – was dictated by the fact that structures already existed on the site and the henge had to encompass them. Aubrey Burl has made a convincing case for an initial design consisting of the two smaller stone circles, the North and South Circles, and a beginning made on a third circle on the site of the North Entrance. In other words the Avebury people were working on an initial design that was more like the Thornborough Circles or Priddy Circles, arranged in lines of three or four, but then changed their minds and made the third encompass the first and second. The surrounding henge bank was built in at least two phases. The visible bank, now 5.5m high, completely smothers a smaller bank half that height. The old ground surface beneath the initial bank is dated to 3000 BC. The North and South Circles may therefore date to 3050 BC. Avebury was a big undertaking, on the same scale as the

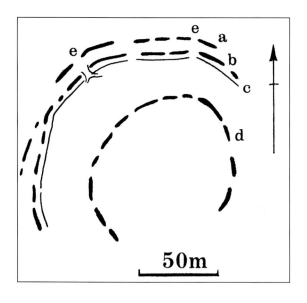

50m

Orsett, a causewayed enclosure in Essex. a = outer ditch; b = middle ditch; c = palisade; d = inner ditch; e = entrance, one with an unusually elaborate timber gateway.

Step Pyramid of Zoser at Saqqara in Egypt, which was built but a short time afterwards.

Just 1,200 metres to the south, in dry open grassland out of sight of the great henge, behind the western flank of Waden Hill, another monument of a very different sort was begun one August some years later. What it had in common with Avebury was its circularity and the fact that it was built in stages, substantial enough even at the start, then later much larger still. It consisted of a 20m diameter circle marked out by a wattle fence surrounding a turf-covered mound of clay and gravel, built over a star-shaped arrangement of grass string. The low turf mound was raised, layer by layer, until it spilt out beyond the wattle fence. The final primary mound was 35m across and 5m high, its creation a series of ritual acts whose meaning is entirely lost to us. It may have been a chief's burial mound – perhaps the chief who organized and coordinated the building of the equally ambitious henge a short walk away, the legendary King Sil[18] – but no burial has yet been found. Alternatively it may have been a harvest hill, a thanksgiving altar to mark the first fruits of the Avebury landscape enriched and fertilized by the huge new henge. Other harvest hills have been tentatively identified elsewhere.[19]

This was Silbury as it stood in 3000 BC – a monstrous grounded flying saucer.[20] During the centuries that followed it would be enlarged to a diameter of 73 metres and a height of 15 metres, then enlarged again to a colossal 37 metres high (just high enough for its summit to be visible from Avebury) and containing 250,000 cubic metres of chalk blocks. Like the henge with its gigantic stone circle, Silbury was a phenomenally ambitious project. Why it was built where it was, in an inconspicuous hollow that would not show the monument to best effect, has never been explained. It may have something to do with commemorating a settlement site; Windmill Hill, the causewayed enclosure, Avebury, the henge, and

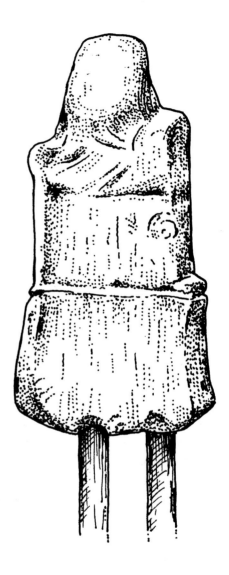

Chalk idol from Maiden Castle, Dorset. The two sockets in the base have been used to reconstruct the stick legs. The front of the head was broken off. Religious ritual was part of the function of the causewayed enclosures (after Piggott 1954).

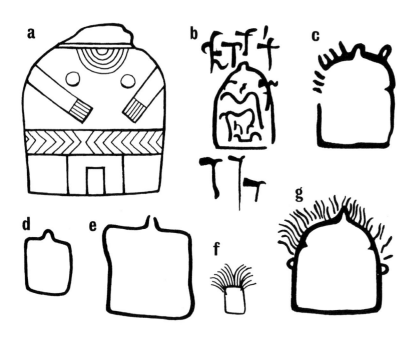

Goddess carvings in Brittany. The cult of the goddess lasted over a thousand years from these early neolithic Breton carvings until the late neolithic box symbols at Stonehenge.
a = Mas d'Asais statue-menhir;
b = Mane-er-Hoek, Locmariaquer;
c = Manio, Carnac;
d = Mane Lud, Locmariaquer;
e and f = Ile Longue, Morbihan;
g = Barnenez, Finistere.

Silbury Hill were all created on or near early neolithic settlement sites,[21] and Avebury had its origins in a woodland hunting camp that existed way back in the middle stone age. The neolithic foci at Windmill Hill, Avebury and Silbury were a slowly evolving glorification of an early woodland hunting camp – all this was made in memory of our hunting fathers.[22] The attractive suggestion that Silbury's location may have something to do with water magic or fertility, as the River Kennet runs past and a spring is close by, seems less likely now that we know that in neolithic times the valley floor here was dry, with neither flooding nor alluviation.[23]

Stonehenge is a curious hybrid, using some of the features of a causewayed enclosure (with its ditch, made of about a hundred adjacent oval pits, and its internal bank) and some features typical of a henge (two, possibly three, entrances only, though not opposite each other, and a circular plan). It was not absolutely unique, though; there were a few other hybrid monuments around, such as the Flagstones enclosure at Dorchester, but the design seems to have been a short-lived experiment.

The layout of the larger monument-complexes was not thought out from the start, but must be seen as an accretion of separate structures, some representing changes of plan. They also varied enormously in scale. The big monuments naturally attract attention, but henges range in overall size from 518m (Marden), its diameter equivalent to three St Paul's Cathedrals, down to 8m (High Knowes in Northumberland), less than a London bus. Although archaeologists have tended to regard earth circles as focal places, they were not foci for settlement and often lay some distance away from habitations. Large-scale feasting went on at certain enclosures,[24] which were visited perhaps only occasionally for ceremonies; people also

Henges (after Wainwright *et al.* 1971 and other sources).

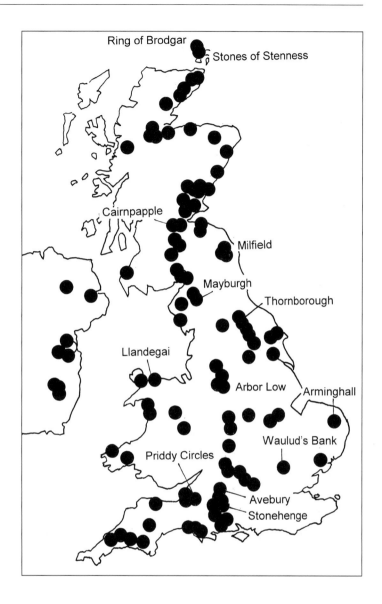

converged on them periodically to repair them. From time to time the ditches needed cleaning out or recutting. In some ways it may be useful to think of the enclosures as occupying much the same relationship with the human community as the hill figures of later prehistory.[25]

STONE CIRCLES

People had been making earth circles for a thousand years before the first stone circles were built. The invention of stone circles in 3000 BC came at a time of astonishing and widespread inventiveness. There was just a century to go before Imhotep designed the first pyramid at Saqqara. In the Middle East people were taming camels for use as beasts of burden and devising three-year crop rotations; they

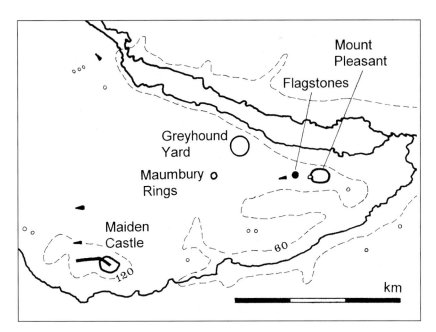

The Dorchester ceremonial complex. The late neolithic Mount Pleasant 'superhenge' replaced the causewayed enclosure at Maiden Castle, though the older enclosure would return to pre-eminence in the iron age.

were about to invent the sickle. The Sumerians invented the helmet, used their new cuneiform script to write down the Gilgamesh epic and devised a numbering system (based on sixty) that is still used today for measuring angles and time. The concepts of yin and yang came into being in China. Clay tokens were made at Susa. Concrete was used in Uruk. In Egypt the first irrigation channels were dug, the first papyrus was manufactured and the first tallow candles were made. In the Indus valley the first cotton fabric was made. The first wheeled wooden carts creaked and wobbled across the new farmlands of Europe.

Just as the Egyptian pyramids developed out of an older monument, the mastaba, simply by stacking successively smaller mastabas on top of one another to make a more conspicuous stepped monument, so stone circles developed out of earth circles to make something taller, more conspicuous, more striking. They were invented in the west of Britain, where soil was thin and rock was hard, and digging out ditches was often daunting.[26]

The stone circles were foci for the axe trade, and it may be that the earliest stone circles were built in Cumbria, on the Langdale axe trade routes. Since many of the axes were transported by sea, it is not surprising that many early stone circles were built on the seaways of the west coast (or not far from them). The inland situation of Rollright looks like an exception, though its location on a scarp-crest with the Kingstone, a conspicuous waymark, close at hand – to help travellers on low ground to the north to find it – does imply that it was on a cross-country route of some kind.[27] The early circles are small, on average about 35m in diameter (Rollright is 33m), but the circles of the next phase are big. They also tend to be low-lying, down on valley floors or river terraces or on low passes; the Ring of Brodgar (104m), Long Meg and

Stanton Drew. Two stones of the Great Circle (centre and right) and an avenue stone (left).

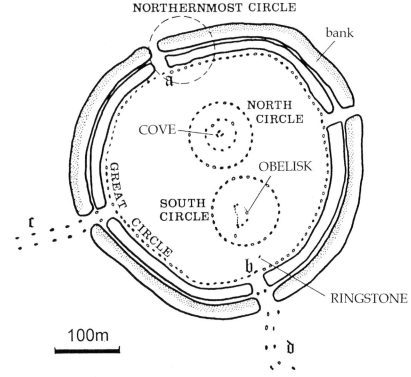

Avebury.
a = north entrance stones;
b = south entrance stones;
c = Beckhampton Avenue (almost
    totally destroyed);
d = West Kennet Avenue (partly
    restored).

Three roughly shaped circle stones at Avebury.

Her Daughters (109m), Stanton Drew (115m) and Avebury (331m) are all giants belonging to this second phase.

Whatever the initial reason for building them, stone circles were soon being built over in 'earth circle country', where some monuments combined earth and stone circles in their design. This is what happened at Stonehenge, where an earth circle made in 3000 BC had stones added centuries later, as a final flourish at the centre of a long-evolving ceremonial precinct. At Avebury the ditch, bank and Great Sarsen Circle were built in quick succession. One by one the big stones were dragged on sledges from the Marlborough Downs in through the east entrance of the huge earthwork, itself newly raised in ungrazed, abandoned pasture that had become thickly overgrown with scrub, and there erected by a combination of pushing with levers and pulling with hawsers until they stood upright in their sockets.[28] The process probably took a fortnight for each stone. There are several thick stake-holes near each stone, showing how each heavy half-raised megalith was left propped up overnight while the work team went home to eat, drink, relax and sleep before returning to the task the next day. When it was finished, it encompassed a precinct big enough to contain the cathedrals of Chichester, Ely, Wells, Canterbury, Winchester and St Paul's – with room to spare. Between its east and west gates the great Temple of Artemis at Ephesus would have fitted comfortably twice over, end to end.

The people living at Barnhouse far away on Orkney imported the idea of the stone circle at the same time as the humble craft of digging ditches. Both the Ring of Brodgar and the Stones of Stenness stand within henges marked by deep rock-cut ditches. Ditches are alien to the islands and were not attempted before the stone circles were built, so it looks as if the design idea for these monuments was imported intact from the south, a stone circle and henge package all in one go, around 3000 BC.[29]

Long Meg and Her Daughters. An attempt was made to explain the curious flattening of the stone circle by means of complex mathematics involving the two axes shown here (Thom 1967). The recently discovered earth enclosure right next to it explains it more simply. The earth enclosure entrance opens directly into the stone circle, which implies that they were in use at the same time.

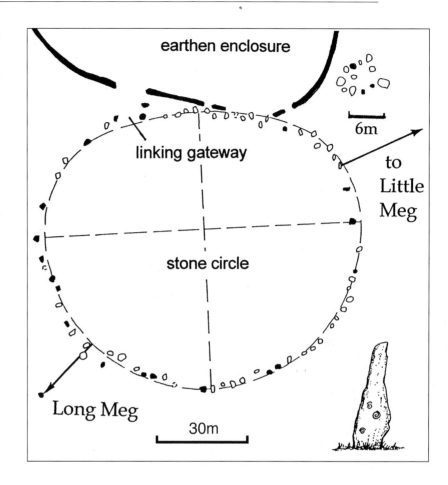

The elaborate Orcadian complex that includes Maes Howe, the Stones of Stenness and the Ring of Brodgar is really a sequence of mainly uncompleted projects. It was the same story at Avebury, Maxey and Dorchester-on-Thames. This appears to open the possibility that we could construct chronological sequences of thought, but a major problem is that where it exists the dating is too coarse; we are still trapped inside the radiocarbon wave. There are also disagreements about sequence. Some see Maes Howe as the culminating achievement of native Orcadian tomb builders, who started with the smaller tombs and worked their way towards the masterpiece. Others see it as an exotic, an importation from Ireland, and the first in a degrading series. Neither radiocarbon nor any other kind of dating has resolved this. Either way, Maes Howe was built in the centuries around 3000 BC. Its mound is 35m across and 8m high, standing on an artificially levelled platform 76m across on a knoll. The encircling bank looks fresh because it is relatively new; it was rebuilt in AD 950, when the tomb was reused probably for the burial of a Viking chief. The entrance passage, oriented to the midwinter sunset, consists of three enormous slabs 7m long, each weighing 3 tonnes. Smaller stones would have done the job, and a huge technical problem was created, apparently just for the pleasure of solving it; it was a display of technique, designed to impress, just like Manhattan skyscrapers. The beautifully crafted entrance passage opens into an unrivalled chamber. It is cavernous, 4.6m square and 4.6m high, with drystone walling corbelled to make a beehive roof. It is one of the defining monuments of the British neolithic – confident, aesthetically compelling and architecturally assured; it is also a wonder of the ancient world and a testament to the power of the old religion. More remarkable still is the thought that it may incorporate an earlier monument on the same site. The huge slabs that have been interpreted as buttresses securing the four corners of the tomb chamber may have been raised before the tomb was built, standing out in the open as a four-stone circle, rather like the free-standing stone setting that once stood at the centre of Mayburgh henge. Beyond that, between mound and ditch, stood another big stone, which may have been part of a surrounding stone circle, demolished at the time when the tomb mound was raised. The complexity of thought and utterance is astonishing.

TIMBER CIRCLES

The later timber circles have been well publicized, but the most famous examples, at Durrington Walls, Woodhenge and The Sanctuary, were built well after 3000 BC. The earliest timber enclosures built around 3000 BC are little known. They represent another of the innovations of this extraordinary moment in prehistory.

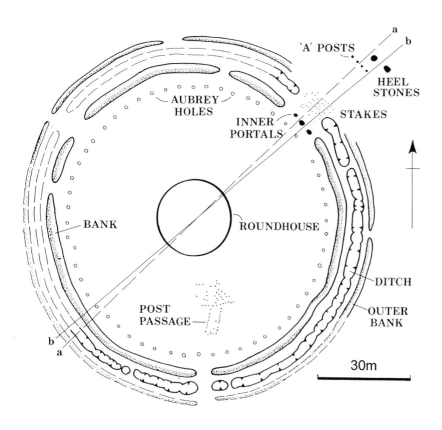

Stonehenge in 3000 BC. The initial lunar axis (a) passed through the centre of the entrance causeway according to Burl (1987); the later solar axis (b) passed between the Heel Stones. It is thought that the Aubrey Holes held small stones or low posts. The only other stones on site at this stage were there to mark the ceremonial north-east entrance.

Three British longhouses? Balbridie was certainly a timber hall. Structures 1 and 2 at Balfarg were probably also roofed longhouses.

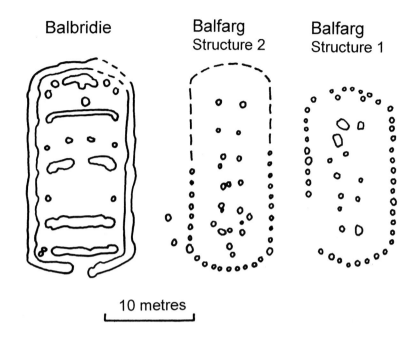

Balbridie

Balfarg Structure 2

Balfarg Structure 1

10 metres

The widely spaced posts that stood in the Aubrey Holes at Stonehenge seem to have been part of the 3000 BC design. The enclosures made of posts set more closely together were built a little later, maybe in 2900–2700 BC, and the enormous Hindwell palisade enclosure was one of these; its perimeter was marked out by 4-tonne timbers 6m high and it enclosed a huge oval space of 34 hectares.[30] Presumably the Hindwell enclosure functioned in the same ways as the earlier earthen enclosures; it was bigger and could have embraced all the functions of a causewayed enclosure.

Many questions remain unanswered about the smaller post-circles, especially those with several concentric circles. Were they mazes of free-standing totem poles, lintelled rings or roofed buildings? At Balfarg there were two large timber structures consisting of four parallel rows of posts, with a curving post row connecting the outermost rows at one end. Some say the two inner rows of posts are too close to the long axis to be well placed to support the weight of rafters.[31] On the other hand, they may mark the upper ends of the rafters; the 'ridge' of the roof could have been left open as a long, narrow skylight or smoke vent. The bowed ends and the close similarity in scale suggest to me that the Balfarg structures were in fact longhouses similar in size to the Balbridie longhouse. Those who want Balfarg to be a ritual structure point to the lack of positive evidence for roof materials, but the same could be said for all the domestic buildings of the period. 'Most archaeologists agree that all buildings in Britain from the Neolithic until the medieval period were thatched',[32] even though there is no direct evidence for neolithic thatch. Does this mean that houses were not thatched, but unroofed? They must have been thatched, and a similar position could be adopted for timber circles. So long as the spans separating one post ring from the

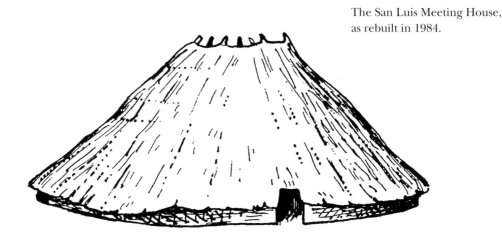

The San Luis Meeting House,
as rebuilt in 1984.

next in the concentric sequence are not too great, there is no reason why the buildings should not be very large. This applies even to very large multiple post circles like the recently discovered one at Stanton Drew.

There are close modern parallels in North America; we know that North American Indians built ambitious rotundas. The San Luis Meeting House in northern Florida was built in the eighteenth century by Appalachi Indians. By the twentieth century only a set of eight concentric rings of post-holes remained, but fortunately it was drawn when complete, so its original appearance is known. In 1984 it was reconstructed and it now stands as it originally looked – a huge and splendid roundhouse, 37m in diameter with a steep conical roof and a skylight 12m in diameter. At the centre was a huge hearth.[33] British neolithic timber circles could also have been huge rotundas like this – even to the big central skylights or smoke-holes.

Some little pottery vessels made as grave goods several centuries later seem to be models of roundhouses. The incense cup from Normanton Down, just a kilometre from Stonehenge, shows a round building with a wall perforated by many windows or doors, a steeply sloping conical roof covered with thatch and a big central skylight.[34] At the centre of Stonehenge there was a timber structure of some kind and, although Rosamund Cleal is sceptical that it amounted to a post circle,[35] there are traces amid the maze of post-holes of a large round structure with at least six concentric rings, even if they were not exactly circular.

If the timber circles were buildings, were they also temples? It is usually assumed so, but some of them could equally have been large communal dwellings. The nuclear or even extended family may not have been the dwelling unit in every region.

The horseshoe settings may be regarded as near-circles and, although they could have been roofed, it seems less likely. The massive setting of eight oak timbers at Arminghall in Norfolk may have been left as an arc of unconnected totem poles, perhaps carved and painted in Native North American style, or they may have been linked together by cross beams in much the same way as the sarsen trilithons at Stonehenge. Another

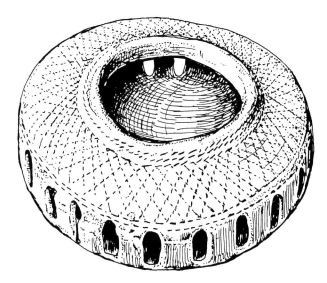

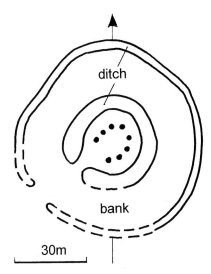

Incense cup from Normanton Down near Stonehenge. A model of a roundhouse? (The original is in Devizes Museum.)

Arminghall. This henge unusually has a ditch outside as well as inside its bank. At the centre was a horseshoe setting of eight massive oak posts, apparently anticipating the much later horseshoe of trilithons at Stonehenge. Arminghall faced the midwinter sunset.

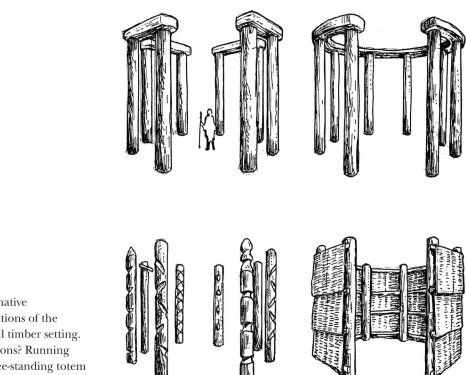

Four alternative reconstructions of the Arminghall timber setting. Four trixylons? Running lintels? Free-standing totem poles? A screened enclosure?

possibility is that they were joined by lighter horizontal planks or by wattles coated with wattle-and-daub to make a wooden tower like a theatrical cyclorama.

All these timber structures are long gone. They are not part of *our* memory of the neolithic, but they were a key element in neolithic community life and must have carried huge symbolic weight in people's minds in the third millennium BC. The roundhouse represented 'home' in the fullest sense, and the sarsen-bluestone structure raised at Stonehenge centuries later would be built in the form of a ruined roundhouse – the long-abandoned but never forgotten image of home.

ASTRONOMY

In modern times people have speculated endlessly about the purpose of the earth, stone and timber circles. Sir Norman Lockyer was among the first, a century ago, to promote the attractive idea that they are temples incorporating astronomical alignments and therefore dedicated to the worship of deities of sun, moon and stars.[36] Some astronomical alignments are very obvious, and the most famous is the one that was identified first – by William Stukeley in the eighteenth century.[37] The main axis of Stonehenge, passing just to the north of the Heel Stone, was deliberately lined up with the place where the sun appeared on the horizon at the summer solstice. The first gleam of the midsummer sunrise is now just in line with the surviving Heel Stone, but in 3000 BC that first gleam would have appeared almost two solar discs to the north. The sun would have floated free of the horizon on a line passing between the two stones marking the midsummer portal, and the full disc would have been perfectly framed by the stones and the horizon. The alignment between the Heel Stones was created to celebrate and salute the full disc of the untrammelled sun just as it floated free of the earth on midsummer morning in 3000 BC.

The entrance passages of Maes Howe and two of the Clava cairns were in a parallel way exactly aligned on the midwinter sunset,[38] and that of Newgrange on the midwinter sunrise; the entrance passage of the initial monument at Howe on Orkney, a stalled cairn, was also aligned on the midwinter sunrise.[39] The rays of sunlight entering the monuments at these pivotal moments in the calendar were probably meant to trigger the next movement in the seasonal cycle, to keep the cycle going and by implication keep the larger cycles of birth, death and regeneration under way. The monuments came to be seen as the engines of terrestrial life, engines that could intercept and harness cosmic forces, and therefore objects of intense mystery and power.

Visitors to Stonehenge in 3000 BC would have seen the two sarsen pillars making a ceremonial doorway for the midsummer sun just outside the earth circle and immediately outside the north-east entrance causeway. Virtually blocking this causeway was a maze of stakes. Each year a new post was added to mark the northernmost position of the moonrise. The sunrise cycle had been easy to unravel; the sun rose in the south-east at midwinter and in the north-east at midsummer, moving gradually and smoothly between these two positions in a cycle that repeated without fail every year. But the moonrise was more mobile and it was only after 18.6 years that the same extreme position was reached. To be sure that this was indeed cyclic and not random, the observers watched several cycles, ending up with an array of posts representing 112 years' worth of observations. The Stonehenge people raised four or maybe five heavy posts summarizing the results of the work with the stakes, which were then pulled out.[40]

Some prehistorians believe the long barrows and other tombs raised before 3000 BC were oriented on the moon. Maybe it was soil depletion and the reduction in food supply that shook people's faith in the power of the moon deity, and it was that which made them abandon the old monuments – the long barrows and causewayed enclosures – in favour of new ones dedicated to whatever deity powered the sun. The sun would have been seen as safeguarding the harvest, the chief governor of the seasons, the protector of the cycles of livestock grazing. At Stonehenge, some claim, there is evidence of an early orientation on the moon and a later orientation on the sun. Perhaps many of the other changes that occurred were also due to this religious crisis – a profound ideological shift.

The lunar and solar orientations at Stonehenge have become world-famous. There are many other contemporary monuments that are rarely heard of, but which have similar alignments built into them. The huge box-shaped enclosure at Godmanchester had six post alignments marking solstice and equinox rising and setting positions of sun and moon. Lunar and solar alignments were firmly embedded in the culture of these islands by 3000 BC.[41]

Throughout the twentieth century prehistorians wrestled with the paradox of barbarians indulging in the scholarly pursuit of astronomy. Gordon Childe admitted to being incredulous in 1930: 'It is fantastic to imagine that the ill-clad inhabitants of these boreal isles should shiver night long in rain and gale, peering through the driving mists to note eclipses and planetary movements.'[42] The paradox remains until you substitute ideology for astronomy, the pursuit of union with the universe for science, intense religious fervour for scholarship. *Then* the nature of the endeavour blends with the archaic culture.

It was not easy to use the megaliths to fix the calendar at the solstices. Fixing specific dates would have been relatively straightforward at the equinoxes, when sunrise and sunset positions move appreciably along the horizon from one day to the next. But at the solstices the sun almost stands still for several days. The fact that many monuments are oriented on the solstice sunrise and sunset positions implies that fixing the calendar was *not* the main motive – rather it was a salutation to the sun at a highly symbolic time of year, a magical and momentous time when the gods relented, when the heavens had a change of heart.

Sometimes the orientation of a monument is more obscure. The (later) recumbent stone circles in Grampian have their altars to the south-south-west. Is this an orientation on a star-rise, as some have thought, or a salutation to the sun where it shines at its most forceful? Stonehenge is oriented to the north-east, the direction of midsummer sunrise, but also, as Aubrey Burl emphasizes, that of the most northerly moonrise. Which? Or which was the more important? It is salutary to remember that when the Globe Theatre was built in 1599 its stage was oriented to the north-east, not to catch the midsummer sunrise but to ensure that the stage remained *out* of direct sunlight, even on a bright summer afternoon.[43]

Sometimes astronomical orientations are used as an argument for regarding a structure as ceremonial, but Colin Richards has recently discovered that they may have been routinely incorporated into domestic buildings too. He noticed that the square hearths at Barnhouse were oddly skewed in relation to the house plans, and all were aligned on midwinter or midsummer sunrise or sunset positions.[44] This observation shows that religion and everyday life were not regarded as separate, and suggests to me a sequence of possible associations and beliefs: that fire and sun were connected,

The Stones of Stenness henge and stone circle, Orkney (Mick Sharp).

The Stones of Stenness, with the bank of the henge visible in the foreground (Mick Sharp).

that the household fire was regarded as a miniature sun, that the house was a microcosm of the larger world outside, and so on.[45] That the domestic hearths at Barnhouse had a symbolic dimension is borne out by the presence of a giant ceremonial stone hearth at the centre of the nearby and exactly contemporary stone circle, the Stones of Stenness. This was, by the way, one of the very first stone circles to be built, and it is perhaps significant that it was fitted with a solar fire-place as if to imitate the sun by sympathetic magic.

The monument builders of 3000 BC were indeed astronomers – to the extent that they observed and respected seasonal changes in the movements of the sun and moon, and built alignments to some of these into their monuments – but the level of their astronomy has been greatly exaggerated by some writers. In the same way, short-distance intervisible alignments were certainly created in the sacred landscapes, but the idea of long-distance alignments, sometimes called ley lines, finds little support among archaeologists. Neolithic people could have made long straight lines across the landscape if they had wished – the technology is not difficult – but on the whole they did not exploit opportunities to do so when they arose; the West Kennet and Beckhampton Avenues are good examples of the non-straight lines the neolithic builders preferred. Some of the cursus ditches were dug straight, but usually for short distances only and when the two ends are intervisible.

MONUMENTAL MAPS

Perhaps we spend too much time looking at the sky, searching for links between monumental architecture and the movements of sun, moon and stars, and not enough time looking at the ground.

Professor Tim Darvill has proposed that Stonehenge symbolically represents the surrounding landscape, the area in which the Stonehenge people lived.[46] His map places Stonehenge at the centre of a circular space about 10km across. The radius of the circle was determined by projecting the main axis of Stonehenge to the north-east until it encountered a substantial boundary, in this case the River Avon. A circle with this 5.2km radius can be imagined to have entrance gaps to the north-east and south. Perhaps by chance the River Avon enters the circle through the north-east entrance gap and leaves by the south entrance gap, while Stonehenge itself, a much smaller circle, also has entrance gaps to the north-east and south. Darvill himself admits this could be coincidental, but comments that when standing at the centre of Stonehenge he has a sense of being at the centre of a circular landscape surrounded by a horizon of low hills, as well as being in a circular monument edged by a bank. In other words, the monument is visibly a microcosm of the macrocosmic landscape outside the bank.

There is evidence in the landscape itself that the neolithic people looked out from Stonehenge into the surrounding landscape and saw some significance in their relationship with that landscape. How far they could see continuously in each direction was significant to them. The continuously visible landscape extends differing

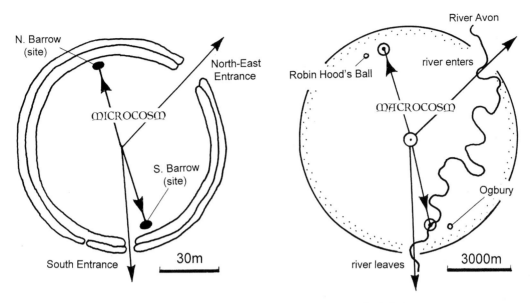

Stonehenge (left) as a map of the landscape outside (right) (after Darvill 1997a).

distances in each direction, reaching a maximum of 1.7 kilometres to the north-east, which is where the Stonehenge people were looking when they observed the northernmost sunrises and moonrises. The maximum distance of the near horizon in that direction is marked by the long barrow at the eastern end of the Greater Cursus. The second longest distance to the local horizon is to the north-west, to a point marked by a round barrow 200 metres from the western end of the Greater Cursus, which runs right along the near horizon to the north. Like a piece of writing decisively ruled off with the stroke of a pen, the continuously visible world in the south was separated by the Stonehenge people from the largely invisible world that lay to the north. The funereal associations of cursus monuments, here and elsewhere, tie in well with this idea and it may be, as several scholars have suggested, that this northern realm, the cursus and beyond, was symbolically associated with death.

Both Aubrey Burl and I sensed that the people who built and used Stonehenge operated within an area extending not more than about 5 kilometres from Stonehenge.[47] Others, working independently on the neolithic settlements of the Tavoliere in southern Italy, came to the same conclusion: that people worked and exploited a roughly circular territory extending not more than 5 kilometres or one hour from their settlements.[48] Burl designed his maps of the Stonehenge 'territory' to show the monuments they built within a circle with a 3 mile (5km) radius; I designed mine to show a square 10km by 10km. Darvill may in fact have noticed the significant relationship between the River Avon and the '5km' circle while studying Aubrey Burl's maps: Burl's book is listed in his references.

The crucial question remains: is the relationship a coincidence, or did the builders of Stonehenge I intend their monument to be in some sense a model of their sacred landscape? Corroboration of some kind is needed. Other features of the Stonehenge I design included the ring of Aubrey Holes, which may originally have held posts. Clearly there are too many of them – fifty-six – to represent significant landscape features beyond the bank, although the North and South Barrows are sufficiently oddly sited to be candidates for landscape feature indicators. The match is not perfect, but the North Barrow indicates the distance, to scale, and the direction, less accurately, of Robin Hood's Ball, the old neolithic causewayed enclosure close to the far horizon to the north-north-west. In the opposite direction, and the same distance away, is Ogbury; again the direction is not quite true.

So there is some corroboration but really, for this idea to have validity, it seems to me that it must be applicable to at least some other monuments of the same period. Contemporary monuments of comparable size and importance existed at Knowlton and, more significantly, because of the use of sarsen stones, at Avebury.

The largest of the Knowlton Circles in Dorset has two entrance gaps, to the north and west. Using Darvill's technique of driving a line from the centre of the circle out through the western entrance until it comes to a significant landscape boundary, we find one relatively quickly, exactly 1 kilometre to the west – the River Allen at the point where it receives the Gussage stream (flowing from close to the western end of the Dorset Cursus) as a tributary. A circle drawn on the outer landscape with this 1,000m radius defines a hypothetical territory. The north entrance gap projected the same distance on to the outer landscape falls close to the point where the River Allen flows into it. In other words, we have a very similar situation to the one that Darvill noticed at Stonehenge: the entrance gaps seem to acknowledge the entrance and exit points for the passage of the sacred stream. The north-western arc of the boundary runs along the western valley side, while the south-eastern arc follows the ridge crest of Knowle Hill, the well-defined local horizon to east, south-east and south. The South Circle at Knowlton can therefore, to this extent, be seen as a 1:8.3 scale model of the landscape around it. It is tempting to wonder whether features outside the South Circle but fairly close to it may also have been intended to represent the locations of more distant features. When a line is drawn to the Great Barrow and the distance between the centre of the South Circle and the Great Barrow is multiplied by 8.3, the point indicated is where the line crosses the River Allen; I am not certain whether that would have been seen as significant in the neolithic.

The Central Circle at Knowlton is like the South Circle in possessing two entrances, though oriented differently. Are they too intended to indicate the relationship between the outer landscape and the passage of the stream? A line projected out through the south-west entrance crosses the River Allen after 1.3 kilometres. A line projected out through the north-east entrance actually follows the river from 1,000 to 1,300 metres; after that the course of the stream veers sharply away to the north. The microcosm of the Central Circle can therefore be seen as another map of the Allen valley, with the entrance gaps marking the ingress and egress of the stream, and the north-western and south-eastern arcs once again indicating the valley sides. The main difference is in scale. The Central Circle is smaller than the South Circle, yet indicates a rather larger area; the Central Circle is drawn at 1:24 scale compared with the 1:8.3 scale of the South Circle.

As in so many other ways, the only worthy analogue for Stonehenge is Avebury. The great embanked and ditched enclosure at Avebury is nearly circular in shape, with an average radius of 175 metres; it also lies in a broad valley floor with low hills marking the horizon all round. Given the position of the local horizon, it is reasonable to suppose that the hypothetical outer neolithic landscape had a radius about ten times larger than this, 1,750 metres. If a circle with this radius is drawn on the Avebury map, its eastern arc closely follows the long smooth skyline of the Ridgeway, while its north-western arc brushes the flank of Windmill Hill and its southern passes close to Silbury Hill. These coincidences with major features of the local horizon suggest that the radius I have selected is close to the one the neolithic Avebury people might also have chosen as the measure of their macrocosm. It may be significant that the three surviving long barrows in the outer landscape all lie on or close to its boundary.

Whereas Stonehenge I had one axis, Avebury had two, with its four entrances oriented north-north-west, east-north-east, south-south-east and west-south-west. At Stonehenge Tim Darvill found that both the north-east and south entrances to the monument indicated significant 'gates' in the wider landscape. Do we find that Avebury's entrances similarly indicate gates in the wider landscape? The River Kennet enters the landscape just 200 metres away from the point where the north-north-west Avebury axis intersects the circumference of the circle, and leaves it just 200 metres from the equivalent intersection in the south-south-east. The south-south-east axis is followed informally but fairly closely by the West Kennet Avenue, which turns markedly to the east as it leaves the outer landscape to ascend the slope to The Sanctuary. The exact point where the south-south-east axis crosses the River Kennet is marked by one of the two newly discovered palisade enclosures, which was actually built astride the stream as if to emphasize that this was a key node in the ceremonial landscape.

The east-north-east axis, which leaves Avebury by its 'east' entrance, is followed very closely by a farm track, the ancient Herepath. Judging from sample geophysical surveys, this was never marked by paired stones or posts, but it is very likely that the entrance attracted a path approaching from this direction right from the time the entrance was created. The track leaves the outer landscape exactly on the east-north-east axis and shortly afterwards joins the Ridgeway.

The west-south-west axis, leaving Avebury by its 'west' entrance, was followed by the destroyed Beckhampton Avenue, a stone-lined ceremonial way similar to the West Kennet Avenue. Only one stone survives, but resistivity surveys have picked up several pairs of stone holes, allowing us to establish the avenue's route. It appears to have terminated at a long barrow, just 1,750 metres from the centre of Avebury and within 200 metres of the intersection of the west-south-west axis and the circumference.

The layout of the wider landscape at Avebury strongly suggests that the builders of Avebury and the surrounding monuments consciously wished to relate the

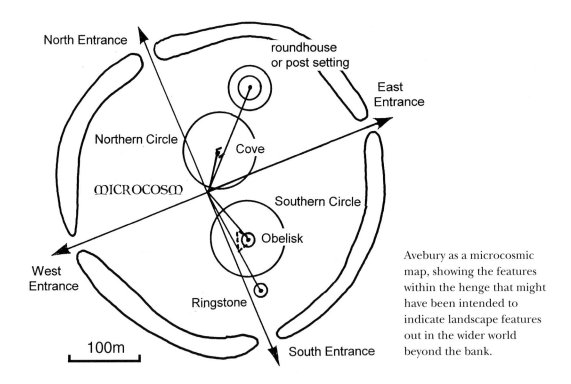

Avebury as a microcosmic map, showing the features within the henge that might have been intended to indicate landscape features out in the wider world beyond the bank.

microcosmic landscape of the monument itself with the macrocosmic landscape beyond the bank. Made and unmade features were interwoven to make the one a scale model of the other.

Further corroboration comes from within Avebury. The South Circle was built round a D-shaped setting of stones that represented the forecourt of a chamber tomb; the focal point of the D-shaped setting was a huge monolith known as the Obelisk. This great stone idol, set at the point where the entrance to the tomb chamber would have been located, and right at the centre of the South Circle, may have been an aniconic epiphany of the goddess who presided over life and death. This major monumental feature was destroyed in the eighteenth century, but its socket has been identified, 90 metres south-east of the centre of Avebury. Given the relative sizes of the microcosmic and macrocosmic landscapes, we might look for an equivalent feature in the macrocosm 900 metres in the same direction from the centre of Avebury. When a line is projected beyond the bank that distance into the outer landscape, it falls within 50 metres of the point where a small stone circle, known as Faulkner's Circle, was built. By a curious piece of sympathetic magic, Faulkner's Circle too has been destroyed.

Just outside the South Circle, 155 metres south-south-east of the centre of Avebury, stands another isolated monolith, the Ringstone. This too may be telling us that some important feature stood at the equivalent location in the wider landscape beyond the enclosure bank, 1,550 metres in the same direction. The Ringstone indicates a point

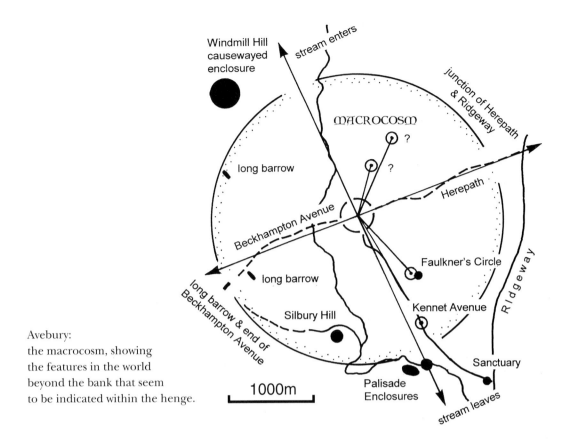

Avebury:
the macrocosm, showing
the features in the world
beyond the bank that seem
to be indicated within the henge.

on the destroyed section of the West Kennet Avenue, perhaps a specific, special stone, perhaps some other marker; nothing survives in the visible landscape to hint at what it may have been. It may alternatively be that the Ringstone simply stands for all the Kennet Avenue stones; its orientation marks a long straight reach of the Avenue.

The idea of the neolithic enclosure as a scale model of the larger landscape is clearly a fruitful one. Finding that it worked at Stonehenge would not mean a great deal. It could have been purely a matter of chance that the River Avon entered and left the macrocosmic landscape at locations on the landscape boundary corresponding to entrance gaps in the Stonehenge bank. Similar relationships recurring at Avebury could really not be attributed to chance. The fact that we have been able to use the location of a major feature within the Avebury enclosure to 'predict' the location of a major feature in the macrocosmic landscape seems to confirm that the neolithic monuments were, at least to some extent, scale models of the wider landscape.

POWER

The place where a monument was built says much about its role. Some monuments were built close to home so that they were conveniently and easily accessible, like the

Machrie Moor stone circles set in the heart of the land of the living on Arran. Others were deliberately located far from dwelling places, inaccessible, difficult to find, hidden away, like the Castlerigg stone circle on the Cumbrian fells, and these were clearly meant to be places of pilgrimage. Some were affected by the availability of raw materials; for all we know, Avebury might have been built anyway, but it was the more easily built for being right next to a stretch of downland where huge sarsens lay waiting to be collected. Others were developed in spite of the absence of local raw materials; the sarsens for the late neolithic phase of Stonehenge were imported from 40 kilometres away – and at great human cost.

In all the monuments, whether of earth, timber or stone, round or linear, there is a sense of a meeting of complementary opposites: natural and made, domestic and wild, visible and invisible, the world of the living and the world of the ancestors, the everyday world and the otherworld, earth and heaven. They are all special places that stand on the edge of our ordinary world and seem to offer the chance of stepping into another world; they are liminal places, places on the boundary of experience, and places of human transformation. It is not by chance that the bounding ditches of ceremonial enclosures often have human remains placed in them, nor that these are often beside the entrance. A female dwarf was sacrificed and buried with a cache of antlers in the deep ditch beside the south entrance at Avebury. The remains are there

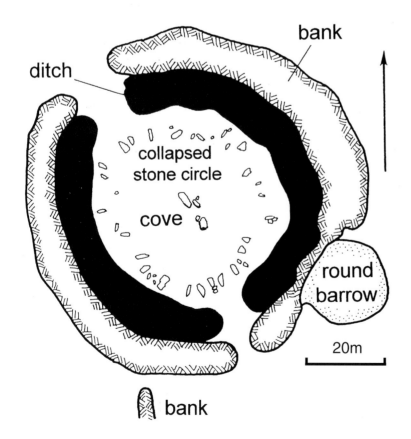

Arbor Low henge in Derbyshire. A bank and ditch surrounded a circle of about thirty weathered limestone blocks, all now fallen. In the middle was a cove, also collapsed, a three-stone setting symbolizing the tomb's heart.

to guard the monument, to make it safe. This is an idea that carried through into the iron age, where enclosures were fitted with ghost fences hung with human heads to frighten away evil spirits, and even into the present, when we encourage children to make pumpkin-head lanterns that will scare off whatever spirits wander abroad at Hallowe'en.

What else can the monuments tell us about neolithic society? It used to be thought that the building of very ambitious, large-scale monuments in the late neolithic was due to the emergence of a powerful central authority – a paramount chief who could command a huge labour force and order constructions such as Silbury Hill. In the 1980s it was suggested that access to the supernatural was a route to political power, and that the building and control of large henges may have been a way for a small élite group – of priests, for example – to exert political power indirectly and unobtrusively; in other words, the superhenges represent a transition to naked secular political power.[49] In the 1990s that idea was taken a step further: the organization and building of large monuments was in itself instrumental in the emergence of a centralized authority.

It seems more likely to me that ambitious undertakings emerged from a common religious ideology, that the plans once agreed generated the common purpose and the organization flowed from a cooperative spirit; we know from sequences of radiocarbon dates that the big monuments took a long time to complete, and it is unlikely that any personal political ambition could have crossed several generations. The long time-scale also means that there is no need to call into play very large labour forces. At each monument we only need to look at the minimum labour force required to achieve the largest single task. For Stonehenge this was dragging Stone 56, the largest of the uprights, from Avebury up a 5-degree slope at Gore Cross in 2400 BC and erecting it at Stonehenge.[50] A small but single-minded community could have built Stonehenge.

It may be that once a visually imposing monument was built it became a source of power for political or religious leaders in the late neolithic and bronze age, and later too. The self-styled druids of the twentieth century rode on the history of Stonehenge, not only claiming the monument as their own but somehow convincing the authorities and the general public that they had some special entitlement to access denied to the rest of us. Monuments built from around 3000 BC onwards would have created new social realities in the later neolithic; they would have changed the human landscape as well as the physical.

Monuments acquired histories of their own; acts of building and destruction added new meanings and connotations, and changed the ways in which they might be experienced.[51] Many monuments, including the long barrows, reconfigured the geography by excavating the soil and underlying rock, putting the substance of the earth itself on display – and in a new and unfamiliar way. Because they functioned as moongates, allowing access to the otherworld, in a sense they enabled people to gain access to the earth itself.[52]

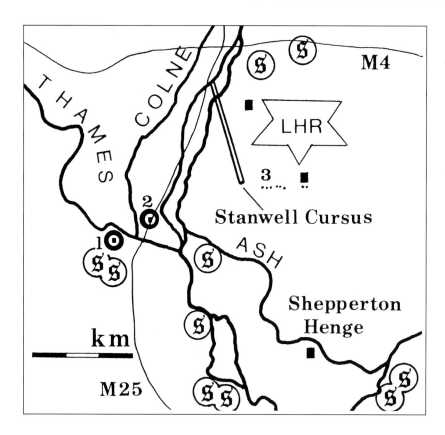

A neolithic landscape in West London.

LHR = London Heathrow Airport (for orientation);

S = neolithic settlement;

1 = Runnymede causewayed enclosure;

2 = Staines causewayed enclosure;

3 = linear cemetery of ring ditches leading towards the southern end of the Stanwell Cursus.

A large ceremonial landscape developed in the Thames valley at what was then, as now, an important route centre.

The most ambitious monuments were designed to make powerful statements. They were statements of power, but whether that power was social, political, economic, religious or a blend of all of these is hard to say. They were communal works, communal identity symbols, and must have attracted visitors from long distances. Thornborough was evidently used more by people travelling across England than by local people. Several ceremonial complexes were developing an importance that reached out to lands way beyond those of the local bands who built them. The evolving pan-British ceremonial centres included Brodgar, Kilmartin, Cairnpapple, Rudston, Thornborough, Dorchester-on-Thames, Stonehenge, Avebury and possibly others such as Staines and Hindwell. These major centres had a number of identifiable characteristics. They consisted of a range of large, awe-inspiring structures; they were often located at awe-inspiring sites; they attracted high-status objects, including valuable trade objects; later, in the late neolithic and early bronze age, they would attract VIP burials; they were long-lasting too, as enduring as medieval cathedrals.

NOT HIEROGLYPHICS BUT 'GEOGLYPHICS'?

A pervasive characteristic of life in the neolithic is the lack of writing. Thought had developed to a level of complexity where 'handing-on' became a priority, yet writing had not yet been developed. Maybe we could coin the word 'geoglyphics' to describe the use of monuments to write on the landscape.

Ritual is an aid to learning and memorizing. In ritual, past reaches through present to future, often by way of an unusual medium, such as song, dance, archaic language or drama. The physical performance is part of the way both the ritual and its content are memorized. The ritual cannot be changed; this protects the belief-system from discussion and dissent, and protects the content from the possibility of change. Monuments have forms inextricably bound up with rituals, and are therefore also mnemonic devices.

Stonehenge was fitted out with a variety of architectural features, many long gone, some still faintly visible, which held meanings for people in the past. The earth circle, with its emphatically unopposed entrance causeways to north-east and south; the northern moonrise stakes and the summarizing A posts; the Heel Stones; the bluestones and sarsens and the stories they told about their journeys to Stonehenge; the horseshoes and circles of stones; the trilithons representing entrances to tomb chambers; the almost chanced-upon summative image of the roundhouse in decay.

Just as a cathedral contains within its architecture a mass of symbolic statements, with every arch, door and pillar carrying meaning – as well as the rituals that take place among them, so it was with neolithic monuments. Stonehenge was a stone, timber and earth mnemonic encapsulating the community's belief-system, its collective identity, its communal pride, its technology, its faith, its past, its tryst with the past, the gods and the tribal ancestors, its status, its ego, its selfhood. In an age before books Stonehenge was an entire library.[53]

The recurring use of the circle – whether in earth, timber or stone – indicates that it had a key symbolic value. The circle symbolized the sun on whose warmth everything depended. The earth banks of a henge represented the world-disc, the crest line simulating in miniature form the far horizon bounding the world of men, the enclosed temenos becoming a microcosm of the world itself. The microcosm was within the priest-magician's power to control; he could gather and focus beneficent forces there; he could also send the gathered forces out like the fertilizing rays of the sun itself into the surrounding fields, meadows and forests.

POINTS OF DEPARTURE, PLACES OF REFUGE

Above all, the ceremonial enclosures, whether made of earth, stone or timber, were special places where people went to escape from the everyday world and approach the world of the ancestors. They were places where whole communities might gather to revise their relationships, perhaps in moots or debates, perhaps performing ceremonies that were rites of passage, initiations and marriages, rituals to avert disasters, rituals of thanksgiving. They supplied opportunities for periodic feasting, and reinforced people's ideas about the way the world worked. They were places of sacrifice, places where the gods were put under an obligation to help. The possibilities multiply.[54]

Those circles with well-defined banks round them, even if only a metre or two high, felt like miniature worlds within the world outside. Because during rituals people met their ancestors, and in some cases the ancestral bones were brought in, they became moongates joining heaven and earth. They also became the hub about which the wheel of neolithic society revolved. Like spiritual tube stations they allowed people to travel to other places, other times.

These many-sided projects incorporate a bewildering matrix of symbols, beliefs and aspirations in their design, but above all they express a holistic and cumulative view of the universe, a view that saw no overriding separation between man and nature, heaven and earth, or the worlds of the living and the dead.

CHAPTER TEN

LANGUAGE, ARTS AND CRAFTS

LANGUAGE AND WRITING

There was no Celtic invasion in 1000 BC. There was no Beaker invasion in 2000 BC. The Norman invaders of 1066 represented a relatively small number of replacement aristocratic landowners. Our family histories are largely uninterrupted, so that many of us living in Britain today are descendants of the megalith builders. This land has been our land for thousands of years longer than is widely believed. We are only now rediscovering something that seems to have been known in the late iron age, when Diodorus Siculus wrote, 'Britain, we are told, is inhabited by tribes that are autochthonous and preserve in their ways of living the ancient manner of life.'[1] Research based on DNA samples supports the idea that a large percentage of the 'apparently English' population of England is actually of ancient British, pre-Anglo-Saxon, stock, so that even the Anglo-Saxon colonization did not break the ancient blood line.

As yet the linguistic implications of this have not been fully grasped, but if modern Welsh has developed from a 'Celtic' language spoken in Wales three thousand years ago then it will probably also have roots in a pre-Celtic language spoken there two thousand years earlier. The surviving 'Celtic' languages must have their origins in languages spoken in 3000 BC. The 'Celtic' languages fall into two groups, Goidelic and Brythonic, sibling proto-Celtic tongues.[2]

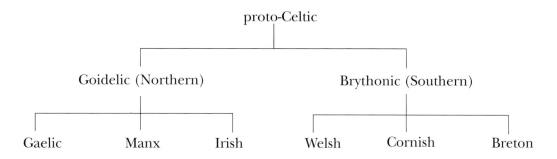

proto-Celtic

Goidelic (Northern)   Brythonic (Southern)

Gaelic   Manx   Irish   Welsh   Cornish   Breton

Maybe, as was suggested long ago, the Romany language Shelta is a 'pre-Celtic' survival from the neolithic,[3] but it would, I think, be very hard to prove.

One broad view of the neolithic in the British Isles is that there were two distinct cultural provinces, represented by heartlands in the north and south. The southern heartland – south Wales and the English chalklands – is characterized by earth burial, leaf-shaped arrow-heads, causewayed enclosures, long barrows with wooden chambers, and large hilltop enclosures. The northern heartland – southern Scotland, the Isle of Man and northern Ireland – is characterized by cremation, kite-shaped arrow-heads, court cairns and a lack of causewayed enclosures and hilltop enclosures.[4] If these heartlands really were culturally distinct, it would not be surprising if they had different languages. The fact that these provinces were later linguistically divided along broadly the same lines suggests to me that there *was* a neolithic language divide, that neolithic people in Scotland, Ireland and the Isle of Man spoke a proto-Goidelic tongue and people in Wales and England a proto-Brythonic one.

There was language, though no fully developed system of writing. It is very hard for me to imagine what life without writing would be like – the neolithic appears starved without it – but it is really *our* age that is unusual in having writing, and the greater part of the human drama has been acted out without it. It was objects, whether as small as stone talismans or as large as Avebury, that were made to carry meaning. It was the artefacts, the artwork, the architecture, that spoke their language, maintaining and communicating their traditions across long reaches of time.[5] Neolithic people had no written literature but, to judge from modern analogues, they are likely to have had stories, poems, songs and sagas. They were as intelligent and as intellectually complex as we are, and a great deal of what is now expressed in literature must then have been expressed through other media. Architecture, and in particular the communal architecture of the monuments, gave scope for expressing in symbolic and metaphorical form the shared ideas and aspirations of the community. It was in clay, wood, stone, and in other media now perished, such as textiles and paint, that ideas, dreams and myths found voice.

Writing as such had not evolved, but the brink was being crossed in eastern Europe and there were marks and signs that recur often enough in the British Isles to show that writing was about to happen. Proto-writing was under way. Most famously, there is the decorative stone carving found in passage graves in the Boyne valley and in other tombs influenced by the Boyne culture. The complete vocabulary of symbols used in the Boyne tombs can be seen, though locally fragmented, all over the British Isles. Passage grave art contains a repertoire of recurring motifs: rayed circles, flowers, serpents, shields, multiple arcs, chevrons, lozenges, triangles, spirals.[6] There are sets of angular motifs (chevron and lozenge) and curving motifs (arc, circle and spiral).[7] Some of the motifs are found on Grooved Ware pottery, which explains how they found their way from place to place – and over long distances at that; pottery is portable. Spirals are found as far afield as Llanbedr in Wales, Templewood in Argyll, Westray in Orkney and Newgrange in Ireland. Right at the source of the Grooved

The Westray Stone, discovered in 1981. A beautiful piece of passage grave art on a lintel from the Pierowall chamber tomb, Orkney. This tomb was dismantled in 3000 BC, so it is remarkable that the most important piece of prehistoric art in Scotland has survived.

Ware style, the same symbols are found on pottery and in tomb art; zig-zags, lozenges and chevrons are carved on a decorated slab that covered a burial on the Ness of Brodgar.

The spiral often occurs at megalithic monuments where the builders have deliberately arranged a solar orientation; Newgrange, for instance, was aligned on the midwinter sunrise. Recently a spiral carving was noticed at Castlerigg stone circle, carved on an easterly stone. Another stone beside it bore a lattice pattern. Together they mark a solar position, the equinox; because the south-eastern horizon is higher than the north-eastern, the midpoint between midsummer sunrise and midwinter sunrise is slightly south of true east. The stone carvings correctly marked the halfway point in time between the sunrises of the midsummer and midwinter. Three anticlockwise spirals carved on Long Meg indicate the sun's journey towards midwinter.[8] The spiral may have been intended to indicate the specific track made by the tip of the shadow as the sun circled round a standing stone; alternatively it may have been intended to symbolize the sun's mazy journey through the heavens and also, in a more general way, through the calendar and the life of the community.

A stone plaque found at the Graig Lwyd axe factory has a double line dividing the space in two; there is a closely worked chevron pattern on one side of the double line but just a few desultory lines on the other, as if the pattern was unfinished. Just as with the monuments, it was the act of making, not the finishing, that counted. A schist plaque from Ronaldsway has bands of chevrons worked more carefully across both flat faces, in such a way that they make lozenges where they touch.

In the northern heartland carved stone slabs were recycled for incorporation into tombs. They began life out in the open, looking across the world of the living, sometimes carved into the living bedrock at viewpoints; then they were grubbed up and built into the fabric of tombs, where they turned inwards towards the world of the dead. Important statements about the relationship between people and landscape were being relayed to the ancestors.[9]

In the southern heartland, the English chalk country, only single ideograms, cryptically carved on plaques of chalk, were deposited at earth circles, in offering pits or in the ditches of long barrows. They represent ritual utterances and, if we could read them, they might tell us much about the beliefs of the neolithic people. The commonest sign is a set of parallel lines.[10] The Butterfield Down plaque has the most orderly sets of parallel lines, framed within rectangles and, unusually, carved on four sides (the two flat faces and 'left' and 'right' edges). A double-sided plaque at Windmill Hill carried something more: two sets of parallel lines separated by an axis, and on the other side a curved line with a number of straight lines and triangles built on to it. At North Marden in West Sussex a series of chalk tablets marked with different signs was laid out in a long barrow ditch, like a row of Scrabble tiles, and suggesting a more complex statement.[11]

No one has yet made any serious attempt to decipher the symbols, which is understandable as there are too few for them to constitute an alphabet. The recurrence of parallel lines suggests to me that they are ideograms, symbolic representations of fundamental ideas. It may be that the parallel grooves refer to or even replicate the act of ploughing. The fact that sometimes the plaque was turned through 90 degrees and a second set of parallel grooves applied is strongly reminiscent of the technique of cross-ploughing and suggests sympathetic magic. This criss-cross pattern was made on a plaque at Whitehawk in Brighton, and was also carved on the wall of a flint mine not far away at Harrow Hill.

At Flagstones near Dorchester a series of symbols was carved into the walls of a ditch surrounding the earth enclosure (dating from around 2750 BC).[12] It may be that the

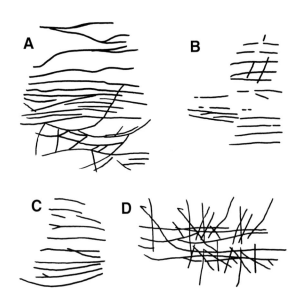

Parallel lines carved in chalk. (a) A talisman probably originally deposited at the Offham causewayed enclosure, and which I discovered five thousand years later built into a river embankment at Newhaven; a chalk quarry has eaten away the eastern half of the Offham enclosure, so it is likely that the chalk rubble and the talisman came from there (published here for the first time). (b) carving found in the Cissbury flint mines by Lane Fox. (c) and (d) carvings in the Grime's Graves flint mines (after Park Harrison 1877, Clarke 1915).

A fertility talisman. The chalk tablet (A) was left at the Whitehawk causewayed enclosure in Sussex. The criss-cross pattern is similar to that of the ard marks (B) found under the South Street long barrow in Wiltshire (after Evans 1971).

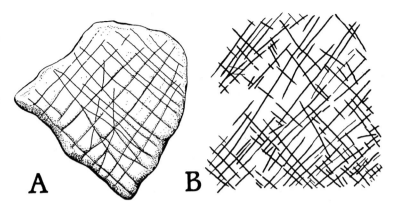

The 'chessboard' carved in chalk in the Harrow Hill flint mine (after Curwen 1936).

positioning of the symbols is significant, and intended to indicate what lay outside the enclosure. Parallel lines and criss-cross lines on the north and west may mean that ploughed fields lay in those directions. A pattern made of discontinuous concentric arcs looks rather like the plan of a causewayed enclosure, and this symbol is marked to the south-west, which is where the old enclosure of Maiden Castle lies, 3 kilometres away. The same symbol is marked in the ditch on the north-west: a spectacular new enclosure lay just a kilometre away in that direction and plainly visible – Greyhound Yard in Dorchester (also built around 2750 BC). Alternatively, given that this was one of the last causewayed enclosures to be built, and to a hybrid, transitional design, the symbols may not be a spatial reference from here to *there*, but a temporal one, from now to *then*, which is a more interesting revelation of neolithic thought – the consciousness of an historic rather than an ancestral past and the desire to commemorate it.

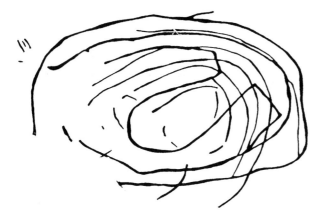

The enclosure carving at Flagstones near Dorchester.

Bryn Celli Ddu: the serpent drawing.

Loose spirals and a wandering sinuous shape that some have described as a serpent can be seen at the Bryn Celli Ddu passage grave on Anglesey. With its long-continuing line and its many changes of direction, wandering from stone to stone, this 'serpent' looks to me more like a narrative than a symbol, like someone trying to tell us a story. Or is someone faking, with failing memory and perhaps without understanding, the beautifully finished spiral carvings seen during a visit to the great Newgrange tomb across the Irish Sea? A more formal spiral at Cauldside Burn in Kirkcudbright is associated with a cup mark, a small circular pit of unknown meaning. More elaborate still is the beautiful spiral design on the Westray Stone, which was part of an Orcadian passage grave.

The symbols were carved on bedrock in some places, on big tomb slabs in others. But they were also carved on small plaques no bigger than your hand, and these may have been purpose-made for people to carry around. These portable symbols were, I believe, talismans – statements about the cosmos that gave the bearer strength and

One of the Maxey batons.

support. We know people carried a lot of equipment about with them, and they might well have included, perhaps in a cloth bag or pouch, a charm that would bring them good luck on a journey.

At Maxey two sceptres or batons made out of red deer antler were carefully inscribed with zig-zags. The carved grooves were filled with red paint made out of red ochre, fat and charcoal. The sceptres, probably of religious or magical significance and used only by the Maxey shaman, were placed in the ditches of the mini-henges, and they are another reminder of the continuity with the remote past; batons of exactly this type were made long before by the hunter-gatherers. They refer back to the hunting fathers, and the red zig-zag was a special statement to, from or about them.[13]

We can be sure that signs and symbols were carved, impressed, woven and painted on materials that have not survived, including people's skin. The Iceman had symbols composed of short straight lines tattooed on various parts of his body, and they are thought to represent instructions from one doctor to another about the acupuncture points that were effective for him; people were walking about with doctors' notes written on them. This confirms what we know from the axe trade, that people travelled, and adds something unexpected: that when they travelled they sometimes asked for medical help from strangers – and presumably expected to receive it.

CRAFTS

In the coastal lowlands of southwest Cumbria lay a small lakeside settlement, home to one or two families. Long after they had joined their ancestors the tarn filled with peat. A nineteenth-century farmer decided to drain the tarn; as his men dug the drains they recovered several stone axes and a collection of wooden artefacts, until that time (1869) the most that had been recovered from the neolithic. This was Ehenside Tarn.[14] Naturally, most wooden artefacts made in 3000 BC have perished. Only a handful of objects have survived, by chance, in waterlogged conditions at sites like Ehenside Tarn, Etton and the Somerset Levels; they represent a small sample of what must have been a large range of artefacts actually made and used.

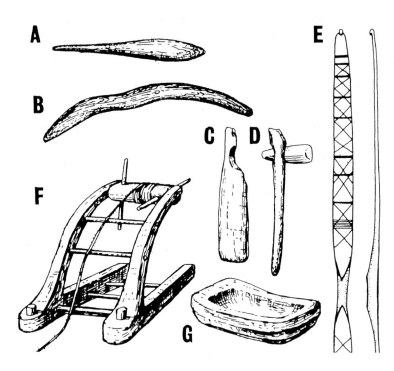

Wooden objects.
A = club;
B = throwing stick;
C = turf spade or paddle;
D = axe handle
(A–D from Ehenside Tarn
  in Cumbria);
E = the Meare bow (from
    the Somerset Levels);
F = windlass (from the
    Humber);
G = bowl (from Ehenside
    Tarn).

A mallet and two bows have been found in Somerset while Cumbria has produced bowls, animal traps, boats and throwing sticks. The scope of neolithic technology was startlingly ambitious. It is impressive that so much could be achieved with such meagre tools. Often the tools were handled with great dexterity and it is difficult to evaluate experiments with facsimile implements because the modern experimenter starts from scratch without the appropriate conditioning, skills or attitudes. One of the two bows from the Somerset Levels, the Ashcott bow (3400 BC), was almost 2m long, very slender, with a square cross-section. The Meare bow (of the same date) was similar in length but had a broad, flat cross-section; it was also elaborately decorated, with carefully carved bands of parallel lines and a complex pattern of horizontal lines and criss-crosses made of rawhide strips.[15] Perhaps the decorated Meare bow was ceremonial and the Ashcott bow functional.

Textiles were probably made from wool and from a range of natural fibres including grasses, though none survives. The carved patterns on the Stonehenge plaques give an idea of the sort of geometric designs that were probably woven and stitched into fabrics.[16]

Most of the inscribed art work is geometric and probably symbolic in character. There is disappointingly little figurative art; this type of art is unambiguous and would give us incontrovertible evidence of the preoccupations of the age. Virtually all we have to go on are two sketches, really little more than cartoons, one of a stag drawn on a flint crust at Grime's Graves, the other perhaps of an ox drawn on a gallery ceiling at the Cissbury flint mine.[17] This may show a secular interest in animals that yielded

Two carved chalk plaques, deposited in a pit on the King Barrow Ridge not far to the east of Stonehenge (Richards 1991).

food, or it may show an interest in them as cult animals. The deer drawing is reminiscent of the cave images painted on the European mainland ten or fifteen thousand years earlier, and very much rooted in the traditions of the old stone age hunters – a useful reminder that older practices and beliefs still continued.

Paint was used to decorate megalithic monuments in Spain and Portugal. One chambered tomb with painted patterns of white, red and black gives the impression of a room hung with tapestries. A red-painted incised drawing on a cist-grave in Germany even more specifically shows an elevation of the decorated wall of a house, with four zig-zag patterned rugs or tapestries hanging side by side.[18] Since houses for the dead often mimicked houses for the living, it may well be that the houses of the living had woven textile hangings or painted walls. The interiors of the Maltese temples were similarly painted with designs in red.[19] Paint has not survived on any British

This delightful stag strolling across a meadow was drawn on a flint at Grime's Graves.

Drawing of an animal head, carved in a flint mine at Cissbury.

monuments, probably because of the damp climate, though we can be fairly sure from the contemporary parallels in Spain and Germany that it was used. Red paint was certainly in use in neolithic Britain, as we know from the Maxey batons. I can see the possibility that not only neolithic tomb interiors but standing stones and stone circles too were painted. The designs were probably similar to those seen on pottery and plaques: a variety of geometric shapes, dots and spirals.

Colour was used symbolically, even in the choice of stone. Pale stones were selected for the main 'altar' stones or sometimes the stones that flanked them at recumbent stone circles. White was chosen for its spirituality – then as in later cultures. At Thornborough Circles the banks of boulders were coated with gypsum crystals, deliberately whitened to make them look more like the earth circles of the chalklands, which were dazzlingly white when freshly made.[20] White quartz was similarly used in the Clava Cairns, where red sandstone was used to face the wall opposite the entrance passage so that when it was lit up by the setting sun at midwinter it would create a red glow in the chamber. The passage grave of Newgrange was also given a dazzling white revetment made mainly of quartz blocks. A Breton passage grave (Jardin aux Moines) has a kerb of alternating red and white boulders.[21] White for sanctity, red for sun.

CHAPTER ELEVEN

peopLe Like us

PATHS INTO A THOUGHT-WORLD

What we see and *who* we see when we look into the remote past depends on how we look, and how we look depends on our vantage point. Our past depends upon our present. Re-presentations of the new stone age continually shift, reflecting the preoccupations of the ever-shifting present, and not necessarily progressing systematically towards the neolithic reality.

Models developed in the 1970s and 1980s lean in part on spatial analysis, for example using Thiessen polygons to infer territorial boundaries from the location of tombs,[1] or calculating community size from monument size, but this approach has been beset by many problems. There is no reason to suppose that functionally central places were central geographically in the past any more than they are in the present: London is not at the geometric centre of the UK, nor are Washington and New York at the centre of the USA. Size of monument may be a poor guide to community size. There is no way of knowing whether a rubble mound took 50 people 2 days to build, or 2 people 50 days. It is difficult to estimate what percentage of the total population the work-force constituted. We can make guesses about the percentage of elderly, infirm and young, but there is no way of knowing whether men and women played equal roles in monument-building, and no way of knowing whether children took part, still less of knowing how childhood was perceived.

It is likely that the closest cultural parallels in the modern world will be found in the least economically developed countries, and in the poorest countries of the world today children work; some Asian children as young as six are made to work all day weaving rugs. This suggests that children *did* take part in communal work, but ritual activity is often surrounded by taboos and rigorously exclusive: certain groups of people may not participate and it may be that some were excluded from creating monuments. My own view is that, given their short life expectancy, people today regarded as children were accorded higher status, that fourteen-year-olds would have been regarded as adults, and that monument-building was an inclusive rather than an exclusive activity. There is one piece of evidence, small but telling, that supports this: an Orkney woman's forehead was dented, showing that she habitually carried or hauled heavy loads with a band wrapped round her head; *one* woman at least was routinely involved in hard physical work.

We can analyse the way people moved through space. At Barnhouse we can reconstruct the paths people habitually followed round the interior of a house. The main access through the single door is marked by a line of paving stones: a great deal of wear was expected there. Within, people either turned right, towards the hearth in the centre of the east room, or walked straight on towards the doorway into the west room, a path also marked by paving. Within the west room people passed to left or right round the central hearth. These are public-access paths. The box-beds were screened off from the central living spaces by big stone slabs. The screens show that individual privacy was required and respected; the routes round the screens, in each case round one edge only, were private-access routes. Often in simple societies, life is communal and there is little regard for individual personal space, but here at Barnhouse we can see indications that the privacy of personal space was respected.[2]

The way bones were separated inside chamber tombs, with skulls grouped together in one place and long bones in another, may have been designed to de-emphasize and conceal the social inequalities that existed in life. The restriction of access seen at a lot of chamber tombs, such as the Breton passage graves, has been taken by some

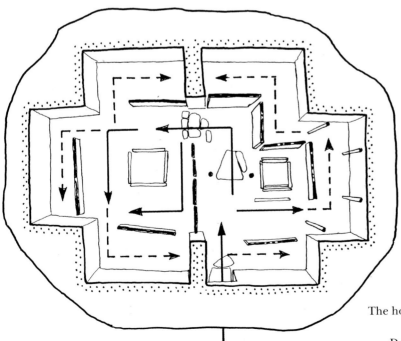

The house with two hearths at Barnhouse.
Solid arrows = public-access routes.
Dashed arrows = private-access routes.

prehistorians to demonstrate that ceremonial practices were controlled by an élite group; conversely the new generation of Breton monuments built around 3000 BC, the gallery graves, were more open structures, accessible and showing little sign of social differentiation.[3] A social change had occurred. Neo-Marxist interpretations of this kind appear to give us access to the social and political psychology of the neolithic, but I wish we had more corroboration: a lot of supposition is involved.

PHYSIQUE

At least we know a good deal about what people looked like in 3000 BC, from their bones. The people of the long barrows were slim, rather delicately built, and generally the men were 1.6 or 1.7m tall (5 ft 3 in to 5 ft 7 in), the women 10cm shorter. It used to be thought that the neolithic people were a distinct type, strikingly different from later people, but now that many more bones have been recovered it has become clear that there were far more noticeable differences between people from place to place; for instance, the people buried in the Coldrum tomb in Kent were shorter than those buried in the West Kennet long barrow in Wiltshire.[4]

The Quanterness and Isbister tombs on Orkney were treasure chests of bones, the remains of entire neolithic communities. The Orcadian women were 1.6m (5 ft 3 in) tall on average, men 10cm (4 in) taller at 1.7m, typical of the British Isles generally. Much has been made of prehistoric people being smaller than modern people. They were only slightly shorter than us, and every day in the street we pass scores of people who are of heights that were normal in the neolithic. The Isbister people were more muscular than the Quanterness people, probably because they regularly climbed up and down the adjacent sea-cliffs on the east coast of South Ronaldsay, foraging for sea-birds and their eggs. There are no cliffs at Quanterness.

The people of Parc le Breos in South Wales were also strong and athletic. Their bones have strong muscle attachments, so they either routinely ran and jumped rather than walked, or stood upright from a squatting position while bearing heavy weights. Pulling bowstrings gave them well-developed arms.[5] The Avebury people were tall, slender, and their faces were child-like, with small concave noses. The same characteristics were shared by people at Littleton Drew, Lugbury and Rodmarton. But the 'child-like' faces may mislead, as their muscles were often highly developed; they had well-developed archer's arms. They may have had the slightness, lightness and fleetness of foot of today's adolescents, but they were much tougher.

The three-age system adopted in Britain in the middle of the nineteenth century was strongly based on an assumption that the three ages were dominated by different races. Wilson divided the past into ages of stone, bronze and iron, and saw a sequence of head shapes characterizing the different ages, but the analysis was based on only thirty-six skulls.[6] It was Lubbock in 1865 who argued most influentially for the three-age system, leaning heavily on the study of skulls. But these theories were based on small samples: a two-volume study in 1865 was still based on only fifty-six skulls.[7] These

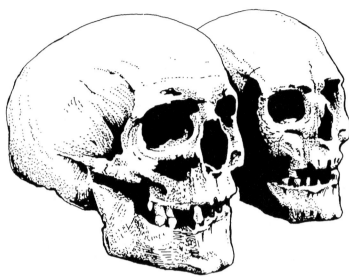

These two people lived in the Isbister community on South Ronaldsay. The stalled cairn in which they were buried was in use for eight hundred years. Their totem animal was the sea-eagle.

early studies left twentieth-century archaeologists with the received wisdom that neolithic people were a race of people with long, narrow skulls. As more skulls are found and measured, we can see that there were quite large regional variations in physical shape and that these passed on into later generations.

The nineteenth-century adage 'long barrows long skulls; round barrows, round skulls' carried with it an unfortunate Darwinian message: that the neolithic people were of a weak and inferior race, swept away by taller, stronger, cleverer bronze age people, perhaps from Scandinavia.[8] That idea fell into disrepute in the wake of eugenics and Nazism, but studies of more skulls in the 1990s suggested that there really *was* a tendency for neolithic skulls to be long and narrow and that head shape *does* vary over long periods. Whether this is to be explained by ethnic variation or by cultural and environmental differences, such as diet or practices like head-binding, is not yet known.

Either way, and this I think is the most significant point, people in 3000 BC were themselves aware of differences in head shape, and presumably of other differences that went with them. At Belas Knap all the skulls in the tomb are long except one; there is just one round skull, which was buried in a special place beneath the portal stone. It is not a later insertion, but dates from the same early neolithic period as the rest. It evidently belonged to someone who was even then seen as different.[9]

People died young, with infant mortality running as high as 50 per cent. According to one calculation the average life expectancy of a fifteen-year-old girl was only nine years, while boys of that age could expect to live another thirteen years. A recent reassessment based on analysis of much later bone material suggests that these figures may be too pessimistic,[10] but even so very few people can have lived beyond forty. As people age they gradually lose the ability to cope with extreme cold, and many older

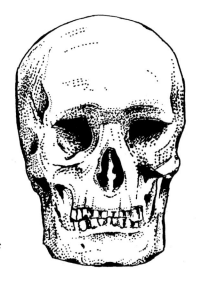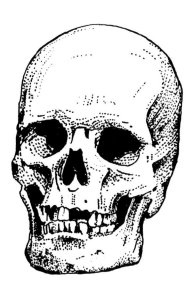

Two skulls buried at Belas Knap. The skull on the left is the single 'round' skull, while that on the right is one of the 'long' skulls.

people must have died on midwinter nights. The small number of people who lived to sixty or seventy must have been seen as rare and remarkable, and were doubtless treated as highly valued links with the community's past.

In most cases we cannot be sure how people died, but the obvious culprits are infectious diseases. It is likely that meals regularly eaten from unglazed pottery that was not properly cleaned actually *strengthened* their immune systems. Even so, occasional food shortages would have weakened their resistance, perhaps seasonally. Eating meat that was not properly cooked doubtless gave them bacterial infections such as salmonella; they would also have picked up weakening parasites such as tapeworms. Population density was still low enough to prevent fast-acting killing infections with short incubation periods like smallpox, rubella, typhoid and plague from sweeping across Europe. Those diseases were beginning to make their mark in the new high-density urban populations of the Middle East, but had not reached Britain.[11] Hunting was full of accidental dangers, and some men probably died peacefully of hypothermia while sleeping rough on hunting trips; others would have died violently, shot with arrows in 'friendly fire' incidents. As far as the men were concerned, life in the farmsteads was far safer, but many women must have died there in childbirth, just as they were to do for centuries to come.

As Aubrey Burl has said: 'Death was no stranger to these people. It was a house-guest.'[12] This helps to explain the neolithic preoccupation with death, the morbid burial practices that included primary and secondary burial, the defleshing of corpses and the repeated handling of human remains.

Death rates were high, but it is difficult to estimate figures. By analogy with communities in the Less Economically Developed World of the nineteenth and twentieth centuries, birth rates and death rates hovered at around forty per thousand per year, keeping population totals low. Aubrey Burl argues, rightly, that even a very small difference between birth and death rates could have serious long-term effects.

An annual increase of 1 per cent in an early neolithic community would have produced a sevenfold population increase over a thousand year period, which would have severely strained resources by 3000 BC. Even so, if we estimate a slightly lower birth rate or a slightly higher death rate, our hypothetical neolithic community only grows at 0.1 per cent.[13]

We are on surer ground when we come to smaller-scale, personal matters. People took care to keep their teeth clean, perhaps by washing, perhaps by systematically rubbing food remnants off with their fingers, or by using toothbrushes made of honeysuckle stems. Their teeth were in excellent condition, far better than most people's teeth today. They were, of course, short of dentists, so the few caries and abscesses they developed must have caused them years of pain.

Nearly half the adults suffered from osteo-arthritis, which most commonly affected their backs. It was brought on by the muscular stress involved in felling trees, ploughing without oxen, dragging logs, carrying heavy loads and building monuments. A boy who ran across the mudflats at Formby had a deformed foot with the second toe missing; a man running with him had rheumatoid arthritis, swollen feet and a limp. Injuries and fractures were common, again as a direct result of hard physical work with big timbers and big stones; inevitably there were accidents. The site that was to become Silbury Hill was awash with chalk mud while work went on, continuously it seems, regardless of the weather. People suffered physically for the neolithic enterprise; like people at other times, they suffered for their ideology.

At any period there is the problem of pain – how to reduce it or how to bear it. Were neolithic people tougher than us, somehow able to stand pain, or did they have ways of reducing it? It is possible that they carried out surgery using a primitive anaesthetic technique that was used in eighteenth-century Italy. It was described as a technique used for castrating boys but could have been used for other operations equally well. The boy's jugular vein was pressed until he fell into a semi-coma. In that state the operation could be performed 'with scarce any pain to the patient'.[14]

There were also herbs that could have been used as pain-killers. Seeds of a known hallucinogen, black henbane, were found in Grooved Ware pottery at Balfarg in Scotland.[15] The tattoos on the Iceman coincide with acupuncture points, in particular with master points against pain and rheumatoid arthritis, so we have good contemporary evidence that acupuncture was used to relieve the pain caused by a widespread neolithic ailment.

THE BACK-PACKERS

There may have been regional variations in dress, determined by local climate and cultural preference, but there is no reason to suppose that people in Britain dressed very differently from the Iceman, then newly frozen in the Alps.[16] Until we have evidence to the contrary, it seems reasonable to assume that people living in Britain dressed similarly, at least in winter, and the few clues we have, such as the cloak-fastening pins found in Scotland and the slightly later belt sliders, point to a similar costume and similar concepts. In summer people probably wore textiles, probably finely woven in two or three colours, to judge from contemporary textiles in Switzerland.

The deerskin tunic, worn knee- or calf-length, was probably standard wear for men, with leather leggings (deer or calfskin) added in winter. Men also wore loincloths, consisting of a length of cloth or sheepskin passed between the legs, drawn up front and back and held in place by a leather belt: the two ends hung down like a skirt. Their moccasins were made in two pieces, uppers and soles, both of leather and sewn together with rawhide.

Winter wear included cloaks made of a variety of materials – animal skins, leather, grass, wool – and a helmet-shaped fur hat. The sleeveless cape or poncho was probably a pan-North European garment, hanging like a portable tent from shoulder to knee to keep the upper part of the body warm. A poncho from neolithic Denmark was made of five big rectangles of fur sewn together leaving a square neck-hole in the middle. Clothes were well-made, often out of a surprisingly large number of strips of leather or skin carefully, evenly and expertly stitched together with thin strips of leather.

Neolithic clothing, based on the Iceman's clothes. Underclothes consisted of a loincloth, belt, suspenders and leather leggings (left). A middle layer consisted of a leather or textile tunic held by a bone pin and a belt with a tool-pouch (centre). The outer layer included leather shoes, a textile or animal skin poncho and a fur hat (right) (after Barfield 1994 and de Marinis and Brillante 1998).

Sometimes light and dark strips were deliberately alternated to create a striking pattern, especially on the front, and it is I think very significant that the (coloured and patterned) fur side was worn facing outwards for show, not inwards for warmth. People evidently cared how they looked. They wore their clothes for a long time, maintained them and repeatedly repaired them, though not always expertly; inevitably their garments became greasy and soiled through long use.[17]

Round their waist they wore a 2m-long belt, which they wound round twice before tying up. On this belt hung a small pouch containing a toolkit of small stone blades, a bone awl and a piece of tinder.

People carried a lot of equipment around with them. In addition to beads and amulets of magic stone for good luck, a hunter had to carry his yew bow and a set of a dozen arrows 87cm long in a leather quiver. He had to repair his own shoes and tunic when he tore them, and therefore took a sewing kit when he travelled. He had to make and trim arrows if he wanted to hunt. He carried a tiny knife in a woven-string scabbard, each tied carefully to his belt to make sure it did not get lost. He also had a retoucher, made of a spine of antler rammed into a hollow stem of limewood, just like a big pencil. This deceptively familiar-looking object had an unfamiliar use. It was used for sharpening the dagger; pressing the antler against the flint blade made a tiny shell of flint snap off, leaving a sharp new edge. When the antler spine wore down, the retoucher itself could be sharpened, just like a pencil. It too was attached by a piece of string to the belt. Several balls of birch fungus were drilled, threaded on to a leather cord and worn like a bracelet on the wrist. This contained antibiotic and acted as travelling medication. A tassel of twisted leather cords was carried for running repairs on clothing. People would have rustled, clattered and clinked as all these odds and ends swung about when they walked.

A backpack was invaluable for carrying a wide range of equipment: dried meat, a net for catching birds, birch-bark containers for carrying hot embers, fire-lighting gear, including dried lichen or grass, a piece of pyrite and a flint core to strike sparks with. The supple but strong birch bark used for making containers was also used to make a glue that could be used for fixing arrow-heads to shafts, and probably had many other uses too.[18] Neolithic people were walking workshops, with bags, pouches, backpacks and dozens of items of equipment clattering about them as they went on their way.

THE BIRTH OF INDIVIDUALITY AND THE BEGINNING OF HISTORY

In Britain 3000 BC people had a different attitude towards dirt. At three Orcadian settlements – Skara Brae, Rinyo and Links of Noltland – old midden material was recycled with some care. Domestic refuse that we unthinkingly throw away and forget about was then regarded as worthy of consideration, even as holding meaning; it was material the community felt it was worth holding some sort of dialogue with, rather like the bones of their long-dead cousins.[19] The midden represented the community's collective past and its capacity to regenerate, in a way parallel to the anonymous mass of human remains buried in the barrows. It was also a very ancient idea reaching back three thousand years deeper into the past.

There was also a brand-new idea, that individual people were of some importance; it was now that the first single burials were made. But what did this sense of individual worth amount to? It may be that individuals were accorded special treatment at death simply because, once dead, they became useful go-betweens with the ancestors. Special treatment need not mean that they were regarded in life as celebrities; they just became messengers after death overtook them.

It was a critical moment, the last moment when a whole-community view held sway; from this time on material culture became more diverse, some individual burials began to look more 'royal' in their resonances and more effort was spent on differentiating people from one another. Arguably that personal, social and economic differentiation was a necessary preamble to the emergence of a more complex society out of which town and city life might grow, but the price paid was considerable. The orientation towards the past that followed would increasingly be preoccupied with particular dead individuals, not all, and claims by the living to descent from those special individuals.[20] The entire relationship between people and time would shift – and contract.

The first burials of single complete human bodies mark the emergence of People-Like-Us. Burials like the primary burial of the chief at Duggleby Howe would have been major events in the life of a community, events that we would now recognize as historic, so it is possible that the concept of history itself was born in 3000 BC. People evidently thought of themselves as beings whose substance was absorbed from animals and from other people, and dissipated through exchanges, sex, arranged relationships and rites of passage and the eventual, staged disintegration of the body after death. This is quite unlike the very 'bounded' self-awareness of human individuality in the West today. The patterns reinforcing the early neolithic mindset were changing, perhaps breaking down, in 3000 BC. People made increasing efforts to differentiate themselves from one another and the material culture became more diverse, with more status objects created to allow this sense of individual selfhood to develop. Having said this, it is clear that much depended on place, context and position in society. For many people, as at most watersheds in history and prehistory, nothing would have changed perceptibly.

Stonehenge was not created in a virgin wilderness in 3000 BC, but at a spot long regarded as special. The first phase of Stonehenge, consisting of a row of totem poles aligned perhaps on a living tree, went up five thousand years earlier, as far back from the Stonehenge earth circle as the earth circle's creation is from us – an unimaginably long span of time. As we saw earlier, the early radiocarbon dates for the totem poles were for a long time not accepted by archaeologists – the dates were perhaps 'contaminated' or the samples were 'poor quality' – because they put the origins of Stonehenge firmly into the middle stone age, a time inconceivably early for monuments.[21] Another route out of the tangle has been to assert that the totem poles are in effect a different site, but the distance between the totem poles and the stones is only the width of the Thames at the Tower of London – too close to ignore.

Conversely, it may be argued that mesolithic economies were mainly immediate-return systems (food and other resources consumed as soon as acquired) and such societies may as a result lack elaborate social systems of rank or descent. In the neolithic a trend towards delayed-return systems began, with associated social evolution. Ideas of rank would lead on to ideas of ancestry and genealogy. These in turn would be likely to favour an interest in the past and the future, and in claiming rights to places via ancestry. Agriculture, with its heavy dependence on seasonality, would also lead to a sharpened sense of time, and the need to track it, and a sharpened sense of place, as different places have differing food-producing potential.

The idea of monument-building, so long thought of as a distinctively neolithic practice, has its roots firmly in the middle stone age. The early totem poles at Stonehenge were raised in 8000–7000 BC. This is echoed elsewhere in mesolithic middens, which acted as imposing foci for communities for very long periods and eventually had cist-burials inserted in them, suggesting that they acquired a kind of sanctity because of their long use; what happened at the middens was not so very different from what happened at neolithic chamber tombs or barrows.

Mesolithic communities elsewhere in the world (such as aboriginal Australia and Brittany) developed monument-building. Early neolithic communities in Britain depended to a great extent on wild food sources and were not very different from their mesolithic predecessors. Many of the earliest European monuments are to be found on the Atlantic margin (notably in Brittany) in areas where there is no evidence for contemporary cultivation.

Monumentality as a concept may have begun long before, but it was only in the centuries running up to 3000 BC that monuments that we can still recognize as monuments came to be built. Monuments create tradition. They ensure the continuity of memory and experience, reaching both backwards and forwards in time. They are statements about the nature of the past and therefore mark the beginning of history. It is no accident that, five thousand years later, we still see those monuments as the beginning of our past; they were built all that time ago as memorials of an ancestral past already then sliding beyond the reach of memory like the receding wake of a ship.

VIOLENCE

Different people see the past in different ways. In the remote past those differences are heightened and for some prehistory is a nightmare of barbaric savagery, while for others it is a fantastic golden age, a paradise lost. We can see from the archaeological evidence that people were emotionally and philosophically different, but it is difficult to argue for violence or non-violence. The very few archaeological traces of group aggression have been made much of, possibly because they speak of the tribal warfare

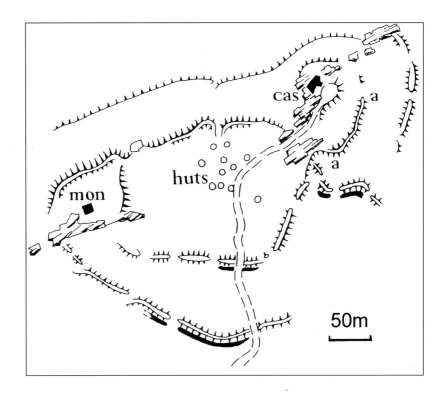

Carn Brea, a fortified tor enclosure in Cornwall. Neolithic walls at (a) have been positively identified. Possibly other defences are neolithic in origin too, as large quantities of pottery have been found across the whole area. Neolithic huts stood between the wall at (a) and the site of the castle. In use for four hundred years, Carn Brea appears to have been destroyed by armed attack.

that some modern people want to associate with cultures they regard as 'backward'. It has recently been asserted that war was endemic in early European farming communities,[22] but there is really far less evidence of war, or even preparation for war, in the neolithic than there is in later prehistory. Evidence for concerted attacks on enclosures at Carn Brea, Hambledon Hill, Hembury and Crickley Hill has been claimed,[23] but the onslaught (with bows and arrows) on Crickley Hill was a few centuries after 3000 BC, putting it into the late neolithic and therefore not appropriate for consideration here. Examples on the European mainland include a further three, one at Talheim in Germany (a mass grave of thirty-four murdered people), one at Roaix in France and one at Trou Rosette in Belgium.[24] There are still only three sites that provide evidence of warfare in middle neolithic Britain.

Hambledon Hill gives conclusive evidence of an attack. A youth was killed while trying to escape from the fiercely burning palisades of the enclosure. After the flames destroyed the outwork revetments, the unsupported rubble banks collapsed; scorched chalk was pushed down into the ditches, which were not recut afterwards. Everything about the site suggests a determined and decisive act of destruction which led to the site's abandonment.[25]

The fortified enclosures frequently offered as evidence of warfare are better evidence of the fear or possibility of attack than of its actuality. The Trundle, Orsett and Whitehawk may have been fitted with palisades, but that does not mean that they were attacked. Lord Palmerston ordered the building of forts along the Channel coast, but there was no invasion; the forts were built for a domestic political reason, to

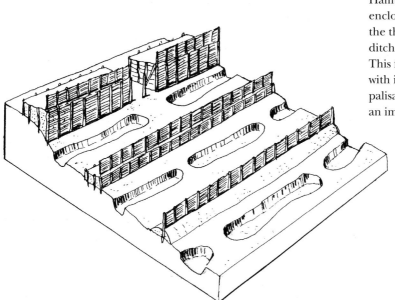

Hambledon Hill causewayed enclosure. A reconstruction of the three circuits of bank and ditch (after Mercer 1980). This fortified hilltop enclosure with its timber gateways and palisades would have been an imposing sight.

make the British *think* that there was a danger of a French invasion. Then again, a palisade may not necessarily tell us that people feared attack, merely that they wanted a decisive and imposing boundary round a separate space.

There are several examples of violent individual deaths, whether accidents, murders or acts of sacrifice, but this is a very different matter from the proposition that there was endemic tribal warfare. The corpses buried with arrowheads inside their ribcages speak of individual murders, which may have been frequent or infrequent – we can't tell. A burial pit close to a house at Fengate contained the remains of four people; it seems likely that the man, woman and two infants were the family who lived in the house. And the man had an arrowhead embedded in his ribs.[26] But the Fengate site was part of a linear ceremonial structure and it could be that the deaths were sacrificial, not murders.[27]

On the other hand, the large cache of bones found in Orcadian tombs revealed that fewer than 2 per cent of the population suffered from broken bones, and those might have been sustained in accidental cliff-falls while collecting birds' eggs.[28] However we explain the individual 'suspicious' deaths, there are very few examples altogether. It looks to me as if this was not a society in which violence played an everyday part.

PEOPLE AND LANDSCAPE

Archaeologists have gradually relinquished ideas of large-scale migrations in the iron age and early bronze age. It is possible that the scale of the Anglo-Saxon migrations of the fifth and sixth centuries AD has also been exaggerated. There is increasing evidence for the survival of 'British' stock in England, and present-day communities in Britain can trace their descent from indigenous neolithic stock. Thus, in spite of the nineteenth-century model of repeated invasions and conquests, the people of the barrows, the people who built Avebury and Maes Howe, were not merely our predecessors but our ancestors in the most literal sense. Changing perceptions of the past go hand in hand with changing perceptions of ourselves. In the nineteenth century it was customary, in England at any rate, to regard the Anglo-Saxons as 'our ancestors'. In the twentieth century, in part because of wars with Germany, the unpalatability of Nazism and the horrors of the holocaust, the German association became far less desirable; it became more fashionable to emphasize the 'Celtic' ancestry. Now that this implicitly European iron age blood line has turned out to be illusory,[29] we must look towards the astonishing alternative – continuity with a still older past. When we compare neolithic feet with much later feet in a particular region, there is a surprising amount of continuity. Neolithic feet from three Wessex locations in Wiltshire and Hampshire have distinctive mid-foot metatarsal areas, which are slightly different in shape from those in the Cotswolds. The distinctive 'Wessex foot' was still evident in the iron age, showing an unexpected continuity of blood line.[30]

Another feature of neolithic Britain that we still see today is pronounced regional differentiation, though different regions emerged then as conspicuous and influential. The great, almost metropolitan, ceremonial centres at Brodgar on Orkney and Callanish on Lewis have no modern equivalents in the far north of Britain. Conditioned by political and economic events of the past two hundred years, there is a tendency not only in the UK but in the EU to see the Highlands and Islands as marginal; indeed in EU parlance the region is officially 'periphery'. In 3000 BC it is clear that there was either no such concept or the periphery was elsewhere. Some regions evidently thought bigger than others. Wessex was a region where projects were conceived on a grandiose scale, where huge monuments were made and made to endure; East Anglia and south-east England apparently were not. So, there was a regional diversity. Equally, there was continual contact between all the regions and a common fund of ideas was available, from which people could draw at will.

Neolithic people were different from their predecessors in developing an acute sense of place. These were people who were making conspicuous changes to the landscape, people who were making their mark. They made very prominent tombs, they laid out fields, they dug out mines and quarries, they built large enclosures, they cleared huge areas of forest for their various projects, for their stone, earth and timber circles.

A hilltop called Caerloggas on the edge of Bodmin Moor shows the connection between people and landscape very clearly. Caerloggas is a tor, a distinctive rocky crag. This landmark was a focus of interest long before, in the mesolithic, but in the neolithic it was deliberately marked with a low ditched enclosure round it. Nature was literally circumscribed and incorporated into the world of human culture.[31]

Above all, it is the monuments that give people of the middle neolithic their distinctive character, marking them out from all other people. They speak with incredible eloquence and directness of the huge human effort involved in their creation. The scale of that effort is plain to see, and much greater than that of any

Bryn Celli Ddu, a monument revisited. In the first phase a henge was built with a fourteen-stone circle inside it. In the second phase a passage grave was built, covering the stone circle, with its revetment wall (crossing the photo) planted in the old henge ditch.

modern equivalent. The Millennium Dome is said to have cost £758 million (excluding decommissioning costs), which sounds a huge sum until it is compared with the current UK GDP, which stands at £811,550 million. In that context, the Millennium Dome – an eloquently meaningless monument – represents less than 0.1 per cent of the national endeavour.

Monument-building imposed itself on human consciousness in a very particular way. A linear monument such as a cursus separated from one another the landscapes on either side, but united the landscapes at either end. Instead of the landscape being an endless two- or three-dimensional continuum, it acquired a distinct man-made boundary, or a distinct pathway, depending on your point of view. Similarly, barrows and henges supplied points to act as man-made foci. A brand-new, self-conscious sense of place emerged; locations could be singled out for enhancement, and the marks became a commentary on the community's evaluation of the landscape; 'this place is important,' 'this place is taboo', 'this place is more important than that.' Because the monuments were self-evidently the work of people, their deterioration would also have become a measure of the passage of time, forging a link between generations and a link between landscape and time. The ageing monuments fed primitive concepts of history and historic time.

People of different times and different cultures have responded to landscape very differently. Until the Romantic movement wild nature was either ignored or frowned upon in Europe. It was only with Rousseau and Wordsworth that mountain scenery was attributed positive virtue – moral grandeur. How did people respond to landscape in 3000 BC? The traditional African response to landscape, except among the pygmies, is negative, even fearful. The traditional Native North American response is positive, even filial. Examples abound of tribes developing elaborate myths to prove their kinship with earth and sky. That the neolithic British were closer to this Amerindian mindset is shown in the way their monuments reflect the surrounding landscape. We saw earlier that Stonehenge, Knowlton and Avebury are maps of the larger landscape. The Castlerigg stone circle is made of lumpen boulders that stand up like miniatures of the real mountains that loom up behind them; the tilt of the Pentre Ifan capstone echoes the slope of Carn Meini in the distance; the Avebury henge bank replicates the flat crests of the chalk ridges in the middle distance; the circularity of Brodgar and Stenness reflects the bowl shape of the basin they stand in.[32]

The Orcadian stone circles are permeable, giving a sense of looking past or over the surrounding water to the distant hills.[33] There is also the extreme sensitivity shown in the siting of tombs. In some areas, as we have seen, people carefully positioned tombs so that they were visible on the skyline when viewed from the fields below.

In all of this, people were showing a heightened awareness of topography, the deepest feeling for landscape. And beyond this, by placing distinctive and enduring monuments at special points in the landscape, they were giving the landscape a sharper definition, making places much more memorable than before.

SUNSUPACHA: THE AGE OF INNOCENCE

Neolithic people were different from their predecessors in having an acute sense of time. The monuments bear witness to a profound awareness of several cycles of time. The orientations on sunrises and sunsets shows a consciousness of the daily cycle of the sun; the emphasis on midwinter and midsummer rising and setting positions shows an interest in marking the passage of the seasons. With this awareness came the capacity to keep a tally of the passing years, though we do not know if they did so. The observations of the moon at Stonehenge and several other sites show that people were interested in the more complex nineteen-year lunar cycle. With this would have come the capacity to count time in units of nineteen years, though again we do not know if they did so. They were concerned with far more than just the passage of secular time, and popular accounts of monuments implying that they are great stone clocks or calendars miss the point.

The poignant concern for the dead, the elaborate two-fold funeral ceremonies and the sometimes astonishingly grandiose tombs – all point to an interest in time on a more profound level than merely crossing off weeks on a calendar until it was time to plough, sow or harvest. The durability of the monuments suggests an interest in the long time-scale, in deep time, though this does not necessarily mean that the builders felt themselves as individuals to be enduring. The monuments that are the most conspicuous survival from 3000 BC were made to link the everyday world to the otherworld where the ancestors existed; they were intended to celebrate the time of the ancestors, deep time. Comparison with our twenty-first-century expectations of our own bodies, our cars, our cats and dogs, suggests that we are all capable of recognizing and accepting different time-scales in different contexts, though we may have lost the ability to function effectively in the longest time-scales.

There are some surviving archaic societies which nurture highly developed concepts of time, and they may throw light on the way people thought in 3000 BC. The Innuit hold the past in high regard, respecting age because it brings experience; the young learn skills by example from their elders, and children are routinely paired with adult mentors to help them learn. There are three Innuit pasts. There is a recent past, which includes time remembered, the years of one's own life. There is an historic past, reaching back to the landmark of the earliest contact with outsiders in AD 1800. Beyond and before that there is unmeasured time, though stories from that time may be detailed and specific.[34]

Bolivian descendants of the Inca in a similar way distinguish several different types of time, which they characterize as world ages. There is a mythic past, a distant time of darkness in which human life originated, followed by *sunsupacha*, an age of childhood or silliness. In this age a distinction between society and nature begins to emerge; it is the time of confrontation between people and animals, explored in myths that show how man and nature establish a new balance with each other. Later comes the colonized age, *jichhapacha*. For the Inca the colonization that began in 1532 meant a loss of control over their own history; time itself had been conquered, the clock of their civilization stopped. These world-ages represent a kind of mythic history of the Inca, in which they are ultimately robbed of their history. Some Bolivians see the present as a new age of disorder and chaos, after which the cycle of time will return things to the pre-colonial order.[35]

I can see in *sunsupacha*, the age of innocence, an equivalent to British neolithic culture in 3000 BC, but I cannot tell how conscious people were at that time of the dynamics of their relationship with nature or where that relationship would lead. It is also easy to see in *jichhapacha*, the colonized age, the arrival of Roman, Anglo-Saxon, Norman and American cultures, though that future could not have been anticipated in 3000 BC. It is, even so, clear from the way the monuments were built, to last for ever, that people must have had some concept of a distant future. That deep future was inseparable from the deep past; it was the time of the ancestors, an over-arching universe which framed all else. That idea of an identity between time past and time future is very different from the way most modern people think.

The many links between the neolithic and the preceding mesolithic ways of life show that there was a mindset geared to tradition. People kept a conscious tryst with the past in other ways too. The year 3000 BC was a pivotal moment, a step change, a

Winterbourne Stoke barrow cemetery near Stonehenge. The big long barrow's axis (74m long) determined where the later round barrows were to be built. Black-filled circle = bowl barrow; crossed circle = bell barrow; open circle = pond barrow; black-filled circle inside open circle = disc barrow.

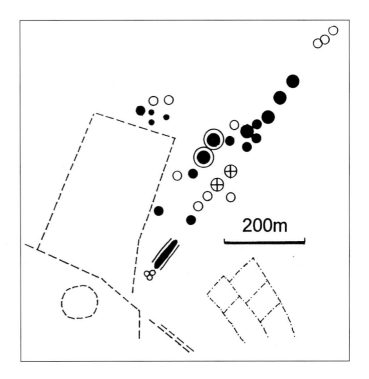

time of many adjustments – the first stone and timber circles were built, collective burial gave way to single graves and long barrows gave way to round – yet in spite of these revolutionary changes people carefully maintained links with the past. A 'disused' long barrow often became the focal point for a cemetery of round barrows. Not only is the long barrow the oldest in the cluster, but its long axis projected out across the landscape determined the line on which all the later barrows were to be built. The Haddenham long barrow 15 kilometres north of Cambridge was the focus for a major barrow field.[36] The finely preserved Winterbourne Stoke barrow cemetery just to the west of Stonehenge has a magnificent long barrow as its focus. The axis of the Alington Avenue long barrow at Dorchester similarly dictated the line of the evolving ceremonial complex that included the Maumbury Rings henge at one end and the Mount Pleasant superhenge at the other.[37] The past shaped the future. Yet linear barrow cemeteries did not evolve everywhere. They were common in the areas round Stonehenge and Maiden Castle, but not, for some reason, round Avebury.[38] The decommissioned monuments were no longer built after 3000 BC, but they were still held in high regard; even in the late neolithic they were respected as great ancient monuments, venerated as fundamental links with the time-world of the ancestors.

The long barrows were themselves falling away into ancestral time, but when built long before they respected still earlier structures and landmarks. The Easton Down long barrow was raised on a knoll which must have been a landmark before the barrow existed; the long barrow incorporated, monumentalized and accentuated the natural landmark. Within the Beckhampton Road long barrow is a lattice of fences marking out the work stints of different families who were responsible for building the mound. One of the fences swerves to pass round a sarsen stone. Even though it was about to be covered up by the fabric of the long barrow mound, its presence in the landscape as, perhaps, a significant landmark, had to be respected.[39] It was a respect for both time and place.

Godmanchester has no long barrow, but the way the ceremonial centre developed shows how the past was remembered and respected, then added to. The huge mid-neolithic enclosure oriented to the north-east was fitted with a cursus, and one bank of this was lined up exactly with the northern side of the enclosure, the other with its central axis. The cursus, as so often, led to the river. In the later neolithic two ring ditches were built, one beside the enclosure, one in the middle of the cursus. In the bronze age a small enclosure was laid out on the site of the large enclosure. Later still, probably during the Roman occupation, a temple was built at the entrance to the now-vanished large enclosure and next to a Roman crossroads, and a shrine was created right in the middle of the enclosure site.[40] It is unlikely that these repeated and insistent accentuations of the same site are accidental; the place was being remembered as a sacred place, in just the same way that the repeated redevelopment at Stonehenge was a series of re-enactments of a tryst with the ancestral past.

Sometimes archaeologists revisiting these places rekindle that tryst, and bring us face to face with a living person, an event, in a way, that melts the span of five thousand years that separates Us from Them. It was in 1978, while excavating one of the three neolithic enclosures on Hambledon Hill, that Roger Mercer found the skeleton of a youth lying face down underneath a spread of chalk just outside the Stepleton enclosure. He had been shot in the back with an arrow and un-ceremoniously buried where he fell. It was a shock to find, as the excavation progressed, that underneath the young man's skeleton was another, the remains of an infant, crushed to death when the young man fell on it.[41]

What had happened here? It may have been a tug of love, the youth attempting to retrieve his child from an estranged wife, only to be pursued and killed by enraged in-laws. Or was he perhaps a criminal, a thief trying to escape from justice by taking the child hostage and using it as a human shield? More likely he was an incidental casualty during a raid on the occupants of the Stepleton enclosure by a hostile tribe – mere collateral damage. He may have been killed when he made a run for it with his family, and found himself fatally slowed down by trying to carry one of his young siblings.

Archaeology can only tell us so much. The rest we are left to imagine.

TIME-PILGRIMS

People then may have looked much as we do today, but much of what went on their minds was different. Their skyward-looking ceremonial complexes, with their celestial alignments and their concern with measuring and celebrating the cycles of passing time, show a people preoccupied with their origins and their future, their place in the cosmos, desperate to make and maintain contact with gods and ancestors. They looked up to the heavens and down into the earth in search of legitimation and support. Each monument was a world pillar locking the three worlds together, the locus of an invisible waterspout that siphoned spiritual power up from deep inside the earth and down from highest heaven, and released it into the world of people.

The architects and custodians of some monuments succeeded in persuading outsiders that *their* monuments were specially sacred doorways to the otherworld offering some special numinous experience, and attracted attention from much further afield; as a result they became holy places of regional significance, and the communities living beside them were opened up to higher networks of exchange. More materials arrived from greater distances; they became foci for exotica.[42] In the remarkable centuries that followed 3000 BC Stonehenge became a spiritual and economic focus as rich and exotic as the shrine of St Thomas of Canterbury in the fifteenth century AD, pulling in pilgrims from far and wide and generating untold wealth.

The long distances involved in these journeys were also highly significant. Travel was slow and took a long time; the monuments you visited were not only remote geographically but remote in time. Journeying to a monument a long way away was in effect making a pilgrimage through time, a way of visiting the time of the ancestors and gaining access to the energizing spiritual forces that gathered about them, before returning renewed and strengthened to your own place and time.

Monuments and even natural landforms treated with monumental respect were set apart and made special. An understanding was evolving that culture and nature were identifiably different, but it is difficult to be sure whether people were acknowledging that the two were separate and divergent, or the converse, that they were asserting that they were inseparable, mutually dependent and convergent; there is also a third possibility, that they were noting that these were two significant aspects of a cosmos that was none the less coherent.[43] By putting together in a simple offering pit a shed antler and a crafted antler pick, people were making a profound and eloquent statement – but what was it? Was it 'Here is what I found, here what I made with it. What I make I can only make if I walk hand in hand with nature'? Or was it 'Here is the world I inhabit, here the better world I replace it with. I surpass nature'? I favour the former, partly because people living in simple societies today, such as the pygmies of the Congo, tend to see themselves and what they do as fully integrated with nature.

On the other hand, the first attempts at agriculture represent a conscious effort to transform nature, and the great monumental complexes transformed the British landscape for ever. The creation of Avebury has made it impossible for those of us who come after to see that location as anything other than a very special place – and that is nothing to do with the natural qualities of the landscape.[44]

Inevitably, we colour the pasts we discover. People have, and always have had, the capacity to rethink the realities which they inhabit. Models and images that are comprehensible to us because they represent the processes we have come across in other periods of history or in other places in our own time have a habit of registering

The Rudston Monolith, 8m tall, the focus of ceremonial activity in the Yorkshire Wolds.

with us, resonating, sounding true. But as our own condition changes, as we pass for instance from imperialism to post-imperialism, different models and images from the past swing into view. Understanding the past requires a critical evaluation of the way we turn it into history. Jean-Paul Sartre's view of the way societies evolve has led some archaeologists to interpret the mid-neolithic crisis in Brittany in dialectical terms.[45] *Society started simple, became more complex, with growing friction between sectional interests as newly-emerging bigmen came into conflict with established elders; this precipitated a mid-neolithic crisis that led to social collapse in the years around 3000 BC.*[46]

This interesting though not necessarily true scenario may bear transference across the Channel to the social, demographic and economic crisis that occurred in Britain at the same time, but only because the analogy is available. Different times produce different ranges of possibilities. What preoccupations have replaced Sartre's? Do we have socio-political agendas that propel us towards new interpretations?

My desire to re-create a neolithic past may originate in a psychological need for ultimate roots, in an extension of an early interest in family history or in the growing awareness that people have been settled in Britain for much longer than historians or prehistorians used to think, and also in a perceived threat – that of the loss of local and national identity with the growth of the European Union, and the loss of regional and continental identity with globalization. The quest for archaic and local roots is entirely explicable and natural in this context, but I need to ensure that it does not distort my view.

A recent and brilliant interpretation of the symbolism built into the architecture of Windmill Hill may be too 'pat',[47] simply because it reads the finished monument as a complete design, when in reality it evolved in stages, with the symbolic gestures – which are surely there – starting in the central arena and spilling over into the surrounding landscape. A perfect unity of interpretation, not only at Windmill Hill but at many other monuments too, may be a projection on the part of modern cultural aliens, who stumble on these sites long after their restless builders have gone under the hill.

Are we any nearer to understanding the nature of the crisis of 3000 BC? The population of Britain rose to around 900,000 in 3000 BC, then crashed to around 500,000.[48] What could have happened to halve the population? Population growth outstripping resources to produce a Malthusian population collapse is possible, though not likely, given the very low population density. An epidemic seems to me more likely; the Black Death of 1349–50 had a similar impact on British population levels, and we know that there were similar earlier plagues, such as the Great Plague of Justinian in AD 541. The problem is that the population density in northern Europe seems to have been too low for the effective transmission of plague in 3000 BC. A third possibility is environmental disaster. A climatic deterioration such as we know occurred at this time could have led to a string of poor harvests, death by famine, the abandonment of farmland and the regeneration of woodland. The effect of such a catastrophe would have been to stimulate an appeal to divine forces to intervene, and this is where the stimulus to build new kinds of monuments may have come from.

This was truly the new stone age. Ambitious and grandiose stone chamber tombs were still being built. Exciting new types of monument, the stone circles and timber circles, were being created for the first time. It was the age of the megaliths.[49] Ceremonial centres that had been evolving for several hundred years took on a new, higher status. A small number evolved into pan-British ceremonial centres, foci that pulled in people and valuable artefacts from a much larger area than before. These sites attracted prestigious trade objects; in the late neolithic and early bronze age they were to attract VIP burials. Often they were awe-inspiring sites; always they were treated to ambitious, original and awe-inspiring structures.

How would it have felt to be one of those privileged few who saw the last stone of Avebury hauled upright to make the design complete, saw the Stonehenge shaman planting a stake to mark the last moonrise in a lunar cycle; to be one of those who watched as willing workers built the opening phase of Silbury Hill? What would it have been like to see all those remarkable monuments when they were new? How would it have felt to walk through that ancient landscape and sense all the ecological wealth of the wildwood at my disposal? Now I walk in an open and hopelessly crowded landscape, with a night sky polluted by the street-lights of half a dozen nearby towns and all but the brightest stars dimmed. I see the whole great bowl of the sky and find my way by the Pole Star. I pick the pointers of the Plough, Merak and Dubhe, follow the invisible line they project across the sky, and five times the distance between them I find the Pole Star. How would it have been then, in Britain 3000 BC?

I walk through a neolithic landscape at nightfall, a quiet and empty forest still largely in its natural state, though with well-worn paths – the ancient wildwood with its deer, boar, woodmice, bats and toads, full of danger and adventure, a place to take you to other times. It is a vast landscape, many shades of green, this constantly changing yet unchanging world of the ancestors, seasonally waking and seasonally sleeping, a land without thought of cities, a land of a hundred homesteads with dimly sputtering fires punctuating the night.

I step into a forest clearing, a hollow crunching of twigs beneath my feet betraying a well-hidden pitfall trap. It would take my weight, though not a deer's. I step round it all the same and peer across the meadow at what at first I take to be a dwarf stone circle, but turns out to be only a group of sheep, the one changing into the other as I stare. I look up at a rag of sky, hemmed in by the forest canopy, a black mirror of the earth below, sparkling with what seem to be the home fires of countless farmsteads, the hearths of unnumbered ancestors.

Across on the far side of the clearing a big thatched log cabin floats in a pall of blue woodsmoke. I can see a flickering hearth fire of the living through the doorway, sending a shaft of light across the grass. A silhouetted woman carries a child across the bright square of the doorway. A boy sits by the fire stroking the elderly pet fox cradled in his lap.[50] Sparks fly up. A yapping terrier sends a couple of long-legged sheep sheltering under the eaves scuttling off across the grass.

Three men arrive, late home from a day's trapping, resplendent in striped fur coats, fur hats and leather leggings. They turn and smile at one another in expectation. Home. I catch their unexpectedly youthful faces and the glint of white teeth as they adjust the weight of their creaking backpacks, fabricators, knives, tools and talismans clinking rhythmically on their belts, arrows rattling softly in their quivers. They trudge across the clearing towards the house, shouting a greeting. The terrier barks.

Above the smoke-wreathed house the dark crowns of oaks move slightly. Above the canopy of foliage a hill rises up, dark against a dark sky, with the ghostly pallor of a long barrow standing prominent on its rim. Next to it is a new round barrow, paler yet, like the crown of a monstrous skull re-emerging from some ancestral burial in deep time. Even on moonless nights like this the barrows can be seen, the bald chalk reflecting every glint of starlight.

The bright ancestral home fires that mark Orion are almost where they will be in five thousand years, but Polaris is not the North Star. The next two stars of the Plough, Phad and Megrez, become the pointers and I follow the invisible line joining them three times the distance between them out into space, to find Thuban in the constellation of the Dragon, a star brighter now than it will be in five thousand years, and held in awe as the pivot of the sky by the city astronomers in Mesopotamia.[51] To King Sargon it will be 'the Crown of Heaven'. The starlight that will glimmer down from Thuban in the twenty-first century will not start on its way towards the Earth until the close of the seventeenth century AD. Much further off, in the next spiral arm of our galaxy, there are stars whose light begins on its way in 3000 BC. When I look, in the twenty-first century, at the Ring Nebula in Lyra, or the Rosette Nebula, or the Poop of the old constellation of Argo with its cluster of five hundred stars near Sirius, or the dying red giant BD+303639, I am seeing the universe as it was in 3000 BC. Images from the Hubble telescope show me gigantic gas clouds in the Omega Nebula

The East Kennet long barrow near Avebury. It was meant to be seen like this, on the skyline.

giving birth to stars in 3000 BC. As I scan the sky, I realise I can *see* the distant past I have been looking for. The idea that to travel through space is to travel through time is a neolithic idea, after all; to travel far is to travel to the time of the ancestors.

The door bangs shut unexpectedly, the square of light is snuffed out and the sound of laughter comes from inside the house. Someone begins chanting a song, a ballad perhaps about the unmeasured time of the ancestors, half-remembered, half-imagined, a keening for a time that somehow transcends the present, enveloping singer and listener in a web that joins distant past to distant future. A baby cries as the song winds on. The homely smells of wood smoke, stew and beer hang on the night air.

NOTES

PREFACE

1. Stuiver and Pearson 1993.
2. Ucko 1995.

CHAPTER ONE

1. Whittle gives 2800–2500 BC as a likely date range for the building of Silbury, but admits that a date as early as 3000 BC is possible for the initial phase.

CHAPTER TWO

1. Parker Pearson 1993, 25.
2. Goudie 1977, 175 shows three different estimates, but all in the range quoted here, 30–40m lower than now.
3. Another is that it was an integral part of the culture of the mesolithic hunter-gatherers that they moved across the tundras and through the forests without significantly altering them. *Their* spoor is hard to detect, unlike that of their neolithic successors.
4. Roberts 1988.
5. Taylor 1980.
6. This is based on a uniquely detailed study of tree-rings from Lancashire for every year for the period 3400–3000 BC: Baillie and Brown 2002.
7. Mitchell 1977 argues from evidence on the east coast of Ireland that there was a high sea level at about +4m in 3000 BC, but other authorities such as Jones and Keen 1993 see the evidence overall as indicating –4m. Some other researchers, such as Schofield 1960 and Morner 1969, argue for –2m or –3m: see Goudie 1977. The Irish evidence is an anomaly and I suggest that it may point to a specific and relatively local event, such as a landslide tsunami in the Irish Sea.
8. Castleden 1996; Robinson 1999.
9. Jones and Keen 1993, 265.
10. Baillie 1989; Baillie and Brown 2002. The major volcanic eruptions indicated by sulphate peaks in ice cores were in 3201, 3192, 3190, 3188, 3184, 3181, 3179, 3177 and 3173 BC – far more frequent than in the previous two hundred years.
11. Roberts 1988, 123.
12. Roberts 1988, 124. Roberts refers to this as 'a switching-off of the Atlantic Ocean conveyor'.
13. Baillie and Brown 2002.
14. Bennett 1989.
15. Roberts 1988, 194–8.
16. Yew charcoal was found in the Quanterness tomb (Renfrew 1979).
17. Renfrew 1979.
18. Roberts 1988, 194–5.
19. Brown 2000, 54–7.
20. Brown 2000, 57.
21. Moore 1997, 34–8.
22. Parker Pearson 1993, 26–7.
23. Castleden 1993, 28–33.
24. Parker Pearson 1993, 27.
25. Piggott 1954; Smith 1981.
26. Allen 2000, 9–26.

27. For example the tombs at Trefignath, Bryn yr Hen Bobl, Barclodiad y Gawres, Dyffryn Ardudwy: see Lynch *et al.* 2000, 45.
28. Austin 2000, 63.
29. Coles 1978.
30. Drewett and Hamilton 1999.
31. Godwin 1944.
32. Evans in Simpson (ed) 1971.
33. As described by Jensen (1982) for the Danish neolithic.
34. The evidence specifically came from Llyn Mire. Pollen evidence from Hockham Mere in East Anglia tells a similar story. Smith 1981; Godwin 1944.
35. www.ifb.net/webit/balbridi.htm.
36. Musty 1991b.
37. Robinson 2000.
38. Roberts 1988, 195.
39. Burl 1979.
40. Whittle 1977; Smith 1981; Thomas 1991, 26.
41. Musty 1985. *Scolytus scolytus* carries the spores of the fungus responsible for elm disease. Robinson in Fairbairn (ed) 2000, 30–1 argues that the closeness of the wing cases to the elm decline horizon has been exaggerated, citing (though courteously not naming) sources where that distance has been minimized. Musty 1985 does indeed give 10cm instead of 20cm – but Robinson's criticism of this 'improving' of evidence misses the more important point, which is that the soil column shows disease-spreading beetles in the right environments at roughly the right times to cause outbreaks of elm disease.
42. Smith 1981; Lynch *et al.* 2000, 44.
43. Field 1996.
44. Thomas 1991.
45. Topping 1996.
46. Loveday 1998.
47. Nash 1997.
48. Austin 2000, 63–78.

CHAPTER THREE

1. Sharples and Sheridan 1992; Whittle 231–3.
2. Parker Pearson 1993, 56.
3. Whittle 1997, 235.
4. It is one of the endless delights of neolithic studies that much of the information can be interpreted in more than one way. The great enigma of Stonehenge is, in this as in so many other ways, a symbol of the period.
5. For details of Auchenlaich see 'Neolithic farmhouse found in Scotland', *British Archaeology* 62, 5.
6. Champion 1984, 14; Hodder 1990, 119–22; Whittle 1996, 232, 238.
7. Curwen 1937, 75-7, 62.
8. Houlder 1976; Lynch *et al.* 2000, 50–1.
9. Anon 2000a.
10. Hodder 1990; Sherratt 1990; Cooney 1997, 25.
11. For example Cowell and Innes 1994 write of neolithic settlements on Merseyside in the same locations as mesolithic.

CHAPTER FOUR

1. For example Burl 1987, 32.
2. Bradley 1993.
3. Pollard 1997, 6–7.
4. Fairbairn 2000, 110–11, 119.
5. Woodburn 1982, quoted in Bradley 1993.
6. Miles 1997.
7. Whittle 1990.
8. A pitfall trap, presumed to be a deer trap, was found in Wigtownshire; it dates to about 2500 BC (Sheridan 1996).
9. Darvill 1982.
10. Jensen 1982, 98.
11. Parker Pearson 1993, 38–40.
12. Jensen 1982, 99.
13. Smith 1981.
14. Thomas 1991.
15. Cross-ploughing was standard, but at Gwithian in Cornwall the furrows were simply reploughed in the opposite direction. The v-shaped furrows that have survived lean to one side; the ploughman was trying to make the soil turn over (Rees 1978).
16. Fowler 1971.
17. Smith 1981.
18. Although no actual remains of pulses have survived anywhere in Britain, the impression of a bean was made out on a late neolithic sherd found at Ogmore in West Glamorgan: so beans were grown. McLaren 2000, 98.
19. Thomas 1991, 20–1.

20. Yarnton in Oxfordshire, Dorney in Bucks and Cople in Beds, quoted by Robinson 2000, 86.

21. Brown 1996, 22. The number of barley impressions on pottery made locally at Windmill Hill was far greater than the number of impressions found on pottery imported from the Bath area (Whittle 1977).

23. Sharples 1992, 323–4.

24. Sharples 1992, 326–7.

25. www.ifb.net/webit/balbridi.htm.

26. Darvill 1982.

27. Evidence from bones at West Kennet long barrow.

28. Simpson 1971.

29. Richards 2000.

30. Anati 1964, 34.

31. Parker Pearson 1993, 40.

32. A neolithic pot base from Italy bears the impression of one of these woven mats, which would have made turning the pot during manufacture much easier (Hurcombe 2000).

33. Hurcombe 2000, 155.

34. We have, for example, evidence of cattle bones at the settlement of Clegyr Boia in Pembrokeshire (Lynch et al. 2000, 45).

35. Pollard 1997, 8–9; there is no trace of bullocks in Denmark either (Jensen 1982, 101). The earliest ox yoke found in Britain, at Loch Neill, dates from 1750 BC (Sheridan 1996).

36. Jensen 1982, 101.

37. Spratt, in Barker 1982.

38. Piggott 1954.

39. Beef at Midhowe, mutton at Blackhammer and Rowiegar, venison at Knowe of Ramsay and Knowe of Yarso (Piggott 1954). Proportions of bones give a rough idea of the relative importance of different stock. At Avebury the proportions were cattle 66 per cent, sheep 16 per cent, pig 18 per cent; it seems to be significant that at lower-status sites, at least in Wessex, there were fewer pigs and at higher-status sites there were more (Smith in Simmons and Tooley 1981).

40. Lynch et al. 2000, 45.

41. Piggott 1954.

42. Piggott 1954.

43. Jensen 1982, 100.

44. Musty 1991a.

45. Parker Pearson 1993, 40.

46. www.eng-h.gov.uk/archrev96_7/hamhill.htm

47. Rackham 1986, 330.

48. Parker Pearson 1993, 40.

49. Thomas 1991, 52–5.

50. Barley cakes radiocarbon dated to 3500 BC (Dinely and Dinely 2000).

51. Musty 1988.

52. Dinely and Dinely 2000.

CHAPTER FIVE

1. Lynch et al. 2000 refers specifically to Wales, but the problem is the same elsewhere in Britain.

2. Lynch et al. 2000, 46–8.

3. Burgess 1980, 161; like all the figures it is highly speculative, but a death rate of 40/1000 is what we would expect in a very poor LEDC (Less Economically Developed Country) today.

4. Brothwell 1971.

5. Quoted by Jensen 1982, 82. Burgess (1980, 162) gives more optimistic figures: 60 per cent surviving to 25, 30 per cent to 40, around medieval levels.

6. Burgess 1980, 162.

7. Burgess 1980, 171.

8. Burgess 1980, 172. But monuments may have been built with far smaller work-forces than is generally assumed; see Castleden 1987, 212; Castleden 1993, 154, 157, 254–5; and see below, Chapter 9 note 50.

9. Burgess 1989. Burgess offers these estimates cautiously, admitting a large error range of +/- 250,000.

10. Eday had a population of 944 in the early nineteenth century. It fell to 198 in 1961. Eday has eleven tombs implying a neolithic population of 220, very close to the 1961 figure (Renfrew 1979).

11. Renfrew 1979.

12. For example Tilley 1996, 163-6.

13. Whittle 1977.

14. Service 1971.

15. Renfrew 1979. Pierpoint (1980) uses the word 'nascent' to describe early neolithic society in Yorkshire.

16. Burgess 1980, 166 is representative of this line of thought.
17. Burgess 1980, 171.
18. Jensen 1980, 110.
19. Pierpoint 1980 describes this society as 'developed', but that term might be better applied to the early bronze age society that emerged at the end of the third millennium.
20. Status is here measured by care in burial, number and type of grave goods, as in Pierpoint 1980.
21. Pierpoint 1980 proposes children, adult men and women and adolescents, and mature men. Children were often sharply distinguished in death, as the provision of entirely separate cists for cremated children at Nympsfield shows (Thomas 1991, 120–2).
22. Morton Fried 1967.
23. Jensen 1982, 109–10.
24. Renfrew 1973; Burgess 1980, 171–5.
25. Burgess 1980, 174–5 suspects a division of power in the late neolithic, with priests taking responsibility for monuments and ritual, leaving the chiefs to deal with socio-political, diplomatic and military matters. I prefer to think of something less formal than the development of two separate power élites.
26. Renfrew 1973.
27. Renfrew 1979.
28. Harding 2000, 31-3; Bell 1992; Osborn 1989.
29. Savory 1980.

CHAPTER SIX

1. Rackham 1980, 249 and 280.
2. Taylor 1979, 2.
3. Wilkinson, Clapham and Clare 1997.
4. Taylor 1979, 8–9.
5. Taylor 1979, 7.
6. Sheridan and Davis 1998, 148–52.
7. Taylor 1969.
8. Taylor 1979, 36–7.
9. Taylor 1979, 19.
10. Rackham 1986, 250–1. The scarp-foot tracks nearly always run along the Upper Greensand outcrop, not the clay as Rackham says. The Greensand roads would have been almost as dry as the chalk roads, but not quite so easy to navigate because they cross more densely forested land. Many of the Anglo-Saxon spring-line villages in south-east England were later founded on the already ancient scarp-foot road.
11. Taylor 1979, 12; Rackham 1986, 251.
12. Waddington 1998.
13. Bradley and Edmunds 1993, 198.
14. Harding 2000b, 33–8, 42.
15. Earle and Sallnow 1991, 6.
16. Taylor 1979, 12–13.
17. Loveday 1998, 27.
18. Barclay et al. 1996, 16.
19. Manley 1989, 62. Similar technical problems often result in similar solutions, as Colin Renfrew reminded me in 1983, but herringbone masonry is relatively uncommon in the neolithic, and in later periods too, so its appearance in different parts of neolithic Britain suggests contact.
20. Bakker et al. 1999.
21. Castleden 1993, 154.
22. Williams and Erlean 2002. The Strangford Lough boat was made around 3200 BC.
23. The crossing places would appear to have been at Owston Ferry on the Trent and Brigg on the Ancholme – Van de Noort and Ellis 1998; Ellis and Crowther, 1990.
24. Castleden 1987, 80–1.
25. Jones 2000.
26. Jones and Brown 2000, 176.
27. Castleden 1987, 81–2.
28. Jones 2000.
29. Jones and Brown 2000, 176: evidence of magnetic susceptibility measurements.
30. Jones and Brown 2000, 177.
31. Thomas 1991.
32. Thomas 1991.
33. Castleden 1987, 83–4.
34. Lynch et al. 2000 gives 3400–2500 BC as approximate dates for the Peterborough style.
35. Castleden 1987, 84.
36. Lynch 2000, 112.
37. Thomas 1991.
38. For example Henshall 1985; Ritchie 1983.
39. Renfrew 2000, 12.
40. Simpson 1999, 148.
41. Renfrew 1979; Renfrew 2000, 8–9; Cleal and McSween 1999.

42. Hedges 1984; Renfrew 2000, 10.
43. Garwood 1999.
44. Cleal and MacSween 1999.
45. Jones 2000.
46. Parker Pearson 1993, 74.
47. Garwood 1999.
48. Castleden 1987, 87.
49. Although there are many disagreements among scholars about Grooved Ware, there is a strong consensus that Orkney was the source of it, for example Cleal and MacSween 1999.
50. Cleal and MacSween 1999.
51. Lynch 2000, 112.
52. Parker Pearson 1993.
53. Parker Pearson 1993; Field 1997, 55.
54. Sherratt 1998, 135–7.
55. Sherratt 1998, 136.
56. Cooney 1998.
57. It is a little like modern Britain; there are those who have honours and privileges, those who expect and seek them, those who bestow them, those who neither have nor expect them. Today there are bewildered outsiders to whom honours mean nothing at all, but outsiders would have had no place in neolithic society; archaic societies do not allow outsiders to exist.
58. Tilley 1994.
59. Cooney 1996 emphasizes this early interest in paths in the context of the Irish neolithic, but what he says is equally applicable to the British.
60. See also Ingold 1986, 153.
61. Aaltonen 2000. The footprints have been dated to 3000 BC by OSL.
62. For example the strip maps of John Ogilby.
63. As a result, imposing triangles or any other geometry on modern maps of journeys undertaken in the neolithic (as in Heath 1998) is, however fascinating, entirely anachronistic.
64. Wallington 1999.

CHAPTER SEVEN

1. Herity and Eogan 1987, 41.
2. One was laid under a piece of wood next to the Sweet Track (Parker Pearson 1993, 34).
3. Parker Pearson 1993, 36.
4. Cooney 1998, 110–13.
5. Herity and Eogan 1987, 39.
6. Cooney 1998, 117.
7. At Boxgrove in Sussex hunters 500,000 years ago left scores of flint tools next to butchered animal bones.
8. Reasons for believing the Windover mines are neolithic: 1) The terraceway leading up the escarpment from the east may be medieval, but it is undated and appears to turn and pass among the flint mines, to gain access to the scarp-crest behind the mines. 2) The road up from the west may have provided access to the late quarry very close to the summit, and be nothing to do with the neolithic pits. 3) The flint mines constitute a cluster of conical pits separated by cones of waste: an 'egg-box landscape' very similar to Grime's Graves. 4) They occupy a classic, dramatic, false-crested location commanding a wide view. 5) There are two long barrows of undisputed neolithic date very close at hand.
9. Technically the Peacehaven Beds of the Newhaven Member.
10. These sheet flint seams lie between the Rottingdean and Old Nore Marls.
11. Whittle 1996.
12. Field 1996.
13. Ashwin 1996.
14. Russell 1996, 73.
15. See map in Russell 1996, 73.
16. Scarre 1998.
17. Champion et al. 1984, 165.
18. Champion 163.
19. Pitts 1996.
20. Bradley and Edmunds 1993, 45.
21. Bradley 1993, 194.
22. Lynch et al. 2000, 55–6; Houlder 1961.
23. Bradley and Edmunds 1993, 45.
24. The calculation is based on the 450 tonnes of worked flakes visible in the scree, and the assumption that 6–10 kg of waste would have been produced in the manufacture of a 1kg axe. Since the estimate is based on the visible industrial debris, it is an underestimate of the factory's output (Quartermaine and Claris 1986).
25. Bradley and Suthren 1990.

26. Some people doubt the ability of our ancestors to organize transport on this scale, and occasionally propose that the Great Langdale rock was spread about the country by an ancient ice sheet. But well-researched maps of glacial erratics from Cumbria are available and they show no relationship at all between the distribution of Cumbrian axes and the distribution of Lakeland erratics (for example Cummins 1978). This controversy bears similarities to the long-running controversy surrounding the Stonehenge bluestones, which mercifully falls in the late neolithic and need not concern us here.

27. Cummins 1974.

28. Lynch *et al.* 2000, 58.

29. Darvill 1989; Lynch *et al.* 2000, 57-8.

30. Sheridan and Davis 1998, 148–52.

31. This is true also in France: Patton 1993.

32. Bradley 1993, 178, 187.

33. The latest radiocarbon date for Langdale is around 3050 BC, for the finishing site on Thunacar Knott (Bradley and Edmunds 1993, 180).

34. Cummins 1978.

35. Houlder 1961, 138; Lynch *et al.* 2000, 56.

36. Cunliffe 2002.

37. Darvill 1982.

38. Herity and Eogan 1987, 93.

39. The idea of a basketwork pannier comes from an axehead that was found in an Irish bog inside an oval basket made of alder rods and probably rushes (Herity and Eogan 1987, 37). The idea of a pannier or backpack comes from the Iceman (Spindler 1994). The likeliest cross-section shape for the backpack is oval.

40. Bradley 1993, 169.

41. Bradley 1993, 177.

42. Burl 1999, 179.

CHAPTER EIGHT

1. Lynch 1998, 62.

2. Parker Pearson 1993, 40.

3. Parker Pearson 1993, 46.

4. Whittle and Wysock 1998. The rapid rates of disintegration were found experimentally, in woodland near Seattle.

5. Margaret Cox's experiment, as described in *Bones of Contention*, broadcast by Channel 4 on 27 February 2001.

6. Parker Pearson 1993, 47.

7. Bradley and Edmunds 1993, 178.

8. Castleden 1987.

9. At Isbister on Orkney people squatted outside the tomb cutting decaying flesh from corpses in preparation for the burial of clean bones inside the tomb; Hammond 2000.

10. Hammond 2000, reporting the work of Mary Baxter. There are modern ethnographic parallels, for example in Madagascar and on the African mainland.

11. Parker Pearson 1993, 41.

12. Bradley 1993, 5.

13. Parker Pearson 1993, 45.

14. Tilley 1994.

15. Hambledon, Abingdon, Maiden Castle, Robin Hood's Ball, Combe Hill, Whitesheet ; see Thomas 1991, 36-8.

16. Parker Pearson 1993, 45.

17. Bradley 1984.

18. Whittle and Wysocki 1998.

19. Tilley 1994.

20. Herity and Eogan 1989, 76–7.

21. Postpit A: pine charcoal HAR-455 9130+180 bc (8820–7730 cal BC). Postpit B: also pine charcoal HAR-456 8090+140 bc (7480–6590 cal BC). See Cleal *et al.* 1995, 7–8 for a summary of the Stonehenge radiocarbon dates. The 'treehole' to the west of pits A, B and C may have been another postpit; it is in the same line and about equidistant.

22. Postpit WA9580: OxA-4920, OxA-4919, GU-5109, three dates giving a mean date midway between the dates of pits A and B. It is some distance to the east of the other postpits and does not lie on the same straight line.

23. Cleal *et al.* 1995, 43–56.

24. Bradley 1993, 35–7. In Denmark it has been noted that neolithic settlements occupy sites that were settled in the mesolithic too (Jensen 1980).

25. A mesolithic settlement dating from 6500 BC was excavated and therefore in a sense discovered by lobsters under 13 metres of water in the Solent. This centre for flint-

working was in a clearing in an oak-hazel forest (Anon 2002: *BA* 64, 5).

26. Bradley 1993, 14.

27. Lynch *et al.* 2000, 63.

28. Thomas 182.

29. Thomas 182.

30. Thomas 1991, 105.

31. Parker Pearson 1993, 41.

32. Lynch *et al.* 1993, 63.

33. As Mike Parker Pearson suggests (Parker Pearson 1993, 50).

34. Parker Pearson 1993, 55.

35. Thomas 1991, 107.

36. Borwick 2001. The Lanhill chambered long mound excavated by Keiller and Piggott in the 1930s was found to contain nine members of one family. Seven of them had the same rare skull features, proving that they belonged to the same family (Hayman 1997, 147).

37. Shand and Hodder 1990.

38. Shand and Hodder 1990.

39. Thomas 1999, 151.

40. Darvill 1982; Saville 1983. Lynch *et al.* 2000, 67 see the lateral or transepted chamber layout as a French import, but the type could as easily have resulted from a cross-fertilization of the earthen long barrow tradition established in Wessex and Sussex and the passage grave tradition that developed in Wales, Ireland and Scotland.

41. Thomas 1991, 32.

42. Lynch *et al.* 2000, 70.

43. For example, the Tumulus-St-Michel at Carnac in Brittany started off as a small round chamber tomb, which then had a secondary long cairn added to it. The tomb of Lont in Denmark consists of a series of four initially separate round chamber tombs finally covered by a large rectangular mound (Bradley 1998, 56 and 65).

44. MacKie 1998.

45. Thomas 1991, 39; Corcoran 1972, 32.

46. Lynch *et al.* 2000, 75.

47. The Alfriston oval barrow in Sussex is, as far as I know, the last of the long barrows to have been built, in 3050 BC (Castleden 1991, 183). This transitional type, halfway between long and round barrow, sometimes had a quarry ditch wrapped round one end, as at Thickthorn Down, Jullieberrie's Grave, Alfriston and Site XI at Dorchester (Bradley and Edmunds 1993, 174–5).

48. Parker Pearson 1993, 48.

49. Brewster 1984. The situation at Garton Slack was slightly different, in that the long barrow there had a round barrow built over it in the bronze age. Brewster 1976.

50. Thomas 1999, 155.

51. Ashwin 1996.

52. Woodward and Woodward 1996; Anon 1979.

53. Thomas 1991, 185–6.

54. Edwards 1985, 19–20.

CHAPTER NINE

1. They are a fairly recent discovery and it is likely that more examples will come to light. In 1950 only eight were known, in 2000 over sixty (Kinnes 1998, 184).

2. Kinnes 1998, 185.

3. The causewayed enclosure idea had been borrowed originally from mainland Europe (Bradley 1993, 73–81; Scarre 255; Whittle 1996, 268).

4. I noticed in 1980 that Colin Renfrew's notional boundaries for Rousay (Renfrew 1973) worked quite well except in the neighbourhood of the Knowes of Yarso, Ramsay and Lairo. These three tombs are very close together, giving Ramsay an impossibly narrow sliver of territory. I visited Rousay in 1985 and in a remarkable piece of synchronicity met Colin Renfrew emerging from the Knowe of Lairo, where he agreed, literally on the spot, that the Thiessen polygons had not given us the answer.

5. Castleden 1996, 127–9.

6. Thomas 1999, 201–2.

7. Peter Drewett interprets the domestic debris in the western ditch as referring to a domesticated landscape that lay to the *east* of the enclosure (1994, 19), which does not seem to me to be at all logical. It also seems to me more natural to assume that the enclosure related to the landscape which it overlooked and from which it was both visible and accessible, i.e. the downland dipslope

valleys to the south-west. But, in any case, Drewett's model is an interesting and useful one, and the time sequence is plausible, with The Trundle in the west yielding the earliest radiocarbon date, 4100 BC, and Combe Hill the latest, 3400 BC.

8. Plans of Hambledon Hill are available in many publications, for example in Manley 1989, 41.

9. Bradley 1986. The interpretation given here is very much Richard Bradley's.

10. Bewley 1994.

11. Bewley 1994, drawing on the work of Roger Palmer.

12. Edmonds 1999, 137.

13. Plan in Burl 1999.

14. Burl 1999, 34.

15. For example Thom 1967.

16. Castleden 1991, 92, 145 and 152.

17. Castleden 1991, 195, 393.

18. John Aubrey (1862) recorded a seventeenth-century local legend that King Sil was buried on horseback under the mound. By the nineteenth century the legend had changed the burial to that of a life-sized gold statue of the king. Many archaeologists nevertheless believe that Silbury *is* a burial mound, among them Stone (1958), Fowler (1968), Dyer and Grinsell (1971).

19. Marlborough Mount (Dames 1976, 135), the Lewes Mount in Sussex (Castleden 1983, 152–6) and Clifford Hill in Northamptonshire (Castleden 1992, 146). Doubt has recently been cast on the antiquity of the Marlborough Mount.

20. A suite of radiocarbon dates shows that the primary mound may have been made as early as 3500 BC, but more likely 3000 BC, with the final mound completed some time after 2500 BC (Whittle 1997a, 25–6; 139).

21. Holgate 1987.

22. Whittle 1990.

23. Dames's attractive fertility hypothesis of 1976 has been upstaged by the palaeo-environmental study of Evans *et al.* 1993.

24. At Maiden Castle and Etton huge numbers of cattle bones, 2,300 and 3,000 respectively, were found (Sharples 2000, 107).

25. Castleden 2000.

26. Though not always. It is remarkable that on Orkney the Ring of Brodgar was fitted with a full-blown quarry ditch, dug painfully out of Old Red Sandstone – more Orcadian showing-off?

27. Burl 1999, 28.

28. Environmental detail from Evans *et al.* 1985.

29. Sharples 2000, 113.

30. Gibson 1998. Gibson has done much to put timber circles on the map as a major class of neolithic monument.

31. Barclay (1996) is a sceptic.

32. Letts 2001.

33. Schreudos 2001.

34. Incense cup from Wilsford G8, Wiltshire, illustrated in Stone 1958, pl. 40.

35. Cleal *et al.* 1995, 150.

36. Lockyer 1906.

37. Stukeley 1740.

38. Scott and Phillips 1999. The chambers of the two Clava cairns were temporarily roofed in to make observation easier. Only the north-eastern cairn was unobstructed by the trees that surround the site, but direct light at the midwinter sunset lit up one complete stone, which seems to have been deliberately selected for its circularity; it is as round as the sun that lights it.

39. MacKie 1998.

40. Newham 1972; Burl 1987, 67–70.

41. Now lost to gravel extraction, this enclosure stood at TL: 255709. The posts were 36 to 38 metres apart. An antler in the ditch provided a radiocarbon date of 2950 BC. Though it could be argued that the many possible lines drawn among twenty-four points are bound to include some that will hit a significant rising or setting position by chance, those that do were marked by special ritual deposits of antlers or ox skulls (Castleden 1992, 22–3).

42. Childe 1930, 164.

43. Wilson 1993, 256.

44. Parker Pearson 1993, 59.

45. This survives as a modern domestic superstition: if you let the sun shine on your fire, it will put it out.

46. Darvill 1997a, 179–80.

47. Burl 1987, 37; Castleden 1993, 33.

48. K. Brown 1997, 134.

49. Bradley 1984.
50. At my (uncredited) suggestion these were the specific tasks undertaken by the team of volunteers gathered for Cynthia Page's award-winning BBC TV programme *Secrets of Lost Empires*, which proved beyond any question that a small community could indeed have built Stonehenge. My contribution to the project also went unacknowledged in Richards and Whitby 1997.
51. Thomas 1991, 182.
52. Thomas 1999, 177–8.
53. Castleden 1993, 223.
54. Whittle *et al.* 1999.

CHAPTER TEN

1. Renfrew 1987, 6.
2. Renfrew 1987, 68.
3. Evans 1933.
4. Herity and Eogan 1989, 54–5.
5. Thomas 1999, 93.
6. Herity and Eogan 1987, 62–4, 73–6.
7. Bradley 1993.
8. Burl 1999, 41.
9. Bradley 1992, 173. The same sort of thing was happening in Brittany, where carved slabs found embedded in the structures of three different tombs 8 km apart can be fitted together to make a single standing stone (Parker Pearson 1993, 34).
10. The Trundle, Flagstones, Thickthorn, ?Offham, Combe Hill.
11. Castleden 1992, 191.
12. Woodward 1988. The radiocarbon date of 4080 bp falls on another ripple in the conversion graph and is therefore ambiguous; it could be as early as 2860 BC or as late as 2600 BC.
13. Pryor 2001, 168–71.
14. Piggott 1954.
15. Clark 1963.
16. Castleden 1993, 71.
17. The stag drawing is illustrated in Shepherd 1980, 60.
18. The German cist-grave is at Leuna-Gohlitzsch, Sachsen-Anhalt, and dates from 3000 BC (Sherratt 1994).

19. Spirals, semi-spirals and tendrils were painted in red on the walls and ceilings of the Maltese Hypogeum (Ridley 1976). Red branching lines were painted on the stones of the Pedralta tomb in Portugal. A hunting scene including deer, archers and dogs is depicted again in red at the Orca dos Juncias tomb (Mohen 1989, 248).
20. Castleden 1992, 254.
21. Lynch 1998.

CHAPTER ELEVEN

1. Renfrew 1973.
2. Parker Pearson and Richards 1994; Richards 1990; Richards 1993.
3. For example Patton 1993.
4. Whittle 1977.
5. Whittle and Wysock 1998. Similar 'archer's arms' were noted in both Wales and Wessex.
6. Wilson 1851, building on Thomsen 1848.
7. Morse 1999.
8. Rolleston and Greenwell 1877.
9. Parsons 2002.
10. Parker Pearson 1993, 52–3.
11. Jones, Martin and Pilbeam 1992, 402.
12. Burl 1987.
13. Burl 1987, 31-32; Jones, Martin and Pilbeam 1992, 402.
14. Kupferberg 1979, 24.
15. Although Long *et al.* 2000 challenge this finding.
16. Spindler 1994.
17. Spindler 1994, 138.
18. Spindler 1994, 86–145.
19. Thomas 1999, 88.
20. Thomas 1999, 229.
21. Vatcher and Vatcher 1973; Castleden 1993, 28–32.
22. Keeley 1996.
23. Manley 1999, 44.
24. Scarre 1998, quoting Wahl and Konig 1987, Courtin 1974 and Polet *et al.* 1995.
25. Edmonds 1999, 141–4.
26. Pollard 1997, 15.
27. Pryor 2001, 55–65.
28. The Iceman died, perhaps of hypothermia and shock, after being wounded in the

shoulder by an arrow – possibly murder, but equally possibly a hunting accident, a death by 'friendly fire'.

29. James 1999.

30. Jackson 1995. Miss Jackson tells me she wanted to test whether the neolithic features were still present in modern Wessex feet, but the local health authority took the view that it would be unethical to let her study patients' x-rays, even anonymously.

31. Bradley 1993, 28–9.

32. Bradley 1998, 122–3.

33. Richards 1996.

34. Anawak 1996.

35. Condori 1996.

36. Hodder and Shand 1988.

37. Castleden 1992, 93.

38. Woodward and Woodward 1996.

39. Thomas 1999, 203–4.

40. Parker Pearson 1993, 65.

41. Parker Pearson 1993, 28.

42. Needham 2000.

43. Bradley 2000.

44. Bradley 2000 as ever provokes an interesting debate on this complex of issues.

45. Sartre 1976.

46. Patton 1993, 191.

47. Whittle *et al.* 1999.

48. Burgess 1989.

49. Cunliffe 2002.

50. Brewster 1984. A child was buried with an aged fox, assumed to be a pet, in the Whitegrounds cairn in North Yorkshire.

51. *Encyclopedia Britannica* entry on precession of the equinoxes. In 13,000 BC Vega was the Pole Star. In AD 13,000 Vega will be the Pole Star once more. Also www.dibonsmith.com.

BiBLiOGRApHy

Abbreviations:

Ant = Antiquity

Arch. J. = Archaeological Journal

BA = British Archaeology

CA = Current Archaeology

HMSO = Her Majesty's Stationery Office

PPS = Proceedings of the Prehistoric Society

PSAS = Proceedings of the Society of Antiquaries of Scotland

RCHME = Royal Commission for Historical Monuments (England)

SAC = Sussex Archaeological Collections

Aaltonen, G. 2000. 'Sands of time', *National Trust Magazine* 91, 36–9

Adkins, R. and Jackson, R. 1978. *Neolithic axes from the River Thames*, London: British Museum

Allen, M.J. 1997. 'Environment and land use: the economic development of the communities who built Stonehenge (an economy to support the stones)', in Cunliffe, B. and Renfrew, C. (eds), *Science and Stonehenge*, 115–44

——. 2000. 'High-resolution mapping of chalk landscapes and land use', in Fairbairn, A. (ed.), *Plants in Neolithic Britain*, 9–26

Allen, T. and Walsh, K. 1996. 'Eton rowing lake', *CA* 148, 124–7

Anati, E. 1964. *Camonica valley*, London: Jonathan Cape

Anawak, J. 1996. 'Inuit perceptions of the Past', in Hodder, I. and Preucel, R. (eds), *Contemporary archaeology in theory*, 646–57

Anon. 1976. 'East Anglia', *CA* 51, 123–4

——. 1979. *Long Barrows in Hampshire and the Isle of Wight*, RCHME, HMSO

——. 1982. 'Balbirnie and Balfarg', *CA* 84, 23–5

——. 1983. 'Sussex prehistory', *CA* 88, 150–2

——. 1985. 'Etton', *CA* 96, 9–10

——. 1988. 'Machrie Moor', *CA* 109, 35–7

——. 1997. 'Barnhouse', *CA* 131, 444–8

——. 1998. 'The Potlock Cursus', *CA* 157, 33

——. 1999. 'Neolithic Orkney', *CA* 160, 137–8

——. 2000a. 'White Horse Stone: a neolithic longhouse', *CA* 168, 450–3

——. 2000b. 'Causewayed enclosures', *CA* 168, 470–2

——.2002 'Mesolithic camp found at the bottom of the Solent', *BA* 64,5.

Armit, I. 1991. 'Loch Olabhat', *CA* 127, 284–7

——. 1992. 'The Hebridean neolithic', in Sharples, N. and Sheridan, A. (eds), *Vessels for the ancestors*, 307–21

Ashbee, P. 1966. 'The Fussell's Lodge long barrow excavation, 1957', *Archaeologia Cantiana*, 1–80

——. 1978. *The ancient British*, Norwich: Geo Abstracts

——. 1984. *The earthen long barrow in Britain*, Norwich: Geo Books

——. 1996. 'Jullieberrie's Grave, Chilham: retrospection and perception', *Archaeologia Cantiana* 116, 1–34

——. 2000. 'The Medway's megalithic long barrows', *Archaeologia Cantiana* 121, 1–41

Ashbee, P., Smith, I. and Evans, J. 1979. 'Excavations of three long barrows near Avebury, Wiltshire', *PPS* 45, 207–300

Ashmore, P. 1996. *Neolithic and Bronze Age Scotland*, London: Batsford

——. 1998. 'Radiocarbon dates for settlements, tombs and ceremonial sites with Grooved Ware in Scotland', in Gibson, A. and Simpson, D.D.A. (eds), *Prehistoric ritual and religion*, 139–47

——. 2000. 'Dating the neolithic in Orkney', in Ritchie, A (ed.), *Neolithic Orkney in its European context*, 299–308

Ashwin, T. 1996. 'Neolithic and bronze age Norfolk', *PPS* 62, 41–62

Atkinson, R.J.C. 1956. *Stonehenge: archaeology and interpretation*, London: Hamish Hamilton

Atkinson, R.J.C., Piggott, C.M. and Sandars, N.K. 1951. *Excavations at Dorchester, Oxon.* Oxford: Oxford Archaeological Unit

Aubrey, J. 1862. *Wiltshire: the topographical collections of John Aubrey (1659–70)*, edited by J.E. Jackson, London

Austin, P. 2000. 'The emperor's new garden: woodland, trees and people in the neolithic of southern Britain', in Fairbairn, A.S. (ed.), *Plants in neolithic Britain and beyond*, 63–78

Baillie, M. 1989. 'Do Irish bog oaks date the Shang dynasty?', *CA* 117, 310–13

Baillie, M. and Brown, D.M. 2002. 'Oak dendrochronology: some recent archaeological developments from an Irish perspective', *Ant* 76, 497–505

Bakker, J.A., Kruk, J., Lanting, A.E. and Milisauskas, S. 1999. 'The earliest evidence of wheeled vehicles in Europe and the Near East', *Ant* 73, 778–90

Barber, J. 1992. 'Megalithic architecture', in Sharples, N. and Sheridan, A. (eds), *Vessels for the ancestors*, 13–32

Barber, M. 1997. 'Landscape, the neolithic , and Kent', in Topping, P. (ed.), *Neolithic landscapes*, 77–85

Barber, M., Field, D. and Topping, P. 1999. *The neolithic flint mines of England*, Swindon: English Heritage

Barclay, G. 1985. 'Balfarg', *CA* 97, 50–2

——. 1996. 'Neolithic buildings in Scotland', in Darvill, T. and Thomas, J. (eds), *Neolithic houses in Northwest Europe and Beyond*, 155–70

Barclay, G. and Grove, D. 1988. *Cairnpapple Hill*, Edinburgh: Historic Scotland

Barclay, G. and Harding, J. (eds), 1999. *Pathways and ceremonies: the cursus monuments of Britain and Ireland*, Oxford: Oxbow

Barclay, G., Bradley, R., Hey, G. and Lambrick, G. 1996. 'The earlier prehistory of the Oxford Region in the light of recent research', *Oxoniensia* 61, 1–20

Barfield, L. 1994. 'The Iceman reviewed', *Ant* 68, 10–26

Barker, G. 1982. *Prehistoric communities in northern England: essays in economic and social reconstruction*, University of Sheffield

——. 1985. *Prehistoric farming in Europe*, Cambridge: Cambridge University Press

Barker, G. and Webley, D. 1978. 'Causewayed camps and early neolithic economies in central southern England', *PPS* 44, 161–86

Barnatt, J. 1982. *Prehistoric Cornwall: the ceremonial monuments*, Wellingborough: Turnstone

Barrett, J.C. 1994. *Fragments from antiquity: an archaeology of social life in Britain, 2900–1200 BC*, Oxford: Blackwell

Barrett, J., Bradley, R. and Green, M. 1991. *Landscape, monuments and society: the prehistory of Cranborne Chase*, Cambridge: Cambridge University Press

Baxter, M. 1999. 'Dancing with the dead in a mass grave', *BA* 48, 6–7

Bayliss, A., Ramsey, C.B. and McCormac, F.G. 1997. 'Dating Stonehenge', in Cunliffe, B. and Renfrew, C. (eds), *Science and Stonehenge*, 39–59

Bedwin, O. 1981. Excavation at the neolithic enclosure on Bury Hill, Houghton, West Sussex 1979', *PPS* 47, 69–86

Bell, C. 1992. *Ritual theory, ritual practice*, Oxford: Oxford University Press

Bell, M. 1977. 'Excavation at Bishopstone', *SAC* 115, 1–291

Bewley, R. 1994. *Prehistoric settlements*, London: English Heritage

Bowden, M., Bradley, R., Gaffney, V. and Mepham, L. 1983. 'The date of the Dorset Cursus', *PPS* 49, 376–80

Bradley, R. 1978. 'Colonization and land use in the late neolithic and early bronze age', in Limbrey, S. and Evans, J.G. (eds), *The effect of man on the landscape: the Lowland Zone*, 95–103

——. 1984. *The Social Foundations of Prehistoric Britain*, London: Longman

——. 1986. 'A reinterpretation of the Abingdon causewayed enclosure', *Oxoniensia* 51, 183

——. 1989. 'Deaths and entrances: a contextual analysis of megalithic art', *CA* 30, 68–75

——. 1992. 'Turning the word: rock-carvings and the archaeology of death', in Sharples, N. and Sheridan, A. (eds), *Vessels for the ancestors*, 168–76

——. 1993. *Altering the earth*, Edinburgh: Society of Antiquaries of Scotland Monographs Series No. 8

——. 1998. 'Stone circles and passage graves – a contested relationship', in Gibson, A. and Simpson, D. (eds), *Prehistoric ritual and religion*, 2–13

——. 2000. *An archaeology of natural places*, London and New York: Routledge

Bradley, R.J. and Chambers, R. 1988. 'A new study of the cursus complex at Dorchester-on-Thames', *Oxford Journal of Archaeology* 7, 271–89

Bradley, R.J. and Edmonds, M. 1993. *Interpreting the axe trade*, Cambridge: Cambridge University Press

Bradley, R.J. and Suthren, R. 1990. 'Petrographic analysis of hammerstones from the neolithic quarries at Great Langdale', *PPS* 56, 117–22

Bradley, R.J., Phillips, T., Richards, C. and Webb, M. 1999. 'Discovering decorated tombs in neolithic Orkney', *CA* 161, 184–7

Brewster, T. 1976 Garton Slack, *CA* 5, 104-16

Brewster, T. 1984. 'Five Yorkshire Barrows', *CA* 94, 328

Briggs, C.S. 1977. 'Stone axe "trade" or glacial erratics?', *CA* 57, 303

Brophy, K. 2000. 'Water coincidence? Cursus monuments and rivers', in Ritchie, A. (ed.), *Neolithic Orkney and its European context*, 59–70

Brothwell, D. 1971. 'Diet, economy and biosocial change in late prehistoric Europe', in Simpson, D.D.A. (ed.), *Economy and settlement in neolithic and early bronze age Britain and Europe*

Brown, A.G. 2000. 'Floodplain vegetation history: clearings as potential ritual space?', in Fairbairn, A.S. (ed.), *Plants in neolithic Britain and beyond*, 49–62

Brown, K. 1997. 'Domestic settlement and the landscape during the neolithic of the Tavoliere, S.E. Italy', in Topping, P. (ed.), *Neolithic landscapes*, 125–37

Brown, N. 1997. 'A landscape of two halves: the neolithic of the Chelmer Valley/Blackwater Estuary, Essex', in Topping, P. (ed.), *Neolithic landscapes*, 87–98

Bunch, B. and Fell, C. 1949. 'A stone axe factory at Pike of Stickle, Great Langdale, Westmorland', *PPS* 15, 1–20

Burgess, C. 1980. *The age of Stonehenge*, London: Dent

——. 1989. 'Volcanoes, catastrophe and the global crisis of the late second millennium bc', *CA* 117, 325–9

Burl, A. 1969. 'Henges: internal features and regional groups', *Arch. J.* 126, 1–28

——. 1976. *The Stone Circles of the British Isles*, London and New Haven: Yale University Press

——. 1979. *Prehistoric Avebury*, London and New Haven: Yale University Press

——. 1981. *Rites of the Gods*, London: Dent

——. 1987. *The Stonehenge People: life and death at the world's greatest stone circle*, London: Dent

——. 1991. *Prehistoric henges*, Princes Risborough: Shire Publications

——. 1993. *From Carnac to Callanish: the prehistoric stone rows and avenues of Britain, Ireland and Brittany*, New Haven and London: Yale University Press

——. 1999. *Great Stone Circles*, New Haven and London: Yale University Press

Campbell Smith, W. 1963. 'Jade axes from sites in the British Isles', *PPS* 29, 133–72

Case, H.J. 1956. 'The neolithic causewayed camp at Abingdon', *Antiquaries Journal* 36, 11–30

Castleden, R. 1983. *The Wilmington Giant: the quest for a lost myth*, Wellingborough: Turnstone Press

——. 1987. *The Stonehenge People*, London and New York: Routledge

——. 1992. *Neolithic Britain*, London and New York: Routledge

——. 1993. *The Making of Stonehenge*, London and New York: Routledge

——. 1996 'Classic Landforms of the Sussex Coast', Sheffield: Geographical Association

——. 1999. 'New views across an old landscape: reassessing Stonehenge (1)', *3rd Stone* 35, 12–8

——. 1999. 'New views across an old landscape: reassessing Stonehenge (2)', *3rd Stone* 36, 31–8

——. 2000. *Ancient British hill figures*, Seaford: SB Publications

Champion, T. , Gamble, C., Shennan, S. and Whittle, A., 1984. *Prehistoric Europe*, London: Academic Press

Charge, B. 1985. 'Archaeology in Haverhill', *CA* 98, 78–80

Childe, V.G. 1930. *The Bronze Age*, Cambridge: Cambridge University Press

——. 1931. *Skara Brae, a Pictish village in Orkney*, London: Kegan Paul, Trench, Trubner

——. 1940. *Prehistoric communities of the British Isles*, London and Edinburgh: Chambers

Childe, V.G. and Grant, W.G. 1939. 'A stone-age settlement at Braes of Rinyo, Rousay, Orkney', *PSAS* 73, 6–31

Clark, G. 1953. *Prehistoric England*, London: Country Book Club

Clark, J.G.D. 1936. 'The timber monument of Arminghall and its affinities', *PPS* 2, 1–51

——. 1938. 'A neolithic house at Haldon, Devon', *PPS* 4, 222–3

——. 1963. 'Neolithic bows from Somerset, England, and the prehistory of archery in north-west Europe', *PPS* 29, 50–98

Clarke, D.V. 1976. 'The neolithic village at Skara Brae: 1972–3 excavations', London: HMSO

Clarke, D.V., Cowie, T.G. and Foxon, A. 1985. *Symbols of power at the time of Stonehenge*, Edinburgh: National Museum of Antiquities, Scotland and HMSO

Cleal, R. and MacSween, A. 1999. *Grooved Ware in Britain and Ireland*, Oxford: Oxbow Books

Cleal, R.M.J., Walker, K.E. and Montague, R. (eds), 1995. *Stonehenge in its landscape: twentieth-century excavations*, London: English Heritage

Clements, J. 1996. 'Drugs and the man', *CA* 148, 158

Clifton-Taylor, A. 1986. *The Cathedrals of England*, London: Thames & Hudson

Clough, T.H. and Cummins, W.A. (eds), 1988. *Stone axe studies.* Vol 2, CBA Research Report No. 67

Coles, B. 1990. 'Anthropomorphic wooden figurines from Britain and Ireland', *PPS* 56, 315–33

Coles, B. and Coles, J. 1986. *Sweet Track to Glastonbury*, London: Thames & Hudson

Coles, J.M. 1978. 'Man and landscape in the Somerset Levels', in Limbrey, S. and Evans, J.G. (eds), *The effect of man on the landscape: the Lowland Zone*

Coles, J.M. and Hibbert, F.A. 1968. 'Prehistoric roads and tracks in Somerset, England: 1. Neolithic', *PPS* 34, 238–58

Coles, J.M., Heal, S.V.E. and Orme, B.J. 1978. 'The use and character of wood in prehistoric Britain and Ireland', *PPS* 44, 1–45

Condori, C. 1996. 'History and prehistory in Bolivia', in I. Hodder and R. Preucel (eds), *Contemporary archaeology in theory*, Oxford: Blackwell, 632–45

Connor, S. 2003. 'Stone age man drank milk, scientists find', *Independent*, 28/01/03

Cooney, G. 1996. 'Images of settlement and the landscape in the neolithic', in Topping, P. (ed.), *Neolithic landscapes*, 23–31

——. 1998. 'Breaking stones, making places: the social landscape of axe production sites', in Gibson, A. and Simpson, D. (eds), *Prehistoric ritual and religion*, 108–18

Corcoran, J. 1972. 'Multi-period constructions and the origins of the chambered long cairn in western Britain and Ireland', in Lynch, F. and Burgess, C. (eds) *Prehistoric Man in Wales and the West*. Bath: Adams and Dart. 31–63

Courtin, J. 1974. 'La guerre au Neolithique', *La Recherche* 15, 448–58

Cowell, R.W. and Innes, J.B. 1994. *The Wetlands of Merseyside*. Lancaster: Lancaster Imprints

Crampton, P. 1967. *Stonehenge of the kings*, John Baker

Cummins, W.A. 1974. 'The neolithic stone axe trade in Britain', *Ant* 48, 201–5

——. 1978. 'Stone-axe trade – or glacial erratics?', *CA* 61, 42–3

——. 1980. 'Stone axes as a guide to neolithic communications and boundaries in England and Wales', *PPS* 46, 45–60

Cunliffe, B. (ed.). 1994. *Prehistoric Europe: an illustrated history*, Oxford: Oxford University Press

——. 2002. 'People of the sea', BA 63, 12–17

Cunliffe, B. and Renfrew, C. (eds), 1997. *Science and Stonehenge*, Oxford: British Academy and Oxford University Press

Cunnington, R.H. 1931. 'The Sanctuary on Overton Hill near Avebury', *Wiltshire Archaeological and Natural History Magazine* 45, 300–35

——. 1931. 'The Sanctuary on Overton Hill. Was it roofed?', *Wiltshire Archaeological and Natural History Magazine* 45, 486–8

Curwen, E.C. 1930. 'Neolithic camps', *Ant* 4, 22–54

——. 1934. 'Excavations in Whitehawk Neolithic camp, Brighton, 1932–3', *Antiquaries Journal* 14, 99–133

——. 1936. 'Excavations in Whitehawk Camp, Brighton, third season, 1935', *SAC* 77, 60–92

——. 1937. *The archaeology of Sussex*, London: Methuen

Dames, M. 1976. *The Silbury treasure*, London: Thames & Hudson

Daniel, G. 1963. *The megalith builders of Western Europe*, Hutchinson

Darvill, T.C. 1982. *The megalithic chamber tombs of the Cotswold-Severn region*, Highworth: Vorda

——. 1989. 'The circulation of Neolithic stone and flint axes: a case study from Wales and the mid-west of England', *PPS* 55, 27–43

——. 1997a. 'Ever increasing circles: the sacred geographies of Stonehenge and its landscape', in B. Cunliffe and C. Renfrew (eds), *Science and Stonehenge*, 167–202

——. 1997b. 'Neolithic landscapes: identity and definition', in Topping, P. (ed.), *Neolithic landscapes*, 1–13

Darvill, T. and Thomas, J. (eds) 1996. *Neolithic houses in Northwest Europe and Beyond*. Oxford: Oxbow Monographs (No. 57)

David, A. 1988. 'Stanton Drew', *Past* 28, 1–3

Davidson, J.L. and Henshall, A.S. 1989. *The chambered cairns of Orkney*, Edinburgh: Edinburgh University Press

de Marinis, R and Brillante, G. 1998. *Otzi: l'uomo venuto dal Ghiaccio*, Venice: Marsilio

Dewar, H.S.L. and Godwin, H. 1963. 'Archaeological discoveries in the raised bogs of the Somerset Levels, England', *PPS* 29, 17–49

Dinely, M. and Dinely, G. 2000. 'Neolithic ale: barley as a source of malt sugars for fermentation', in Fairbairn, A.S. (ed.), *Plants in neolithic Britain and beyond*, 137–53

Dixon, P. 1972. 'Excavations at Crickley Hill', *Ant* 46, 49–52

Downes, J. and Richards, C. 2000. 'Excavating the neolithic and early bronze age of Orkney: recognition and interpretation in the field', in Ritchie, A. (ed.), *Neolithic Orkney in its European context*, 159–68

Drewett, P. 1975. 'The excavation of an oval burial mound of the third millennium bc at Alfriston, East Sussex, 1974', *PPS* 41, 119–52

——. 1977. 'The excavation of a neolithic causewayed enclosure on Offham Hill, East Sussex, 1976', *PPS* 43, 201–41

——. 1977. *Neolithic and bronze age settlements and their territories. Rescue Archaeology in Sussex*, Institute of Archaeology Bulletin No. 14

——. 1994. 'Dr V. Seton Williams' excavations at Combe Hill, 1962, and the role of neolithic causewayed enclosures in Sussex', *SAC* 132, 7–24

Drewett, P. and Hamilton, S. 1999. 'Marking time and making space. Excavations and landscape studies at the Caburn hillfort, East Sussex, 1996–8', *SAC* 137, 7–37

Dyer, J. and Grinsell, L.V. 1971. *Wessex*, London

Edmonds, M. 1999. *Ancestral geographics of the neolithic landscape, monuments and memory*. London: Routledge

Edmonds, M. and Richards, C. (eds), 1998. *Understanding the Neolithic of north-western Europe*, Glasgow: Cruithne Press

Edwards, I.E.S. 1985. *The pyramids of Egypt*, Harmondsworth: Penguin

Ellis, S. and Crowther, D.R. 1990. *Humber perspectives: a region through the ages*, Hull: Hull University Press

Evans, A.A. 1933. *On foot in Sussex: a loiterer's notebook*, London: Methuen

Evans, J.G. 1971a. 'Notes on the environment of early farming communities in Britain', in Simpson, D.D.A. (ed.), *Economy and settlement in neolithic and early bronze age Britain and Europe*, 11–26

——. 1971b. 'Habitat change on the calcareous soils of Britain: the impact of neolithic man', in Simpson, D.D.A. (ed.), *Economy and settlement in neolithic and early bronze age Britain and Europe*, 27–73

——. 1975. *The environment of early man in the British Isles*, Elek

Evans, J.G., Limbrey, S. and Cleere, H. 1975. *The effect of man on the landscape of the Highland Zone*, Council for British Archaeology Research Report No. 11

Evans, J.G., Limbrey, S., Mate, I. and Mount, R. 1993. 'An environmental history of the Upper Kennet valley, Wiltshire for the last 1,000 years', *PPS* 59, 139–95

Evans, J.G., Pitts, M.W. and Williams, D. 1985. 'An excavation at Avebury, Wiltshire, 1982', *PPS* 51, 305–20

Fairbairn, A.S. 2000. 'On the spread of plant crops across neolithic Britain, with special reference to southern England', in Fairbairn, A.S. (ed.), *Plants in neolithic Britain and beyond*, 107–21

——. (ed.). 2000. *Plants in neolithic Britain and beyond*, Neolithic Studies Group Seminar Paper 5. Oxford: Oxbow Books

Field, D. 1997. 'The landscapes of extraction', in Topping, P. (ed.), *Neolithic landscapes*, 55–67

Field, N.H., Matthews, C.L. and Smith, I.F. 1964. 'New neolithic sites in Dorset and Bedfordshire, with a note on the distribution of neolithic storage-pits in Britain', *PPS* 30, 352–81

Fleming, A. 1973. 'Tombs for the living', *Man* 8, 177–93

Fowler, P.J. 1968. *Regional archaeology of Wessex*, London

——. 1971. 'Early prehistoric agriculture in Western Europe: some archaeological evidence', in Simpson, D.D.A. (ed.), *Economy and settlement in neolithic and early bronze age Britain and Europe*, 153–82

Fried, M.H. 1967. *The evolution of political society*, New York

Fox, A. 1973. *South-West England, 3500 BC–AD 600*, Newton Abbot: David & Charles

Gibson, A. 1992. 'Sarn-y-Bryn-Caled, Welshpool', *CA* 128, 341–3

——. 1995. 'Walton', *CA* 143, 444–5

——. 1998. *Stonehenge and timber circles*, Stroud: Tempus

——. 2000. 'The Walton Basin, Radnor, Powys: explorations in a neolithic landscape', in Ritchie, A. (ed.), *Neolithic Orkney in its European context*, 31–46

Gibson, A. and Simpson, D.D.A. (eds), 1998. *Prehistoric ritual and religion*, Stroud: Sutton

Glass, H. 2000. 'White Horse Stone: a neolithic longhouse', *CA* 168, 450–3

Godwin, H. 1944. 'Age and origin of "Breckland" heaths of East Anglia', *Nature* 154, 6–7

——. 1960. 'Prehistoric wooden trackways of the Somerset Levels: their construction, age and relation to climatic change', *PPS* 26, 1–36

Goudie, A.S. 1977. *Environmental change*, Oxford: Clarendon Press

Green, M. 1994. 'Down Farm', *CA* 138, 216–25

Haggarty, A. 1988. 'Machrie Moor', *CA* 109, 35–7

Hammond, N. 2000. 'Gruesome burial practices of the Neolithics fascinate archaeologists today', *The Times* 3/01/00, 18

Harding, A.F. 1981. 'Excavations in the prehistoric ritual complex near Milfield, Northumberland', *PPS* 47, 87–135

Harding, J. 1999. 'Pathways to new realms: cursus monuments and symbolic territories', in Barclay, A. and Harding, J. (eds), *Pathways and ceremonies: the cursus monuments of Britain and Ireland*, 30–8

——. 2000a. 'Henge monuments and landscape features in northern England: monumentality and nature', in Ritchie, A. (ed.), *Neolithic Orkney in its European context*, 267–74

——. 2000b. 'Later neolithic ceremonial centres, ritual and pilgrimage: the monument complex of Thornborough, North Yorkshire', in Ritchie, A (ed.), *Neolithic Orkney in its European context*, 31–46

Harrison, J. 1877. 'On marks found upon chalk at Cissbury', *Journal of the Royal Anthropological Institute* 6, 263–71

Hawkins, G.S. 1966. *Stonehenge decoded*, London: Souvenir Press

Hayman, R. 1997. *Riddles in stone: myths, archaeology and the Ancient Britons*, London: Hambledon Press

Heath, R. 1998. *Sun, Moon and Stonehenge: high culture in ancient Britain*, Cardigan: Bluestone Press

Hedges, J.W. 1984. *Tomb of the Eagles: a window on stone age tribal Britain*, London: John Murray

Hedges, J. and Buckley, D. 1978. 'Excavation at a neolithic causewayed enclosure, Orsett, Essex', *PPS* 44, 219–308

Heggie, D. 1981. *Megalithic science*, London: Thames & Hudson

Helm, P.J. 1971. *Exploring prehistoric England*, Robert Hale

Henshall, A. 1963. *The chambered tombs of Scotland*, Edinburgh: Edinburgh University Press

——. 1970. 'The long cairns of eastern Scotland', *Scottish Archaeological Forum* 2, 29–49

Herity, M. and Eogan, G. 1978. *Ireland in prehistory*, London: Routledge

Hey, G. 1997. 'Neolithic settlement at Yarnton, Oxfordshire', in Topping, P. (ed.), *Neolithic landscapes*, 99–111

Hodder, I. 1990. *The Domestication of Europe*, Oxford: Blackwell

Hodder, I. and Preucel, R. (eds), 1996. *Contemporary archaeology in theory*, Oxford: Blackwell

Hodder, I. and Shand, P. 1988. 'The Haddenham long barrow: an interim statement', *Ant* 52, 349–53

Holgate, R. 1985. 'Neolithic settlement in the Upper Thames', *CA* 95, 374–5

——. 1987. 'Neolithic settlement patterns at Avebury, Wiltshire', *Ant* 61, 259–63

Hornsey, R. 1987. 'The Grand Menhir Brise: megalithic success or failure?', *Oxford Journal of Archaeology* 6, 185–217

Houlder, C.H. 1961. 'The excavation of a neolithic stone implement factory on Mynydd Rhiw in Caernarvonshire', *PPS* 27, 108–43

——. 1976. 'Stone axes and henge monuments', in Boon, G.C. and Lewis, J.M. (eds), *Welsh Antiquity: Essays presented to Dr H.N. Savory*, Cardiff: National Museum of Wales, 55–62

Hurcombe, L. 2000. 'Plants as the raw materials for crafts', in Fairbairn, A.S. (ed.), *Plants in neolithic Britain and beyond*, 155–73

Ingold, T. 1986. *The appropriation of nature. Essays on human ecology and social relations.* Manchester: Manchester University Press

Jackson, P. 1995. 'Footloose in archaeology', *CA* 144, 466–70

James, S. 1999. *The Atlantic Celts: ancient people or modern invention?*, London: British Museum Press

Jensen, J. 1982. *The Prehistory of Denmark.* London: Methuen

Jessop, R. 1970. *South East England,* London: Thames & Hudson

Johnson, R. 1999. 'An empty path? Processions, memories and the Dorset Cursus', in Barclay, A. and Harding, J. (eds), *Pathways and ceremonies: the cursus monuments of Britain and Ireland,* 39–48

Jones, A. 2000. 'Life after death: monuments, material culture and social change in neolithic Orkney', in Ritchie, A. (ed.), *Neolithic Orkney in its European context,* 127–38

Jones, G. 2000. 'Evaluating the importance of cultivation and collecting in neolithic Britain', in Fairbairn, A.S. (ed.), *Plants in neolithic Britain and beyond,* 79–84

Jones, R.E. and Brown, B. 2000. 'Neolithic pottery-making in Orkney: a new look', in Ritchie, A (ed.), *Neolithic Orkney in its European context,* 1–20

Jones, R.L. and Keen, D.H. 1993. *Pleistocene environments in the British Isles,* London: Chapman & Hall

Jones, S., Martin, R. and Pilbeam, D. 1992. *The Cambridge encyclopaedia of human evolution,* Cambridge: Cambridge University Press

Keeley, L.H. 1996. *War before civilization. The myth of the peaceful savage,* Oxford: Oxford University Press

Kinnes, I. 1998. 'From ritual to romance: a new Western', in Gibson, A. and Simpson, D.D.A. (eds), *Prehistoric ritual and religion,* 183–9

Kinnes, I., Schadla-Hall, T., Chadwick, P. and Dean, P. 1983. 'Duggleby Howe reconsidered', *Arch. J.* 140, 83–108

Kupferberg, H. 1979, *Opera,* New York: Newsweek Books

Lane Fox , A.H. 1869. 'An examination into the character and probable origins of the hillforts of Sussex', *Archaeologia* 42, 27–52

Last, J. 1999. 'Out of line: cursuses and monument typology in eastern England', in Barclay, A. and Harding, J. (eds), *Pathways and ceremonies: the cursus monuments of Britain and Ireland,* 86–97

Lawson, A.J. 1997. 'The structural history of Stonehenge', in Cunliffe, B. and Renfrew, C. (eds), *Science and Stonehenge,* 15–37

Leslie, K. and Short, B. 1999. *An historical atlas of Sussex,* Chichester: Phillimore

Letts, J. 2001. 'Thatch through history', *BA* 58, 13

Limbrey, S. 1978. 'Changes in quality and distribution of the soils of lowland Britain', in Limbrey, S. and Evans, J.G. (eds), 1978. *The effect of man on the landscape: the Lowland Zone,* CBA Research Report No. 21

Lockyer, N. 1906. *Stonehenge and other British Monuments astronomically considered.* London: Macmillan

Long, D.J., Tipping, R., Holden, T.G., Bunting, M.J. and Milburn, P. 2000. 'The use of henbane as a hallucinogen at neolithic "ritual" sites: a re-evaluation', *Ant* 74, 49–53

Loveday, R. 1998. 'Double entrance henges – routes to the past?', in Gibson, A. and Simpson, D.D.A. (eds), *Prehistoric ritual and religion,* 14–31

—, R. 2000. 'Aston: a barrow preserved', *CA* 167, 438–9

Lubbock, J. 1865. *Pre-historic times, as illustrated by ancient remains and the manners and customs of modern savages,* London: Williams & Norgate

Lugli, P.M. 1967. *Storia e cultura della citta Italiana,* Bari: Editori Laterza

Luning, J. 1982. 'Siedlung und Siedlungslandschaft in bandkeramischer und Rossener Zeit', *Offa* 39, 9–33

——. 1988. 'Zur Verbreitung und Datierung bandkeramischer Erdwerk', Archäologisches Korrespondenzblatt 18, 155-8

Lynch, F. 1975. 'The impact of landscape on prehistoric man', in Evans, J.G., Limbrey, S. and Cleere, H. (eds), *The effect of man on the landscape of the Highland Zone*

——. 1998. 'Colour in prehistoric architecture', in Gibson, A. and Simpson, D.D.A. (eds), *Prehistoric ritual and religion*

Lynch, F., *et al.* 2000. *Prehistoric Wales*, Stroud: Sutton Publishing

McInnes, I.J. 1971. 'Settlements in later neolithic Britain', in Simpson, D.D.A. (ed.), *Economy and settlement in neolithic and early bronze age Britain and Europe*, 113–30

MacKie, E. 1977a. *The megalith builders*, London: Phaidon

——. 1977b. *Science and society in prehistoric Britain*, Elek

——. 1998. 'Continuing over three thousand years of prehistory: the "tell" at Howe, Orkney', *Archaeological Journal* 78, 1–42

McOmish, D. 2003. 'Cursus: solving a 6,000-year-old puzzle', *BA* 69, 8–13

Malim, T. 1999. 'Cursuses and related monuments of the Cambridgeshire Ouse', in Barclay, G. and Harding, J. (eds), *Pathways and ceremonies: the cursus monuments of Britain and Ireland*, 77–85

Malone, C. 1989. *Avebury*, London: English Heritage and Batsford

——. 2001. *Neolithic Britain and Ireland*, Stroud: Tempus

Manby, T.G. 1970. 'Long barrows of northern England; structural and dating evidence', *Scottish Archaeological Forum* 2, 1–28

——. 1976. 'Excavation of the Kilham Long Barrow, East Riding of Yorkshire', *PPS* 42, 111–59

Manley, J. 1989. *Atlas of prehistoric Britain*, Oxford: Phaidon

Mercer, R.J. 1980. *Hambledon Hill: a Neolithic landscape*, Edinburgh: Edinburgh University Press

——. 1986. 'The Neolithic in Cornwall', *Cornish Archaeology* 25, 35–80

——. 1990. *Causewayed enclosures*, Princes Risborough: Shire Publications

——. 1992. 'Cumulative cairn construction and cultural continuity in Caithness and Orkney', in Sharples, N. and Sheridan, A. (eds), *Vessels for the ancestors*, 49–61

Midgley, M. 1992. *TRB Culture: the first farmers of the North European Plain*, Edinburgh: Edinburgh University Press

Miles, D. 1997. 'Conflict and complexity: the later prehistory of the Oxford region', *Oxoniensia* 62, 1–19

Mitchell, G.F. 1977. 'Raised beaches and sea levels', in Shotton, F.W. (ed.), *British Quaternary Studies*, 169–86

Mohen, J.-P. 1989. *The world of the megaliths*, London: Cassell

Moore, J. 1997. 'The infernal cycle of fire ecology', in Topping, P. (ed.), *Neolithic landscapes*, 33–40

Morgan, F. 1959. 'The excavation of a long barrow at Nutbane, Hampshire', *PPS* 25, 15–51

Morner, N.A. 1969. 'The Late Quaternary history of the Kattegatt Sea and the Swedish west coast', *Sveriges Geologiska Undersokning* Series C, NR. 640, Arsbok 63, NR. 3

——. 1971. 'The Holocene eustatic sea level problem', *Geol. en Mijn* 50, 699–702

Morse, M. 1999. 'Craniology and the adoption of the Three-Age system in Britain', *PPS* 65, 1–16

Musty, J. 1984. 'Mesolithic arable?', *CA* 94, 344

——. 1985. 'Elm decline: axeman or beetle', *CA* 98, 77

——. 1988. 'New beer', *CA* 109, 55

——. 1991a. 'Fleeced sheep', *CA* 124, 182

——. 1991b. 'Early woodland', *CA* 124, 183

——. 1992. 'Dating the neolithic', *CA* 131, 470

——. 1995a. 'Footprints in time', *CA* 142, 393

——. 1995b. 'The oldest wheel', *CA* 143, 433

Nash, R.J. 1997. 'Archetypal landscapes and the interpretation of meaning', *Cambridge Arch. Journal* 7, 57–69

Needham, S.P. 2000. 'Power pulses across a cultural divide: cosmologically driven acquisition between Armorica and Wessex', *PPS* 66, 151–207

Neighbour, T. and Crawford, J. 2001. 'Bernera: reconstructing a figure-of-eight house at Bosta', *CA* 175, 294–300

Newham, C.A. 1972. *The astronomical significance of Stonehenge*, Leeds

North, J. 1996. *Stonehenge: neolithic man and the cosmos*, London: HarperCollins

O'Connell, M. 1986. 'The Heathrow/Stanwell Cursus', *CA* 99, 122–5

O'Kelly, M.K. 1982. *Newgrange: archaeology, art and legend*, London: Thames & Hudson

Osborn, A. 1989. 'Multiculturalism in the eastern Andes', in Shennan, S.J. (ed.), *Archaeological approaches to cultural identity*, 141–56

Oswald, A., Dyer, C. and Barber, M. 2001. *The creation of monuments. Neolithic causewayed enclosures in the British Isles*, Swindon: English Heritage

Palmer, R. 1976. 'Interrupted ditch enclosures in Britain: the use of aerial photography for comparative studies', *PPS* 42, 161–86

Palmer, S. 1977. *Mesolithic cultures of Britain*, Poole: Dolphin Press

Park Harrison, J. 1877. 'On marks found upon Chalk at Cissbury', *Journal of the Anthropological Institute* 6, 263–71

Parker Pearson, M. and Richards, C. 1994. *Architecture and Order: Approaches to Social Space*, Routledge

Parsons, J. 2002. 'Great sites: Belas Knap', *BA* 63, 18–23

Patton, M. 1993. *Statements in stone*, London and New York: Routledge

Pearson, M.P. 1993. *Bronze Age Britain*. London: Batsford

Pierpoint, S. 1980. *Social patterns in Yorkshire prehistory*, BAR British Series 74

Piggott, S. 1954. *The neolithic cultures of the British Isles*, Cambridge: Cambridge University Press

——. 1962. *The West Kennet long barrow*, London: HMSO

——. 1965. *Ancient Europe*, Edinburgh: Edinburgh University Press

——. 1973. 'Dalladies long barrow, north-east Scotland', *Ant* 47, 32–6

——. 1947–8. 'The excavations on Cairnpapple Hill, West Lothian, 1947–8', *PSAS* 10, 68–123

Pitts, M. 1996. 'The stone axe in neolithic Britain', *PPS* 61, 311–71

Pitts, M. and Whittle, A. 1992. 'The development and date of Avebury', *PPS* 58, 203–12

Polet, C., Dutour, O., Orban, R., Jadin, I. and Lourgon, S. 1995. 'Note sur une neolithique mosan blesse par une pointe de fleche', *Notae Praehistoricae* 15, 105–11

Pollard, J. 1992. 'The Sanctuary, Overton Hill, Wiltshire: a re-examination', *PPS* 58, 213–26

——. 1997. *Neolithic Britain*, Princes Risborough: Shire Publications

Pryor, F. 1974. 'Excavations at Fengate, Peterborough. The First report', *Royal Ontario Mus. Arch.* Monograph 3

——. 1999. *Etton: excavation at a Neolithic causewayed enclosure near Maxey, Cambridgeshire, 1983–7*, London: English Heritage

——. 2001. *Seahenge: new discoveries in prehistoric Britain*, London: HarperCollins

Quartermaine, J. and Claris, P. 1986. 'The Langdale axe factories', *CA* 102, 212–13

Rackham, O. 1980. *Ancient Woodland: its history, vegetation and uses in England*. London: Edward Arnold.

——. 1986. *The history of the countryside*, London and Melbourne, Dent

Rees, S. 1978. 'Tools available for cultivation in prehistoric Britain', in Limbrey, S. and Evans, J.G. (eds), *The effect of man on the landscape: the Lowland Zone*

Renfrew, C. 1973. *The explanation of cultural change: models in prehistory*, London: Duckworth

——. 1974. *British prehistory: a new outline*, London: Duckworth

——. 1979. *Investigations in Orkney*, London: Society of Antiquaries/Thames & Hudson

——. (ed.). 1981. *The megalithic monuments of western Europe*, London: Thames & Hudson

——. 1985. *The Prehistory of Orkney*, Edinburgh: Edinburgh University Press

——. 1987. *Archaeology and language: the puzzle of Indo-European origins*, London: Jonathan Cape

——. 2000. 'The auld hoose speaks: society and life in stone age Orkney', in Ritchie, A (ed.), *Neolithic Orkney in its European context*, 1–20

Richards, C. 1990. 'The late neolithic house in Orkney', in Samson, R. (ed.), *The Social Archaeology of Houses*, Edinburgh: Edinburgh University Press, 111–24

——. 1991. 'Rethinking the neolithic of Orkney', *BA* 42 (www.britarch.ac.uk/ba/ba42)

——. 1992. 'Barnhouse and Maeshowe', *CA* 131, 444–8

——. 1993. Monumental choreography, architecture and spatial representation, in late neolithic Orkney, in Tilley, C. (ed), *Interpretative archaeology*. Oxford: Berg 143–78

Richards, J. 1990. *The Stonehenge Environs Project*, London: English Heritage

——. 1999. *Meet the ancestors*, London: BBC

——. and Whitby, M. 1997. 'The engineering of Stonehenge', M. Cunliffe, B. and Renfrew, C. (eds) *Science and Stonehenge*, 231–56

Richards, M.P. 2000. 'Human consumption of plant foods in the British neolithic: direct evidence from bone stable isotopes', in Fairbairn, A.S. (ed.), *Plants in neolithic Britain and beyond*, 123–35

Ridley, M. 1976. *The megalithic art of the Maltese islands*. Poole: Dolphin Press

Ritchie, A. 1995. *Prehistoric Orkney*, London: Batsford and Historic Scotland

——. (ed.). 2000. *Neolithic Orkney and its European context*, Cambridge: McDonald Institute Monographs

Ritchie, G. 1976. 'The Stones of Stenness, Orkney', *PSAS* 107, 1–60

Roberts, N. 1988. *The Holocene: an environmental history*, Oxford: Blackwell

Robertson-Mackay, R. 1987. 'The Neolithic causewayed enclosure at Staines, Surrey: excavations 1961–3', *PPS* 53, 23–128

Robinson, D. 1999. 'The coast and coastal changes', in Leslie, K. and Short, B. (eds), *An historical atlas of Sussex*, 8–9

Robinson, M.A. 2000. 'Further considerations of neolithic charred cereals, fruit and nuts', in Fairbairn, A.S. (ed.), *Plants in neolithic Britain and beyond*, 85–90

Rolleston, G. and Greenwell, W. 1877. *British barrows*

Ruggles, C. 1997. 'Astronomy and Stonehenge', in Cunliffe, B. and Renfrew, C. (eds), *Science and Stonehenge*, 203–29

——. 1998. 'Ritual astronomy in the neolithic and bronze age British Isles: patterns of continuity and change', in Gibson, A. and Simpson, D.D.A. (eds), *Prehistoric ritual and religion*, 203–8

Ruggles, C. and Barclay, G. 2000. 'Cosmology, calendars and society in neolithic Orkney: a rejoinder to Euan MacKie', *Ant* 74, 62–74

Russell, M. 1997. 'Neo-"Realism"?: an alternative look at the neolithic chalkland database of Sussex', in Topping, P. (ed.), *Neolithic landscapes*, 69–76

——. 2000. *Flint mines in Neolithic Britain*, Stroud: Tempus

Sahlins, M. 1972. *Stone age economics*, London: Tavistock

Samson, R. (ed.). 1990. *The Social Archaeology of Houses*, Edinburgh: Edinburgh University Press

Sartre, J.-P. 1976. *Critique of dialectical reason*, London: Verso

Saville, A. 1983. 'Hazleton', *CA* 87, 107–12

——. 1990. *Hazleton North, Gloucestershire, 1979–82: the excavation of a neolithic long cairn of the Cotswold-Severn group*, London: English Heritage Archaeological Report 13

Savory, H.N. 1980. 'The neolithic in Wales', in Taylor, J.A. (ed.), *Culture and environment in prehistoric Wales*

Scarre, C. 1983. *The neolithic of France*, Edinburgh: Edinburgh University Press

——. 1998. 'Arenas of action? Enclosure entrances in neolithic western France, *c*. 3500–2500', *PPS* 64, 115–37

Schofield, J.C. 1960. 'Sea level fluctuations during the past four thousand years', *Nature* 185, 836

Schreudos, T. (producer). 2001. *Miami Circle*, BBC Horizon broadcast, 25/01/01

Scott, J.G. 1988–9. 'The stone circles at Templewood, Kilmartin, Argyll', *Glasgow Archaeological Journal* 15, 52–124

——. 1992. 'Mortuary structures and megaliths', in Sharples, N. and Sheridan, A. (eds), *Vessels for the ancestors*, 104–27

Scott, R. and Phillips, T. 1999. 'Clava: light at the end of the tunnel', *CA* 165, 332–5

Service, E.R. 1971. *Primitive social organization: an evolutionary perspective*, New York

Shand, P. and Hodder, I. 1990. 'Haddenham', *CA* 118, 339–42

Sharples, N. 1992. 'Aspects of regionalisation in the Scottish neolithic', in Sharples, N. and Sheridan, A. (eds), *Vessels for the ancestors*, 322–31

——. and Sheridan, A. 1992. *Vessels for the ancestors*. Edinburgh: Edinburgh University Press

Shee Twohig, E. 1981. *The megalithic art of western Europe*, Oxford: Clarendon Press

Shennan, S.J. 1989. *Archaeological approaches to cultural identity*, London: Routledge

——. 2000. 'Antlers and Orcadian rituals: an ambiguous role for red deer in the neolithic', in Ritchie, A. (ed), *Neolithic Orkney in its European context*, 107–16

Shepherd, R. 1980. *Prehistoric mining and allied industries*. London: Academic Press

Sheridan, A. 1996. 'The oldest bow and other objects', *CA* 149, 188–90

Sherratt, A. 1990. 'The genesis of megaliths, monumentality, ethnicity and social complexity on neolithic north-west Europe'. World Archaeology 22 (2), 147–67

Sherratt, A. 1998. 'Points of exchange: the later neolithic monuments of the Morbihan', in Gibson, A. and Simpson, D.D.A. (eds), *Prehistoric ritual and religion*, 119–38

Shotton, F.W. (ed.). 1977. *British Quaternary studies*, Oxford: Clarendon Press

Simmons, I.G. and Tooley, M.J. (eds). 1981. *The environment in British prehistory*, Duckworth

Simpson, D.D.A. (ed.). 1971. *Economy and settlement in neolithic and early bronze age Britain and Europe*, Leicester: Leicester University Press

——. 1996. Balleygalley houses, Co. Antrim, Ireland, in Darvill, T. and Thomas, J. (eds) *Neolithic houses in Northwest Europe and Beyond*. Oxford: Oxbow Monographs

Smith, A.G. 1981. 'The neolithic', in Simmons, I.G. and Tooley, M.J. (eds), *The environment in British prehistory*, 125–209

Smith, I. 1965. *Windmill Hill and Avebury*, Oxford: Clarendon Press

Smith, R. 1984. 'The ecology of neolithic farming systems as exemplified by the Avebury region, Wiltshire', *PPS* 50, 99–120

Spindler, K. 1994. *The man in the ice*, London: Weidenfeld & Nicolson

Spratt, D. 1985. 'The North Yorkshire Moors', *CA* 98, 86–9

Stone, J.F.S. 1958. *Wessex before the Celts*, London: Thames & Hudson

Stuiver, M. and Pearson, G.W. 1993. 'High-precision calibration of the radiocarbon time-scale AD 1950–400 BC and 2500–6000 BC', *Radiocarbon* 35, 1–23

Stukeley, W. 1740. *Stonehenge, a temple restor'd to the British druids*. London

Swogger, J. 2000. 'The altering eye: reconstructing archaeobotany', in Fairbairn, A.S. (ed.), *Plants in neolithic Britain and beyond*, 175–86

Taylor, C. 1979. *Roads and tracks of Britain*, London: Dent

Taylor, J.A. 1980. 'Man-environment relationships', in Taylor, J.A. (ed.), *Culture and environment in prehistoric Wales: selected essays*

——. (ed.). 1980. *Culture and environment in prehistoric Wales: selected essays*, BAR British Series 76

Thom, A. 1967. *Megalithic science in Britain*, Oxford: Oxford University Press

Thomas, J. 1991. *Rethinking the Neolithic*, Cambridge: Cambridge University Press

——. 1992. 'Monuments, movement and the context of megalithic art', in Sharples, N. and Sheridan, A. (eds), *Vessels for the ancestors*, 143–55

——. 1996. 'Neolithic houses in Britain: a sceptical view', in Darvill, T. and Thomas, J. (eds), *Neolithic houses in northwest Europe and beyond*, Oxford: Oxbow Books

——. 1999. *Understanding the neolithic*, London: Routledge

——. 2000. 'The identity of place in neolithic Britain: examples from southwest Scotland', in Ritchie, A. (ed.), *Neolithic Orkney and its European context*, 79–87

Thomas, N. 1955. 'The Thornborough Circles, near Ripon, North Riding', *Yorkshire Archaeological Journal* 38, 425–45

Thomsen, C.J. 1848. *Guide to northern antiquities*, London.

Tilley, C. 1994. *A phenomenology of landscape*, Oxford: Berg

Tilley, C. 1996. *Landscapes of the mind*, Oxford: Blackwell

Topping, P. 1997. 'Different realities: the neolithic in the Northumberland Cheviots', in Topping, P. (ed.), *Neolithic landscapes*, 113–23

——. (ed.). 1997. *Neolithic landscapes*, Oxford: Oxbow Monographs 86

Tratman, E. 1967. 'The Priddy Circles, Mendip, Somerset, henge monuments', *Proceedings of the University of Bristol Speleological Society* 11, 97–125

Trick, S. 1999. *Virtual Barnhouse*. www.cf.ac.uk/hisar/people/sgt/index

Ucko, P.J. 1995. *Theory in archaology*. London: Routledge

Ucko, P.J., Hunter, M., Clark, A.J. and David, A. 1991. *Avebury Reconsidered: from the 1660s to the 1990s*, London: Unwin Hyman

Van de Noort, R. and Ellis, S. 1998. *Wetland heritage of the Ancholme and Lower Trent valleys*, London: English Heritage

Varndell, G. and Topping, P. (eds). 2002. *Enclosures in neolithic Europe: essays on causewayed and non-causewayed sites*, Oxford: Oxbow Books

Vatcher, F. 1961. 'The excavation of the long mortuary enclosure on Normanton Down, Wiltshire', *PPS* 27, 160–73

Vatcher, L. and Vatcher, F. 1973. 'Excavation of three post-holes in Stonehendge car park', *Wiltshire Archeological Magazine* 48, 57–63

Vayson de Pradenne, A. 1937. 'The use of wood in megalithic structures', *Ant* 11, 87–92

Vyner, B. 1984. 'The excavation of a neolithic cairn at Street House, Loftus, Cleveland', *PPS* 50, 151–96

Waddington, C. 1998. 'Cup and ring marks in context', *Cambridge Arch. Journal* 8, 29–54

Wahl, J. and Konig, M.G. 1987. 'Anthropologischtraumatologische Untersuchung der menschlichen Skelettreste aus dem bandkeramischen Massengrab bei Talheim, Kreis Heilbronn', *Fundberichte aus Baden-Wurttemberg* 12, 65–193

Wainwright, G. 1989. *The henge monuments – ceremony and society in prehistoric Britain*, London: Thames & Hudson

Wainwright, G.J., Evans, J.G. and Longworth, I.H. 1971. 'The excavation of a late neolithic enclosure at Marden, Wiltshire', *Antiquaries Journal* 51, 177–239

Wallington, R. 1999. 'More bluestones', *BA* 49, 14

Warren, S.H. 1922. 'The neolithic stone axes of Graig Lwyd, Penmaenmawr', *Archaeologia Cambrensis* 77, 1–35

Wheeler, M. 1943. *Maiden Castle, Dorset*, London: Society of Antiquaries

Whittle, A. 1977. *The earlier neolithic of Southern England and its continental background*, BAR Supplementary Series 35

——. 1978. 'Resources and population in the British Neolithic', *Ant* 52, 34–42

——. 1988. *Problems in Neolithic archaeology*, Cambridge: Cambridge University Press

——. 1990. 'A model for the mesolithic–neolithic transition in the Upper Kennet valley, North Wiltshire', *PPS* 56, 101–10

——. 1991. 'Wayland's Smithy, Oxfordshire: excavations at the Neolithic tomb in 1962–3 by R.J.C. Atkinson and S. Piggott', *PPS* 57, 61–101

——. 1996. *Neolithic Europe: the creation of new worlds*, Cambridge: Cambridge University Press

——. 1997a. *Sacred mound, holy rings*, Oxford: Oxbow Monograph 74

——. 1997b. 'Moving on and moving around: neolithic settlement mobility', in Topping, P. (ed.), *Neolithic landscapes*, 15–22

Whittle, A. and Wysock, M. 1998. 'Parc le Breos transepted long cairn, Gower, West Glamorgan: date, contents and context', *PPS* 64, 139–82

Whittle, A., Pollard, J. and Grigson, C. 1999. *The harmony of symbols: the Windmill Hill causewayed enclosure*, Oxford: Oxbow Books

Wilkinson, D.M., Clapham, A.J. and Clare, T. 1997. 'The ground flora of the British wildwood', *Quaternary Newsletter* (Quaternary Research Association) 83, 15–20

Williams, B. and Erlean, M. 2002. 'Maritime archaeology in Northern Ireland', *Ant* 76, 505–11

Wilson, D. 1851. *The archaeological and prehistoric annals of Scotland*, Edinburgh: Sutherland & Knox

Wilson, I. 1993. *Shakespeare: the evidence*, London: Headline

Wood, J.E. 1978. *Sun, Moon and Standing Stones*, Oxford: Oxford University Press

Woodward, A.B. and Woodward, P.J. 1996. 'The topography of some barrow cemeteries in bronze age Wessex', *PPS* 62, 275–91

Woodward, P.J. 1988. 'Pictures of the neolithic: discoveries from the Flagstones House excavations, Dorchester, Dorset', *Ant* 62, 266–74

Zvelebil, M. and Rowley-Conwy, P. 1984. 'Transition to farming in northern Europe: a hunter-gatherer perspective', *Norwegian Archaeological Review* 17, 104–28

INDEX